IBM

International Technical Support Organization

**Global Development and Delivery in Practice:
Experiences of the IBM Rational India Lab**

May 2007

SG24-7424-00

Note: Before using this information and the product it supports, read the information in "Notices" on page vii.

First Edition (May 2007)

Contents

Notices

This information was developed for products and services offered in the U.S.A.

IBM may not offer the products, services, or features discussed in this document in other countries. Consult your local IBM representative for information about the products and services currently available in your area. Any reference to an IBM product, program, or service is not intended to state or imply that only that IBM product, program, or service may be used. Any functionally equivalent product, program, or service that does not infringe any IBM intellectual property right may be used instead. However, it is the user's responsibility to evaluate and verify the operation of any non-IBM product, program, or service.

IBM may have patents or pending patent applications covering subject matter described in this document. The furnishing of this document does not give you any license to these patents. You can send license inquiries, in writing, to:
IBM Director of Licensing, IBM Corporation, North Castle Drive, Armonk, NY 10504-1785 U.S.A.

The following paragraph does not apply to the United Kingdom or any other country where such provisions are inconsistent with local law: INTERNATIONAL BUSINESS MACHINES CORPORATION PROVIDES THIS PUBLICATION "AS IS" WITHOUT WARRANTY OF ANY KIND, EITHER EXPRESS OR IMPLIED, INCLUDING, BUT NOT LIMITED TO, THE IMPLIED WARRANTIES OF NON-INFRINGEMENT, MERCHANTABILITY OR FITNESS FOR A PARTICULAR PURPOSE. Some states do not allow disclaimer of express or implied warranties in certain transactions, therefore, this statement may not apply to you.

This information could include technical inaccuracies or typographical errors. Changes are periodically made to the information herein; these changes will be incorporated in new editions of the publication. IBM may make improvements and/or changes in the product(s) and/or the program(s) described in this publication at any time without notice.

Any references in this information to non-IBM Web sites are provided for convenience only and do not in any manner serve as an endorsement of those Web sites. The materials at those Web sites are not part of the materials for this IBM product and use of those Web sites is at your own risk.

IBM may use or distribute any of the information you supply in any way it believes appropriate without incurring any obligation to you.

Information concerning non-IBM products was obtained from the suppliers of those products, their published announcements or other publicly available sources. IBM has not tested those products and cannot confirm the accuracy of performance, compatibility or any other claims related to non-IBM products. Questions on the capabilities of non-IBM products should be addressed to the suppliers of those products.

This information contains examples of data and reports used in daily business operations. To illustrate them as completely as possible, the examples include the names of individuals, companies, brands, and products. All of these names are fictitious and any similarity to the names and addresses used by an actual business enterprise is entirely coincidental.

COPYRIGHT LICENSE:

This information contains sample application programs in source language, which illustrate programming techniques on various operating platforms. You may copy, modify, and distribute these sample programs in any form without payment to IBM, for the purposes of developing, using, marketing or distributing application programs conforming to the application programming interface for the operating platform for which the sample programs are written. These examples have not been thoroughly tested under all conditions. IBM, therefore, cannot guarantee or imply reliability, serviceability, or function of these programs.

Trademarks

The following terms are trademarks of the International Business Machines Corporation in the United States, other countries, or both:

Redbooks (logo) ®	IBM®	RequisitePro®
iSeries®	Lotus®	RUP®
AIX®	MQSeries®	Sametime®
AS/400®	ProjectConsole™	System i™
Build Forge®	Quickr™	System z™
ClearCase MultiSite®	Rational Suite®	Tivoli®
ClearCase®	Rational Unified Process®	Trigo®
ClearQuest®	Rational®	WebSphere®
DB2®	Redbooks®	Workplace™

The following terms are trademarks of other companies:

Ascential, are trademarks or registered trademarks of Ascential Software Corporation in the United States, other countries, or both.

Java, and all Java-based trademarks are trademarks of Sun Microsystems, Inc. in the United States, other countries, or both.

Microsoft, Visual Basic, Windows, and the Windows logo are trademarks of Microsoft Corporation in the United States, other countries, or both.

UNIX is a registered trademark of The Open Group in the United States and other countries.

Linux is a trademark of Linus Torvalds in the United States, other countries, or both.

Other company, product, or service names may be trademarks or service marks of others.

Preface

IBM® Rational® is the leading software development brand that supports Global Development and Delivery (GDD) (also known as Geographically or Globally Distributed Development). At Rational Bangalore, we not only practice GDD ourselves, but we also help our customers overcome their GDD challenges. This IBM Redbooks® publication presents our collective experiences with GDD: the common problems, the tailoring of Rational tools to solve the problems, and best practices and case studies.

This book is intended to help both new and experienced practitioners of GDD by addressing the pain points of GDD and providing solutions.

The team that wrote this book

This book was produced by a team of developers at the IBM Rational Lab in Bangalore, India.

Kamala Parvathanathan is an Engineering Manager at the IBM Rational India Lab. She has experience working with different multinationals, in various domains, such as databases, application servers, and desktop products. She has extensive experience in distributed development, including setting up a team and processes and collaborating with teams located in various geographies, such as the United States, the United Kingdom, and India. Kamala has a Master of Computer Science degree from Madurai University.

Anindya Chakrabarti is a Senior Software Engineer at the IBM Rational India Lab. He has worked on Rational Purifyplus development and has experience in Rational Application Developer (RAD). Anindya is currently working in the change management (CM) tools team for ClearQuest® development. He has also been involved in the implementation of the software configuration management (SCM) process for the team.

Priti P Patil is a Software Engineer for the IBM Rational India Lab. She has experience in software development in various domains such as Project/Portfolio Management and Interactive Voice Response Systems (IVR). Her areas of expertise include Rational Unified Process® (RUP®), XML databases, and service-oriented architecture (SOA). Priti holds a Master of Computer Science degree from the Indian Institute of Science (IISc) in Bangalore.

Sreerupa Sen is a Senior Software Engineer at the IBM Rational India Lab. She is an architect in the analysis, design, and construction group and is currently designing and developing components for IBM Rational Software Architect, the latest modeling tool offering from Rational. Sreerupa has worked in various geographies and practiced GDD for over ten years. She holds a Bachelor of Computer Science degree.

Neeraj Sharma is a Senior Software Engineer at the IBM Rational India Lab. His primary role is to manage quality engineering for the ADC suite of products, interfacing with customers around the globe, and helping them to use Rational tools. Neeraj holds a Bachelor of Electronics degree and a Master of Software Systems degree. He is also a certified software tester (CSTE), certified analyst (CSQA) and holds two file rated patents.

Yessong B Johng is an IBM Certified IT Specialist at the IBM International Technical Support Organization, Rochester Center. He started his IT career at IBM as an IBM S/38 Systems Engineer in 1982 and has worked with the S/38, AS/400®, iSeries®, and System i™ platform for 20 years. He writes extensively and develops and teaches IBM classes worldwide in the areas of IT optimization, covering such topics as Linux®, AIX®, and Microsoft® Windows® implementations on the IBM System i platform. His other areas of expertise include TCP/IP, networking security, high availability, and system area network (SAN).

We are especially grateful to the following people:

Pawan Rewari
Director, Rational India Lab

Lawrence J. (Jeff) Smith
RUP Method Architect and Author, IBM Software Group

We also thank the following people for their contributions to this project:

Brad T. Adams
David L. Brown
Manjeri Dharmarajan
Daniel Diebolt
Mark T. Duquette
Doug Fierro
Kathryn Fryer
Eric Funk
Ana M. Giordano
Celso Gonzalez
Mats Gothe
Kurian John
Sandeep Kohli
Amitava Kundu
Sharoon S. Kuriyala
Eric Larsen
Kevin Lee
Martin R. Levesque
Lu Li
Patrick Mancini
Manjari Mansingh
Brian Massey
Steven Milstein
Lynn Mueller
Sanjeev K. Nair
Khurram Nizami
Wendy Page
Catherine Radatus
Greg Rader
Balasubramani Radhakrishnan
Sharmila Ramesh
Cathy Reinhart
Aniruddha Roy
Anil Sarin
Murray Schwartz
Bikram Sengupta
Sefa Sevtekin
Farshad Shadpey

Ankur Sharma
Nansi Stretcher
Rajesh Thakkar
Malcolm D. Thomas
Daniel Toczala
Tanuj Vohra
Ueli Wahli
IBM Worldwide

Become a published author

Join us for a two- to six-week residency program! Help write an IBM Redbooks publication dealing with specific products or solutions, while getting hands-on experience with leading-edge technologies. You'll have the opportunity to team with IBM technical professionals, Business Partners, and clients.

Your efforts will help increase product acceptance and customer satisfaction. As a bonus, you will develop a network of contacts in IBM development labs, and increase your productivity and marketability.

Find out more about the residency program, browse the residency index, and apply online at:

ibm.com/redbooks/residencies.html

Comments welcome

Your comments are important to us!

We want our Redbooks to be as helpful as possible. Send us your comments about this book or other Redbooks in one of the following ways:

► Use the online **Contact us** review form at:

ibm.com/redbooks

► Send your comments in an e-mail to:

redbooks@us.ibm.com

► Mail your comments to:

IBM Corporation, International Technical Support Organization
Dept. HYTD Mail Station P099
2455 South Road
Poughkeepsie, NY 12601-5400

Foreword

After 20 years in the U.S., primarily in Silicon Valley, in July 2006, I moved to Bangalore, India, to run the IBM Rational India Lab. This Lab has been in India for 14 years. During that time, we have built strong technical and product leadership in the Lab. Now we have a team with significant combined experience in successful global development and delivery of software products. Over the past year, we have seen a steady flow of global customers who want to visit the India Lab and understand our experiences and practices in global software development. In parallel, IBM Rational has been changing its business model toward a much stronger solutions orientation, with one of the key solutions being Global Development and Delivery (GDD).

GDD is an area where we, in the Rational India Lab, have unique experiences to share with our customers. It presents us with an opportunity to start building business leadership in this Lab. Many of IBM Rational's global customers and partners now have significant teams in India. Most of the largest Global System Integrators (GSIs), including the Indian SIs, are IBM Rational customers. This is a great opportunity to learn from our customers. We can drive innovation in a customer-centric setting, and in turn, contribute our learned knowledge and innovations back to our customers and partners worldwide.

As a lab, we have embraced the GDD solution and decided to share our real-world experiences in this publication. While we have tried to make this book broadly applicable, it clearly reflects the experiences of its authors, all of whom are current employees of the IBM Rational India Lab. While this book focuses on software product development, many parts may be equally useful to services and outsourcing. It emphasizes the IBM Rational tools and solutions we use for GDD, although some of the guidance should be equally applicable to open source and other non-IBM products. Finally, while we have captured experiences across multiple IBM Labs in the U.S., Canada, U.K. (Hursley), China, and various labs in India, this book is primarily reflective of the unique experiences that we have had at the IBM Rational India Lab.

We invite our global customers to visit us so we can share and learn from each other. We also invite our local customers to leverage the geographical proximity of the IBM India Labs. Today the IBM India Software Lab is located in Bangalore, Hyderabad, New Delhi, Pune, and Mumbai, in addition to new locations to come.

We hope you find this book helpful and welcome your feedback.

Pawan Rewari
Director, IBM Rational India Lab
prewari@us.ibm.com

Part 1

Setting the stage

This part provides an overview of Global Development and Delivery (GDD), with a focus on jump-starting a GDD project. The following topics are discussed in this part:

► Introduction to GDD and discussion of related terms and concepts
► Transitioning products from one location to another
► A distributed development process from the Rational Unified Process (RUP) perspective

Introduction to Global Development and Delivery

The last two decades have witnessed a fundamental paradigm shift in the operation of the software development teams worldwide. Application development, maintenance, and management, which used to be concentrated at a single site, are now dispersed across the globe. Globalization has had a major impact on almost everything, from society to world economy to politics. In the world of business, it has become a means of survival.

Global Development and Delivery (GDD), which is also known as Geographically or Globally Distributed Development, comes with its own share of complexity. In order for GDD to deliver the desired value, it has to be done right. To be successful, organizations must treat GDD as an ongoing initiative with a focus on repeatability.

IBM has been one of the pioneers of GDD and is one of the early adapters and practitioners. IBM Software Group has used its collective experiences and expertise to build tools designed for GDD that help you produce high quality software while giving you the flexibility to leverage global teams to meet your business objectives.

At IBM India Software Lab (ISL), we have been practicing distributed development for years, building high quality large-scale software applications that collaborate across the globe. In this book, we bring IBM software tools and our GDD experiences together and discuss all aspects of GDD, and present our best practices, examples, and tips and techniques.

1.1 Document roadmap

This book has been divided into three parts:

- ► Part 1, "Setting the stage" on page 1 is more of an overview of GDD, with a focus on jump-starting a GDD project. This section consists of three chapters:

    - Chapter 1, "Introduction to Global Development and Delivery" on page 3, introduces GDD and discusses related terms and concepts, reference architectures, benefits, and pitfalls. If you have been practicing GDD for a while, you may want to just skim through this chapter. Pay particular attention to the scenario description, though. The scenario introduced in 1.7, "Scenario description" on page 17 is used in case study examples throughout the rest of the book.

    - Chapter 2, "Work transfer to subsite" on page 25, discusses the transitioning of development activities from one location to another. Many GDD projects start with transitioning work to a different location. This chapter discusses the challenges and process considerations during product transition.

    - Chapter 3, "GDD process guidance" on page 43, discusses the need for a unified process for GDD and how IBM Rational Unified Process (RUP) can be used for distributed development.

- ► Part 2, "Running the show" on page 57, takes you through the various phases of software development, with a strong focus on GDD. From requirements management to architecture management to change and release management, Part 2 covers it all for new product or feature development projects. For maintenance projects, Part 2 additionally discusses triaging of defects. Reporting and defect tracking are also discussed at length. Here is a more detailed breakdown of the chapters in this part:

    - Chapter 4, "Requirements analysis and design" on page 59, discusses requirements management and software design in a distributed development. If your team does either new product development or development of major enhancements to an existing product in a distributed fashion, then this chapter will be helpful for you. It describes GDD specific issues in requirements analysis and software design, and how to mitigate such issues. However, if your team is primarily responsible for maintenance and defect fixes, then you may want to quickly skim through or skip this chapter and move on to next chapter.

    - Chapter 5, "Change management and reporting" on page 83, focuses on how to do efficient change management and planning in order to fix defects or features in time, with optimum utilization of resources in geographically dispersed teams. This chapter is especially useful for program managers and project managers.

    - Chapter 6, "Software configuration management" on page 113, discusses software configuration management in distributed projects as well as how it can be integrated with defect tracking. This chapter is a must read for development tools administrators. Architects, developers, and build engineers will also find it useful and informative.

    - Chapter 7, "Build and deployment" on page 151, focuses on typical issues that distributed teams face with build and deployment. Build and release engineers will find this chapter useful. It will also be an interesting read for program managers, development tools administrators, and developers.

- Chapter 8, "Test management" on page 167, is about geographically distributed software quality management. This chapter discusses distributed test management. It talks about test tools, test reporting and tracking, and traceability in testing, with an emphasis on the distributed development aspects. Test managers, test engineers, and test architects will find this chapter useful. The management aspects of this chapter will also appeal to program and project managers.

► Part 3, "Connecting the dots" on page 179, discusses behind the scenes GDD requirements, especially some "soft" requirements. These requirements are spread across all phases of globally distributed software development, and are considered important enough to be discussed in a separate section of the book:

- Chapter 9, "Success factors for GDD" on page 181, takes a high-level look at some of the key success factors for GDD, such as global project management, collaboration across distributed sites, and global access to artifacts.

1.2 What is GDD

The term Global Development and Delivery describes almost any software development that involves teams that are spread across geographies and share workflows or deliverables. By development, we mean the entire software life cycle, including requirements analysis, design, implementation, testing, deployment, maintenance, and support.

For example, if a company builds software in San Jose, California, and tests it in Beijing, China, then it is doing distributed development. Similarly, a company may do requirements gathering and high-level architecture building in Ottawa, Canada, and then develop the software modules across several sites in Canada, India, and China. In this case, the software development for this company is also globally distributed. In another example, if a company in the United Kingdom contracts the maintenance of its mature products to a company in the United States, then it is also involved in GDD.

GDD is a natural choice for companies worldwide considering the following factors:

► The improvement in high bandwidth networks and global communications
► The availability of skilled engineers worldwide
► The drive to stay on top in a fiercely competitive business
► The necessity of globalization

It is important to keep in mind that collaboration in a team of engineers from different cultures, speaking different languages and working in different time zones is a highly challenging task. To be successful, a GDD venture requires effective communication, effective management skills, and most importantly, the right processes with the right set of collaborative tools.

1.3 Historical perspective

Distributed development started primarily with software organizations offshoring projects to contractors in regions where skilled labor was less expensive. A lack of skilled labor, the need for efficiency, and a variety of other reasons led software houses to open development centers around the world.

Gartner Dataquest forecasts the global application outsourcing market to be USD39 billion in 2005, growing at a five-year CAGR of 7.7%, to reach USD57 billion in 2010.[1]

---

[1] Gartner, Inc. "Gartner on Outsourcing, 2006-2007" by Lorrie Scardino et. al., December 19, 2006.

IBM, one of the pioneers of GDD, is an excellent example of a company that does successful distributed development across the globe. One of its GDD initiatives is its India operations, which showcases how an organization establishes its presence in a country or region and then gradually expands it into a major business center (Figure 1-1).

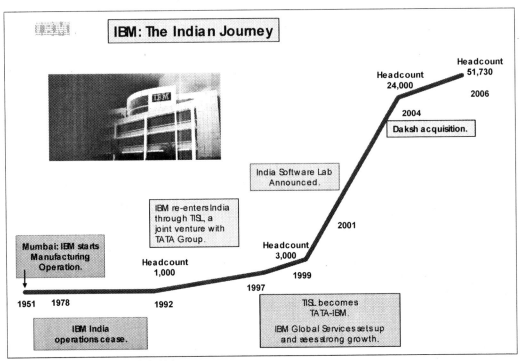

Figure 1-1   IBM India - a brief history

The history of IBM in India originally began as early as 1951 with manufacturing operations in Mumbai. India operations ceased in 1978, and the IBM South East Asian headquarters shifted its base to outside India.

IBM India operations restarted in 1992 as a joint venture with TATA, one of the most respected business houses in India. TATA Information Systems Limited (TISL) was launched, with IBM and TATA having a 50:50 stake in it. Starting its India operations as a partnership with TATA helped IBM gain its foothold in India.

In 1997, TISL became TATA IBM Ltd. At the same time, IBM Global Services were launched as an 80:20 joint venture between IBM Corporation and TATA.

In 1998, IBM Global Services achieved SEI CMM level 4 Certification. At the same time, the IBM India Solutions Research Center was launched in Delhi.

In 1999, IBM offered to buy out the stake from TATA, as per an IBM global directive. The TATA group divested its equities in the IBM companies in India and IBM India was launched as a fully owned subsidiary of IBM in India. This was followed by the establishment of IBM Software Labs in Bangalore in 2000.

Over the years, IBM has made acquisitions to add to its portfolio of software products. In many cases, these acquisitions have had an impact on IBM in India. The acquired companies have had captive or outsourced Indian operations, which had to be brought into the IBM fold. Two examples of this type of acquisition are Trigo® and Ascential™. In the case of Trigo, the India-based organization Symphony was building a captive unit for it in India. With the acquisition, its employees moved into IBM.

Thus, starting as a joint venture, the presence of IBM in India has progressed to the point that India is one of the key business centers for IBM. Primarily concentrated on services in its early years of operation in India, and then evolving to a strong focus on research and software development, IBM in India has gone from 1,000 employees to more than 50,000 in 15 years. The experiences and lessons learned over this period have been invaluable to IBM India in maturing its GDD capabilities.

1.4 Why GDD: The business factors

Cost containment, speed of execution, and gaining a competitive edge in the industry are some of the goals that drive software companies worldwide. To achieve expected results, companies need to look at a variable staffing model that provides a wide range of development skills, reduces costs, and ensures a global effectiveness. Many companies are focusing on GDD as a fundamental component of their IT strategy to accelerate their progress toward these results (Figure 1-2).

The explosive growth of the Internet and the infrastructure of IT have also played a major role in GDD. In today's networked world, collaboration has become much easier through real-time chats and Web conferences. Information sharing has improved with wikis and team rooms. Thanks to the Internet, people around the world have access to the same information at comparable speeds and at the same time, which has accelerated global communication.

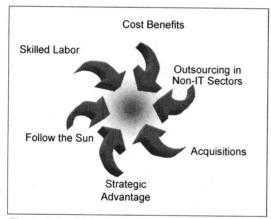

Figure 1-2   GDD accelerators

In the following subsections, we take a more detailed look at some of the factors behind GDD.

1.4.1 Cost benefits

One of the most commonly perceived benefits that popularized GDD among software companies is the reduction of IT costs associated with software development and maintenance.

The largest software-related expense for companies is the long-term maintenance of their applications in production. This includes the people, the infrastructure, and the tools required to keep the software current and operational. For example, 49% of enterprises and 29% of small-to-midsized businesses say that they run their applications for more than five years.[2]

---

[2] From "Saving Money from Outsourcing Beats Expertise", *Application Development Trends* Magazine, August 31, 2005

Global distribution of software development reduces such labor and infrastructure costs. Hiring across borders takes advantage of low labor rates in developing nations, even for the highly specialized skills that are required for software engineering.

However, the cost advantage only helps companies that are offshoring and outsourcing in a well-defined and planned way. Although cost benefits were one of the primary drivers behind GDD when it started, the drive toward GDD is increasingly focused on the strategic advantages that it provides rather than just the cost benefits.

The significant potential cost benefits offered by offshoring imply that software organizations can afford to improve and enhance their application portfolio rather than addressing only the most essential updates. This increases the ability of a software organization to compete in the market.

1.4.2 Skilled labor

Another important driver for GDD is to find the correct resources to staff a project. To meet the ever increasing demands of the software industry, companies must look outside of local labor pools. The demand for trained software professionals falls far short of the supply, especially in the developed world. Companies in the U.S. and worldwide are adding jobs and having a difficult time finding qualified professionals to fill them. According to the vice president of the IBM Academic Initiative, the supply of IT professionals is not keeping pace with demand. In one estimate of the future workforce gap, an additional 2.2 million people will be needed in IT-related professions by the year 2010.[3]

This situation makes it clear that countries that constitute the biggest markets and the biggest producers of software can no longer rely on local skilled labor to meet their needs. To execute their IT strategy, companies must equip themselves with the flexibility to source qualified personnel wherever they may be available in the world.

Also, resources with specialized technical skills are often scarce and difficult to allocate. Instead of hiring and training local people to fill the needs of a project, it is now possible to bring highly skilled and experienced resources onto a project without relocations. Using the right resources reduces training costs and improves productivity.

1.4.3 Follow the sun

To reduce the time to market, companies seek to accelerate the development process. If a company has development centers in different countries, at different time zones all around the world, then it is possible, at least theoretically, to work on a product around the clock. This creates a "virtual workday" where work is transferred from one development center to another at the beginning of their respective work days. The potential reduction in the development cycle makes GDD an attractive proposition.

1.4.4 Strategic advantage

Globalization has been one of the key accelerators in distributed development of software. With globalization, newer markets for software have opened up all over the world. Formerly low-cost geographies such as the BRIC countries are offering new markets for growth. Establishing strong development centers in such countries can accelerate the growth.

Localization of product offerings may be needed, and this may lead to a reengineering of the product. In some countries, government regulations mandate the setting up of such centers

---

[3] Career Resource Center: http://www.acm.org/careernews/issues/v1_i9.html#story_2

as well. When such centers are set up, software development was the next predictable step to be taken.

1.4.5 Mergers and acquisitions

In order to increase their market share and provide new technologies as early as possible, traditional firms acquired upcoming firms for specialized skills and competencies, to diversify product lines, or to complement existing offerings. This resulted in a flood of mergers and acquisitions through the 1990s, as new sites across the globe were added to a parent company.

Mergers and acquisitions have accelerated in recent years to all time highs. The global mergers for 2006 reached an all-time high of over USD3.8 trillion, topping the high set in the 2000 IT boom of USD3.332 trillion. This has resulted in mega multinational corporations.[4]

Today as well, mergers and acquisitions are a strategic initiative for many software companies.

1.4.6 Outsourcing in non IT sectors

Non-IT sectors have also contributed significantly to the spread of globalization. Sectors like banking, finance, and retail have set up IT centers all over the world. These service oriented sectors have huge older applications that require maintenance and occasional enhancements and re-engineering. Many companies in these sectors have outsourced most of their operations all around the world, while maintaining small in-house teams with project, product or application management, and coordination roles.

For example, finance and banking companies, such as Amex, Citibank, Deutsche Bank, and Merrill Lynch, and retail giants, such as Tesco and Target, have either opened IT centers in India or have outsourced to Indian IT companies.

1.5 Reference architectures

Software development is a complex process. Performing it in a distributed fashion increases the complexity manifold. That is why having a clear distribution rationale is vitally important for GDD to succeed.

GDD teams may have different types of topologies. There may be one central site with many satellite sites, or there may be sites operating quite independently. Teams may operate on a peer to peer fashion or a centralized control fashion. Distributed projects may be executed across the world in a phased fashion or in a 24x7 fashion.

The following sub-sections talk about various topologies in distributed projects. While these are not necessarily the only topologies, we have described those that occur most frequently in the software industry.

1.5.1 Organization-based models

Often times the development of a software product or application is distributed across companies or organizations. Outsourcing and insourcing are two terms related to such distribution.

---

[4] From Dealogic: http://www.boston.com/business/articles/2006/12/18/merger_boom_shows_no_sign_of_slowing

Outsourcing

Outsourcing refers to sharing organizational control with a different company, irrespective of where that company is located. Outsourcing may therefore be onsite, nearshore, or offshore. Offshore outsourcing in countries with lower labor costs, if done right, can provide the maximum cost benefits to a company. However, it is also the one that involves a lot of risks in terms of effective collaboration and management, quality of service, and security.

For example, if company A in San Jose, California, contracts out the development of the user interface for its product to company B in Bangalore, India, and the quality engineering of the overall product to company C in San Jose, California, then company A is outsourcing to companies B and C.

Insourcing

Insourcing refers to re-ownership of previously outsourced services done to regain control over critical products or competencies. It is also the practice of doing work in-house that would ordinarily have been contracted out.

For example, company A contracts out the development of its user interface to company B. The first prototypes of the UI are developed and fall short of customer expectations. Company A then decides to insource some of the critical UI components that need a lot of rework based on customer feedback.

1.5.2 Geography- or location-based staffing model

This section discusses the various ways in which a distributed project may be staffed across geographies.

Onsite

Onsite staffing may be internal or outsourced. Outsourced resources are provided through a contract with a service supplier that supplies supplemental resources or assumes responsibility for all or part of the software development life cycle.

For example, if company A in San Jose, California, contracts out the testing of its products to company B, who then performs the tests at company A's site, then that would be considered onsite outsourcing.

Nearshore

Nearshore refers to a satellite office usually in a neighboring country or in the same region. Geographic proximity reduces travel costs and communication is expected to be easier than in the offshore model.

For example, if a company in Raleigh, North Carolina, sets up an office in Toronto, Canada, to do technical support and quality engineering for its products in North America, then it is nearshoring some of its software development.

Offshore

In this model, a company may directly own facilities in a foreign country or region, in the form of a subsidiary or a joint partnership. Employees of the new center are termed *offshore resources*. Offshore staffing may be outsourced as well, through a low cost service supplier that assumes responsibility of all or part of the software development cycle.

Some companies also do "offshore outsourcing" on a project-by-project basis, to leverage the benefits of offshore development, without transferring any product ownership.

For example, if a company in Boston, Massachusetts, opens an office in Bangalore, India, and starts sharing the development of some features of its product with its Bangalore team, then it is offshoring some of its product development. If it contracts the maintenance of its product to a company in Bangalore, India, then it is doing offshore outsourcing.

1.5.3 Operational model

The operational model described in the following subsections discuss the various ways that GDD manifests itself in the software development domain. It can help you frame the architecture of your GDD initiatives using a common vocabulary.

Core site

A core site can be described as a physical location that is central to the business of the software organization. A core site serves as a data center for the organization and has a concentration of hardware and infrastructure resources.

A core site also has a concentration of software development resources, including stakeholders in the requirements management, development, test management, change management, and deployment processes.

Projects executed in the core site may involve development resources not only from that site but also from other sites.

Subsite

A subsite can be described as a physical location that plays a particular role in the execution of some portion of the business of the software organization. A subsite serves as a local data center for the organization and have hardware and infrastructure resources.

A subsite also has a concentration of software development resources.

Subsites work on projects in a collaborative fashion with other subsites or in conjunction with core sites. There may be contractual agreements between these sites if they are in different business organizations or companies. Projects only use local development resources, who collaborate with development resources at other locations. For example, a subsite may work on delivering a new component for the core product.

Subsites need to communicate development and business metrics to senior management located at the core site.

A subsite may be *trusted* or *untrusted*. A trusted subsite is within the corporate network. An untrusted subsite is outside of the corporate network. Users from an untrusted subsite have restricted access to corporate IT assets.

Independent site

An independent site can be described as a physical location that is central to some portion of the business of the software organization. Independent sites serve as a local data center for the organization and have hardware and infrastructure resources.

An independent site also has a concentration of software development resources.

Independent sites work on localized projects that are intended to support the local site. They do not contribute to core site projects.

Projects only use local development resources. Independent sites need to communicate development and business metrics to senior management located at the core site.

An independent site may be *trusted* or *untrusted*. A trusted independent site is within the corporate network. An untrusted independent site is outside of the corporate network. Users from an untrusted independent site have restricted access to the corporate IT assets.

Remote site

A remote site is as a collection of single users, at a variety of physical locations, which play specific roles in the execution of some portion of the business of the software organization. A small team collocated at an offshore location could be thought of as a collection of remote sites. What characterizes remote sites is the lack of server infrastructure and a lack of infrastructure for the storage of software development assets. Remote sites usually have minimal hardware and infrastructure resources, personal workstations and network connections to core/independent/subsites, with limited or no server hardware.

A remote site also has a concentration of software development resources.

Software development resources at remote sites collaborate with development resources at other locations. No projects are done completely at such sites. Users at these sites perform specific system development tasks or phases of a project. There is a kind of contractual or business arrangement with these sites. Remote sites need to communicate development and business metrics to senior management located at the core site.

A remote site may be *trusted* or *untrusted*. Users from a trusted remote site have accounts within the corporate domain and use the corporate network. Users from an untrusted remote site do not have accounts within the corporate domain and may or may not use the corporate network. They are not trusted with unrestricted access to the corporate IT assets.

1.5.4 Team topologies

Most GDD efforts start with the centrally controlled development model. In this model, the core site plays the most crucial role. It is responsible for all deliverables and the overall project schedule. It controls the initial phases of software development, analyzing requirements and creating the high level design. The low level design and implementation phases are then distributed between the core site and other sites. A program manager at the core site tracks the schedules and deliverables. Integration and system testing are done at the core site.

In this model, other sites are integrated tightly into the development teams at the core site and extend the core site in the form of virtual teams. The core site may also contract out well defined pieces of work to the other sites. Work done is tracked and monitored closely by the core site. Teams are tightly coupled, and managed by the core site. Work distribution is usually fine-grained.

As organizations mature in their GDD practice, and become more comfortable with collaborations across distributed teams, the core site may start delegating more responsibilities to the other sites. Stakeholders from different sites may start participating as early as in the requirements analysis phase, though the overall responsibility of project deployment and delivery may still be with the core site. Teams are more loosely coupled, working closely in the early phases of development, and then more independently, with well-defined points of integration. There is still a substantial amount of collaboration across sites, in the form of design and code reviews, integration testing, and status meetings, but each team manages its own modules on the whole.

1.6 Risks to consider

Many of the risks associated with adopting GDD come from people-related issues, such as management, collaboration, communication, and cultural differences. Security, sharing of knowledge, and protection of intellectual property are among the biggest technological challenges. This section discusses some of the potential pitfalls that organizations must watch for when doing distributed development (Figure 1-3).

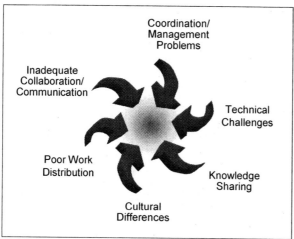

Figure 1-3   GDD risks

1.6.1 Coordination and management problems

In any GDD project, coordination is one of the biggest challenges. The different sites involved in a distributed project have different management hierarchies, with functional managers across sites.

Unless there is continuous collaboration and cooperation at all management levels in the organization, teams can run into a lot of problems in such situations.

► Resources may be unsure of their work priorities unless they have been dedicated for a specific GDD project. Dedicated involvement in a project is the recommended option for GDD, since it is difficult to coordinate with shared resources in distributed projects. If dedicated involvement does not work, then time and effort allocation for multiple projects must be clearly defined and abided by. Managers from the collaborating sites should jointly review and decide on the division of work at the outset of the project, and review it periodically.

► Resources may be unwilling or apprehensive of taking functional direction from a manager they have not met or to whom they do not report.

► Managers may find it easier to rely on local employees whose working styles they are familiar with, and who they see everyday, rather than on team members in remote offices with whom they are not familiar. This may result in role allocations and work distribution that are deemed unfavorable by remote team members.

► Participation in local projects gains more visibility locally, and may be more attractive, so resources may be more interested in such projects.

► Working on GDD projects means working on a global schedule. Apart from the day job, a member of a distributed team is expected to participate in status meetings, teleconferences, and so on, beyond office hours. This can make the prospect of working on a distributed project an unattractive one.

- Tracking the work done by a team member from a different geography is more difficult, especially if the time zones are wide apart, and common status meetings are few and far between.

- There are often some ownership issues at different sites with managers wanting their teams to work on higher visibility or technically more interesting modules, to keep the team motivated. Unless handled with sensitivity, this may lead to cross team interaction and collaboration issues.

- Accountability issues are also more common in distributed projects than collocated ones. In a distributed environment, organizations may sometimes spend a lot of time on product development, without accomplishing business objectives. Often there is not clear responsibility or accountability for project milestones and groups may spend time and effort on unproductive tasks.

1.6.2 Inadequate collaboration

Teams from different sites may not always collaborate well. Often times, there are work ownership issues, where some of the stakeholders have not accepted the idea of distributed development and are not willing to collaborate with other teams.

Getting the right information to the right people is a challenge sometimes as well. Often developers receive a lot of information from remote sites, most of which is redundant from their perspective. As a result they soon start ignoring such messages, thereby running the risk of missing pertinent information as well.

Inadequate collaboration can pose serious challenges to a distributed project, in terms of unexpected rework, mismatched processes, and poor project synchronization and team dynamics.

Unexpected rework

Teams may have to rework on product components if:

- Teams have not understood the requirements correctly.

- There were mistakes in the work transfer.

- Common interfaces were not designed correctly, leading to poor integration of software developed by distributed teams.

Project schedules may not have sufficient slack to accommodate such delays, ultimately increasing costs for a project.

Mismatched or misunderstood processes

Another source of friction and confusion is attempting to have software organizations using different processes for software development to collaborate and communicate. For example, one team may follow a waterfall model, while another team pursues iterative development. They use the same terminology, but have a different understanding of the terms used, leading to confusion and delays in project execution, and often decreasing the quality of the developed software.

Roles and responsibilities may not be clearly defined or understood. For example, the core team may not have a dedicated test organization and may rely on rigorous developer testing instead. The remote team may assume that dedicated test engineers will do rigorous testing of the product and consequently carry out only limited unit testing, which reduces product quality. When GDD teams have a clear understanding of each others' roles and responsibilities, gaps like this can be avoided.

Poor project synchronization/team dynamics

Collocated teams have the advantage of being able to communicate constantly, formally or informally. Such communication, for example, chats by the coffee machine, at lunch, during chance meetings in the hallway, and so on, play an important role in project synchronization. Design decisions are made and project status is discussed. Such discussions help in familiarizing individuals with the working styles of others, and often reduce the time in problem solving and defect fixing as well.

Informal communication also goes a long way in improving team dynamics. Team outings, lunches, chats across cubicle walls, and so on, all build a rapport among team members, that has a positive influence on collaboration and team synergy. In remote teams, where the members are sometimes hard pressed to even put faces to names, this sort of social networking is much harder to build. As a result of this, remote co-workers are often perceived as less helpful than local ones.

1.6.3 Poor distribution of work and responsibilities

Poor planning is a risk that all projects face. To make a distributed project successful, work distribution must be planned carefully at the inception of a project phase. Distribution is based on the following factors:

- ► Teams should have the right set of skills and maturity to take on the allocated work.

- ► The right sets of people should be collocated. As an organization's experience with and expertise in GDD increases, its success with virtualized teams increases as well. But organizations at a lower maturity level may need to collocate teams with tightly coupled project responsibilities.

- ► Lack of challenging work, poor visibility to management, poorly defined career growth path, and so on may lead to retention issues in non-core sites. This should be taken into account while planning the responsibilities and roles across sites.

1.6.4 Cultural differences

Cultural differences between geographically distributed teams may further widen the communication gap. The primary spoken language may vary from one site to the other and even words in a common language such as English often have subtle differences in meaning from one country or region to another.

Cultural differences may run much deeper than linguistic differences. A person who is considered a go-getter in their own geography may be perceived as aggressive in a different culture. In some cultures, people are more open and freely speak their minds, while in a different culture it may be considered impolite to openly disagree with anybody. People from different geographies do not share the same sense of humor either. A joke at one site may be an insult at another. Even working styles of team members may be culture dependent. Distributed teams that are divided by culture may therefore not be as cohesive as local ones, and this may lead to less trust, poor cooperation, and ultimately, conflicts.

Corporate cultures followed at various sites may be quite different as well. Some offices follow a hierarchical management structure with its associated protocols, while others may have relatively flat organizational structures. This can create confusion during team collaborations.

1.6.5 Knowledge sharing

Sharing of knowledge is more difficult and less effective in a distributed project than in a local one, due to reduced collaboration and reduced informal discussions, as seen in the earlier sub sections. Added to that are lack of formal project documentation, and lack of well-defined processes in transitioning a product, or in the joint ownership of a product.

1.6.6 Technical challenges

A company's enterprise architecture and supporting infrastructure have a strong correlation to their capability and flexibility in GDD. Geographically distributed software projects can be severely impacted by poor technical infrastructure.

Remote teams often need to share or exchange large data volumes, in the form of source code, documents, binaries, and so on. Poor bandwidth and network problems in these cases mean that effective collaboration is impossible.

In a distributed environment, shared source code needs to be managed across distributed teams with rapid propagation of changes. The effectiveness and efficiency of this process would depend on how well the repositories are configured, how well they can synchronize, and so on. Defect tracking and updates across sites are also less efficient if replication across sites is slow.

Tools that work well in a single-site scenario may not scale well for distributed development. They may not support remote access or global workflows or may not integrate well with other tools used across the organization. They may not scale to the expectations and requirements of 24x7 availability or to the size of the team or the size of the interconnected projects in the enterprise.

Finally, there are security challenges. Often times organizations outsource work, and the contracting company needs to have well-defined access permissions to the source repositories, requirements, project documents, and defect and test management systems. If access rights are not in place, security and confidentiality issues may result in a negative and lasting impact on the organization that is sponsoring the GDD project.

1.6.7 Other challenges

The success of a distributed development project also depends on such factors as predictability of software delivery, sustainability of the developed software, process metrics, and so on.

Predictability
In a GDD environment, aggressively selecting different strategies/vendors can drastically affect the predictability of delivering software on time and to budget.

Sustainability
Any development that has the potential to be outsourced must be done using predefined standards through processes, controls, and tools. Otherwise, the future development of existing applications may be severely compromised. For example, poorly designed/documented software can be expensive and in some cases impossible to offshore/outsource.

Lack of processes and metrics
For a distributed project to be successful, there should be uniform processes and metrics implemented across all sites that can proactively assess and measure performance.

1.7 Scenario description

In this book, we discuss GDD in the context of ITSO Inc., a fictitious software company creating software for the retail sector.

This section lays the groundwork for the rest of the chapters, by introducing ITSO Inc. and its distributed teams, and the division of work and roles across the organization. In the rest of the chapters, we explain how ITSO Inc. does product transitioning, requirements analysis, design, development, testing and deployment, how it maintains existing applications, and how it performs portfolio and people management.

ITSO Inc.'s distributed development scenarios are based on our collective experiences in GDD. ITSO Inc.'s usage of our tools to effectively practice GDD is based on our collective experiences in using our tools in a distributed environment.

1.7.1 ITSO Inc. products

ITSO Inc. has been in business for approximately five years. Its targeted customer base consists of small and medium retailers.

ITSO Inc. has a suite of products for the retail sector. The *ITSO Inc. Retail Cash Console* and the *ITSO Inc. Retail Manager* are the most successful of the company's products.

► ITSO Inc. Retail Cash Console is a typical cash console used in retail stores.
► ITSO Inc. Retail Manager is a warehouse for retailer specific information.

Figure 1-4 shows some of the products and product components that are of interest to us in this book.

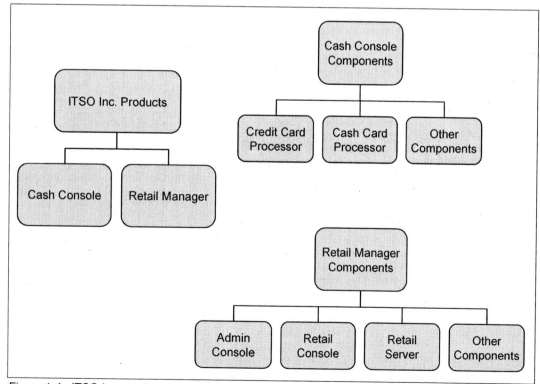

Figure 1-4   ITSO Inc. products

ITSO Inc. Retail Cash Console and ITSO Inc. Retail Manager are at Version 5.0.

1.7.2 Distributed development for ITSO Inc.

ITSO Inc. started with a team of 20 people in Santa Clara, California, and grew to have a medium sized software development team of about a 100 people in 2005.

A year ago, ITSO Inc. decided to expand its development and testing teams.

Key factors considered during ITSO Inc.'s expansion

The key factors that ITSO Inc. considered during its expansion are as follows:

► ITSO Inc. wanted to double its current size. It wanted qualified software professionals who could ramp up quickly, but without going through a long interview process for each candidate they hired.

► ITSO Inc. wanted to establish its presence in emerging markets such as India and China.

► ITSO Inc. did not want to double its expenditure while doubling its size.

► ITSO Inc. wanted to increase its business revenue in Europe.

ITSO Inc. wanted to gradually transition the older products and components to its expanded teams, while the core team concentrated on new products and features.

ITSO Inc. in India and China

In keeping with its business and technical considerations, ITSO Inc. decided to first expand in India and China.

In late 2005, ITSO Inc. acquired a medium size software company of around 100 people in Bangalore, India, to augment development resources.

Around the same time, they also opened a center in Beijing, the People's Republic of China. The China lab has about 20 people and is an extension to ITSO Inc.'s test team in Santa Clara.

ITSO Inc.'s Bangalore operations started with the transitioning of some components of its products. Now ITSO Inc. Santa Clara also shares some new product development with ITSO Inc. Bangalore. ITSO Inc. Bangalore has set up a small satellite office in Gurgaon, India, to manage the inflow of work.

ITSO Inc.'s operations in Ireland

Recently, ITSO Inc. has decided to outsource translations, translation verification testing, and product support for the European market to a company called YBJ Consulting, based out of Dublin, Ireland.

ITSO Inc. teams

Figure 1-5 shows the locations of the sites. In our scenario, the ITSO Inc. office in Santa Clara, U.S., is the core site. The company has outsourced and offshored translation and globalization testing, as well as translation of the product, to YBJ, in Dublin, Ireland. YBJ is an untrusted subsite for ITSO Inc.

ITSO Inc. in Bangalore, India, and ITSO Inc. in Beijing, the People's Republic of China, are both trusted subsites for ITSO Inc. in the U.S. The U.S. location of ITSO Inc. offshores development and testing work to these sites. ITSO Inc. Gurgaon is a trusted remote site.

Project execution is done across all sites of ITSO Inc. Although the bulk of program management and business analysis is performed at the core site in Santa Clara, both the Bangalore and Beijing sites participate in architecture, design, and implementation. Similarly, the Beijing site executes system tests independently.

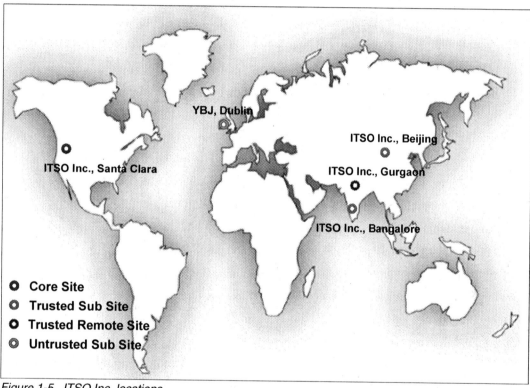

Figure 1-5   ITSO Inc. locations

Cross-team collaboration

Figure 1-6 illustrates how each site collaborates with each other. The ITSO Inc. Santa Clara team needs to help the other teams in Beijing, Bangalore, and Dublin to understand the product, be it requirements, architecture decisions, models, code changes, test cases, and so on. The collaboration will be across time zones and may be complicated by language barriers.

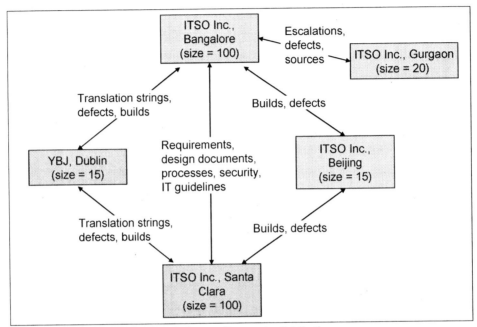

Figure 1-6   ITSO Inc. site descriptions, with people distribution

ITSO Inc. development teams

ITSO Inc. Santa Clara and ITSO Inc. Bangalore need to:

► Share and modify common artifacts, such as requirements, models, source code, and so on.

► Ensure a common understanding of the requirements and architecture.

► Make sure that changes to shared sources are controlled.

ITSO Inc. test teams

ITSO Inc. Santa Clara and ITSO Inc. Beijing need to collaborate:

► With the distributed development teams to make sure that all defects get resolved.

► With each other to make sure that all components get tested and that duplicate defects do not get filed.

ITSO Inc. and YBJ

For security reasons, ITSO Inc. wants to provide YBJ access to only what they need for translation:

► The translation strings and translation test cases for the existing/new release

► Builds for the next release to enable the execution of the translation and globalization tests

► Builds for the current release to help them provide technical support

► Restricted access to the defect management system so that they can log defects for technical issues that they find during support, and track such defects, but not see information about the other defects in the system

Roles and responsibilities across sites

This section gives the outline of the roles and responsibilities of each site.

Responsibilities

Table 1-1 describes the responsibilities across distributed sites for ITSO Inc.

Table 1-1   Responsibilities of each site

ITSO Inc., Santa Clara, U.S.	ITSO Inc., Bangalore/Gurgaon, India	ITSO Inc., Beijing, the People's Republic of China	YBJ, Dublin, Ireland
► Overall project delivery ► Requirements management ► Overall solution architecture ► Architecture, code, and unit/function test for all components developed in the U.S. ► Builds ► Solution deployment ► Defining common development processes across ITSO Inc. sites ► Security policies, access rights, IT guidelines for all ITSO Inc. assets/sites	► Development management for site contributions ► Requirements management for localized enhancements ► Application maintenance ► Enhancements to current product ► Architecture, code, and unit test for all components developed in Bangalore ► Any local IT guidelines in addition to those defined by ITSO Inc. Santa Clara	► Component testing for all components developed out of Bangalore ► System, regression, and integration testing	► Translation and globalization testing for all components ► Translation for all UI screens and messages that the customer sees ► Security policies, access rights, and IT guidelines for YBJ

Roles

Table 1-2 describes the roles across distributed sites for ITSO Inc.

Table 1-2   Roles of each site

ITSO Inc., Santa Clara, U.S.	ITSO Inc., Bangalore/Gurgaon, India	ITSO Inc., Beijing, the People's Republic of China	YBJ, Dublin, Ireland
► Program manager ► Project manager ► Business analyst ► Systems analyst/architect ► Developer ► Test architect ► Test engineer ► Release/build engineer ► Enterprise/security architect ► IT administrator ► Development tools administrator	► Project manager ► Business analyst (for India market) ► Systems analyst/architect ► Developer ► IT administrator ► Development tools administrator	► Project manager ► Test manager ► Test architect ► Test engineer	► Translator ► Test manager ► Test engineer ► Customer support manager ► Customer support engineer

1.8 A comprehensive list of tools described in this book

IBM Rational provides a software delivery platform that is well suited to distributed development. In each of the chapters in Part 2, "Running the show" on page 57 and Part 3, "Connecting the dots" on page 179, we have discussed the appropriate Rational tool, with emphasis on how it can help distributed teams.

In this section, we give you a brief overview of the recommended tools, that is, a kind of summary list of tool recommendations for the entire life cycle of your project. These tools integrate well with each other, providing solutions for a distributed development environment, that takes care of the development process all the way from requirements analysis to product deployment.

Figure 1-7 gives a quick view of the tools that we describe throughout this book and use in our case study example.

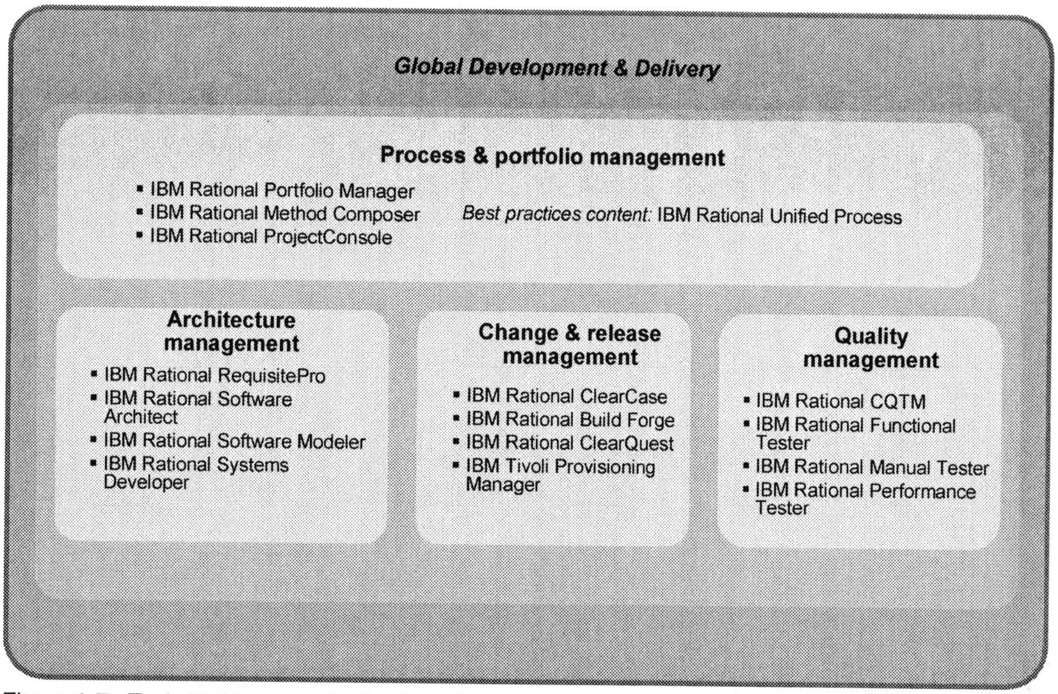

Figure 1-7 Tools that help you in distributed development

You can learn more about the tools shown in Figure 1-7 in the following chapters:

► Chapter 3, "GDD process guidance" on page 43 discusses how *IBM Rational Unified Process/IBM Rational Method Composer* can be tailored for distributed development.

► In Chapter 4, "Requirements analysis and design" on page 59, for requirements analysis, we have used *IBM Rational RequisitePro®*.

► *IBM Rational Software Modeler/IBM Rational Software Architect* is our design tool of choice in Chapter 4, "Requirements analysis and design" on page 59.

► We have used *IBM Rational ClearQuest* for triaging and defect tracking in Chapter 5, "Change management and reporting" on page 83.

► We have implemented software configuration management using *IBM Rational ClearCase®* in Chapter 6, "Software configuration management" on page 113.

► In Chapter 7, "Build and deployment" on page 151, we have discussed a build strategy using *IBM Rational Build Forge®, IBM Rational ClearCase, IBM Tivoli® Provisioning Manager*, and *IBM Rational ClearQuest*.

► In Chapter 8, "Test management" on page 167, we have discussed several test tools, such as *IBM Rational ClearQuest Test Manager, IBM Rational Functional Tester, IBM Rational Manual Tester*, and *IBM Rational Performance Tester. IBM Rational ProjectConsole™* provides the quality dashboard.

► For project and portfolio management in Chapter 9, "Success factors for GDD" on page 181, our tool of choice is *IBM Rational Portfolio Manager* along with *IBM Rational ProjectConsole*.

Work transfer to subsite

GDD is initiated with the transfer of a particular discipline in the life cycle of an existing product or a component, except perhaps in the case of mergers and acquisitions. There are several inhibitors in the initial projects done in a GDD model, such as rework, productivity loss, project management overhead, and so on. The impact of these factors can only be addressed with effective work transfer.

In this chapter, we discuss the planning, deployment, success criteria, and the best practices to contain risks and make an effective transfer of responsibilities from one geographical location to another. We approach it in phases:

► Initiation: The business case and definition of the viability and scope of the transfer

► Preparation: Assessment of the capabilities needed for the transfer

► Implementation: The specifics of the transfer and the best practices to be followed

► Execution: Post transfer development

2.1 Introduction to work transfer

As discussed in Chapter 1, "Introduction to Global Development and Delivery" on page 3, organizations may choose to adopt a GDD model due to various motivations. Whether it is a tightly controlled subsites model or completely independent peer site model, successful transfer of responsibilities from one site to another is one of the crucial challenges most development organizations face.

Depending on the complexity of the product, transfer in itself can be a major challenge. In our experience, on one end of the spectrum, there have been transitions that involved a two member team of products that are nearing end of life, to the other end of the spectrum, where we have had transitions of strategically important products that included various life cycle disciplines such as development, testing, and project management with several hundred members.

Whatever the complexity, following well defined methods to do the transfer controls the risks. In this chapter, we discuss the implementation strategies, best practices, and recommendations.

One could say that the success of the transfers and the continued effective management of the transferred projects to some extent reflect the GDD maturity of the product development organization.

Certain topics, such as the hiring and setting up processes that we discuss here, are applicable for cases where a subsite is being setup for the first time, perhaps without a transfer involved.

2.2 Initiation phase

The objective of this phase is to establish the opportunity for change in terms of a high level business proposition and agree on the viability, scope, and value of such an initiative. This section talks about the important factors to be considered to do a detailed assessment of the particular product, component, or discipline for GDD.

2.2.1 Scope assessment

While the general benefits of GDD may be apparent, it is crucial to take a look at how worthwhile and amenable a particular project is for distributed development and how well the general benefits are applicable to the particular case. Some of the factors to be assessed are:

► Viability: One of the first questions that has to be answered is if it is viable to transfer or initiate the specific responsibility to a remote location. With the flattening of the globe and with development being distributed all over the globe, viability seems to be the least of the problems associated with work transfer. Yet the location of choice might cause potential issues.

– Does the setup require special domain expertise or specific talent that is hard to find at the target location that has been scoped out? Even if the target location is not identified, are there any specific requirements in terms of resources that would prevent the responsibilities being carried out effectively from any other location other than the current one?

– Are there any export restrictions or security or legal concerns that would prevent exposure of certain assets crucial to the responsibility that is being considered?

- ► Return of Investment: Cost comes up repeatedly as the most crucial factor for the GDD setup and transition. However, the process of transition in itself·adds cost and has a potential impact on immediate deliverables. It takes time for the target location to start performing at the same level as the source location. Thus, it is important to understand the return of investment to determine whether the transfer is worthwhile.

  - – Is this the right time to do it? For example, is the risk of a delayed release due to the transition considerable?

  - – Is there potential for the target location to not just deliver this particular project, but also enhance and add to the responsibilities it has taken up? If not, the ROI may turn out to be short term.

  - – Is there a way to exploit the modularity of the product or divide the distribution based on the life cycle? If possible, this would reduce the overhead on day to day communication.

  - – Are there any other climate issues? For example, rampant piracy, lack of data security, unclear IP laws, and so on that may need more attention and investment.

- ► Strategic Importance: Again, apart from cost, there are also long term benefits to be considered. In the near term, transitions incur more cost with respect to visits for relationship building, process reorganization, and investment on tools that support GDD. Without strategic importance and an eye on the long term, the transition may have more pains than gains depending on the complexity of the product being transitioned. Some relevant factors are:

  - – Transitioning a product to free up the resources to concentrate on the next generation of the product.

  - – Transferring a product to a location where the growing market is.

  - – A key partner is in the target region.

  - – Availability of right skills and domain expertise. For example, if the target location has a strong testing competency, it may make sense to move testing discipline to the target location. In some locations, there is an inadequate skilled labor supply that falls short of demand, and it makes sense in the long term to distribute work.

Expected results

At the end of the assessment, an agreement among the executive management stakeholders to go ahead with the transition is expected. A business proposal with the expected ROI that would be refined after the elaboration should be started. The proposal should include location of choice, viability, assessment of risks, expected time for transfer, and estimated or expected ROI.

Case study

In the case study sections of this chapter, we follow a work transfer that was done in ITSO Inc. that was introduced in 1.7, "Scenario description" on page 17.

ITSO Inc. Cash Console component is not only a top product, but is also one of the earliest products of the company. Lately, the company has been considering rearchitecting the product to address some of the performance issues and to support Web-based cash console operations. To be able to do this without multiplied costs, ITSO Inc. decided to look into distributing the work.

The responsibility of the maintenance release of ITSO Inc. Cash Console that was developed in Santa Clara, U.S. was to be transitioned to Bangalore, India and the Systems Verification Testing (SVT) of the same to Beijing, China. There were no legal restrictions for the transfer.

Specific skill sets were required but were considered to be predominantly available and at strong competency levels in the target locations.

While cost benefits were definitely a consideration, in this case there were also a few other factors. The target locations had already established credibility and demonstrated success with similar responsibilities with a comparable product. The Bangalore team was working on certain modules of the new development, for example. The trust that was built by the initial forays enabled the locations to contemplate the next steps. Apart from this, the GSIs in India were emerging as a potential influence in the market for the retail product that was being developed. An engineering team in the same location could tap into potential benefits, such as customer engagements, testing scenarios, and so on.

ITSO Inc. development center in China had a strong testing competency and had great potential for hiring skilled test engineers.

By moving the maintenance responsibility to India and testing to China, ITSO Inc. hoped to cut down on costs and reuse the investment on the enhancements for the new release.

Specific goals
► Must deliver ITSO Inc. Cash Console 5.3 in Q2.
► Must increase investment in ITSO Inc. Cash Console Perf.
► Must Deliver ITSO Inc. Cash Console Perf by Q4.
► Must keep overall development investment relatively flat.

Recommendation
► Transition ITSO Inc. Cash Console development work to India and SVT to China.

► Begin to staff and transition the appropriate ITSO Inc. Cash Console resources to ITSO Inc. Cash Console Perf over the course of Q1/Q2.

Planned investment profile
Table 2-1 shows a planned investment profile for each project. The reduction in investment for Cash Console by the end of the transition is to meet the goal of overall flat investment.

Table 2-1 Planned investment profile in USD1000

Project	2006	2007
ITSO Inc. Cash Console	$7000	$2500
ITSO Inc. Cash Console Perf	$500	$5000

2.2.2 Success criteria

Before delving into the next steps, first we have to define the success criteria for the transfer. Some of the general factors to be considered are:

► Preserve the quality of the development processes and thus the quality of the product itself.

► Establish effective communication channel with all the key stakeholders, such as release management, customer support, product management, and so on, by the time of transfer completion.

► Ability of target site to be able to enhance product/process in the long term, after successful initial deliverables.

Apart from general considerations as mentioned previously, the product-specific detailed goals must be spelled out.

Clearly the success criteria can be achieved only by an effective knowledge and asset transfer and on how well the target team is set up and grown.

Expected results

A top priority is that the goals that are hoped to be achieved after transition should be clearly understood and defined. In essence, these goals define the success of the transfer.

Case study

In our sample scenario, the success criteria were:

- Staffing and beginning knowledge transfer to India and China teams by Q1
- Delivery of Cash Console V5.2 as a combined effort of U.S., India and China teams by Q2 with no P1 or P2 defects
- Ability of India development center to build and deliver any supported version of Cash Console by Q3
- Ability of India development to enhance and innovate with respect to product features and deliver Version 5.3 by Q4
- Ability of the China team to execute already defined tests and evolve new tests, enhance test harness and automate tests, and test Version 5.3 independently by Q3
- Ability of the China team and India team to engage with stakeholders such as product management, customer support, and sales by Q3
- Ability of the Santa Clara team to move fully on to Cash Console Perf by Q3

2.2.3 Leadership skills

While dynamic leadership is important for any product development organization, it becomes a particularly crucial factor due to the difficulties and challenges GDD brings. Proportional to the complexity of the discipline in transition, a strong leader is a must for its success. While general traits such as excellent project management experience, domain knowledge, and so on are a good starting point, there are also several other needed traits, such as:

- Established trust with the core site or at least the key stakeholders in the core site.
- Experience in working across geographies with excellent collaboration and communication skills.
- Understanding of the business goals and the ability to impart them to the remote site.
- Ability to be a long term leader for the project being transitioned or at least shepherd the team through the first few releases. This is especially crucial when most of the disciplines of a product are transferred along with the accountability.
- Understanding and, if possible, experience in both geographies. Understanding of the local difficulties is important in estimation.
- Ability to bridge team issues effectively.

In the case of smaller components where it does not warrant a senior level leader, it could be addressed with a liaison or a point of contact in charge of the training and transfer.

In cases where the locations are quite apart in terms of culture, there may be a tendency to choose someone with similar background. But it is much more important to choose a leader with proven management and collaboration skills. Culture clash is only one of the risk factors, but can be learned if other leadership skills are strong and mature.

Expected results

Identification of the project leader as early as possible. Establishment of the project leader's goals aligned with the success criteria of the product transfer.

Case study

In the sample scenario, a leader was identified early on. Jay had experiences in working in Santa Clara and had an understanding of the target location difficulties. He had domain expertise and a proven record of managing similar project and working on distributed development. He took up an international assignment and relocated to Bangalore, India for a time period that would span various phases.

Yao, the leader chosen for testing project in China development center, had experience of working extensively in the U.S. and the U.K and was known for his project management skills and domain knowledge.

John's mandate for the year was set clearly. As the Santa Clara team's lead, it was his responsibility to make sure the two transfers succeeded. It was also his responsibility to make sure the existing resources moved on to the new project.

2.3 Preparation phase

When there is a business case for the transfer, it is time to assess the distributed development readiness of the processes, tools, and people, and analyze and estimate the work involved. Based on this assessment, the business case is refined and a clearer project schedule can be achieved. While the primary business need is reduced cost, improper assessment and underestimation of the overhead could result in limited or no cost savings and in the worst case more expenses.

2.3.1 Processes definition

Extensive verbal communication may have compensated for risky and costly *ad hoc* processes in a single site localized development. But the problems get exacerbated as soon the complexity of GDD comes into picture.

Standard, repeatable, and well documented processes are a major asset to any transition. Lack of such processes affects the effectiveness of the transition and severely handicaps the target location's ability to set up and start contributing. In many real case examples, target locations end up spending time in reinventing standard procedures due to lack of adaptable processes in the source location or due to inefficient transfer.

By the end of the assessment, recommendations based on the gaps found should be made. For example, a better level of communication model may have to be achieved. It might also be worthwhile to roll out Rational Unified Process (RUP) across the board with an eye for the long term benefits. Chapter 3, "GDD process guidance" on page 43 describes the benefits of RUP and touches upon the excellent resilience of RUP in a GDD environment. However, any such process change done simultaneously while transitioning to a GDD model would have to be planned carefully since it would introduce risks.

Some points to analyze include:

► Is there a standard iterative development model with milestones?

► Build management is a predominantly weak area that works even with informal processes in a single site but could cause innumerable delays in a distributed scenario. Is there a clear build process?

- Are there well defined workflows for change management? Are the roles and activities clearly defined as to who assigns the change requests? How is its source controlled? How is it deployed?

- Are there good processes to convey requirements?

- Are the release cycles and patch deployment well understood?

- What is the status of the backlog of defects? Are there any customer commitments with respect to them?

- What are the disciplines that are going to be distributed, for example, where is product management going to be located, and where will documentation be?

- How much of the workflows are automated? Heavily manual processes are risky in distributed teams.

- Is there good induction material for new members?

After analyzing various processes and auditing to make sure the processes are indeed being practiced, we would get a clear idea of the bottlenecks and an understanding of which processes have to be analyzed in-depth with respect to the development disciplines and associated responsibilities being transitioned.

Expected results

After this exercise, we should develop a process content document with activities done by various roles, templates used, and other artifacts.

A clear understanding of the current view and the target view has to be formed.

A GDD usage model or workflow that depicts the location of the various roles and the activities performed would be helpful.

Case study

In our scenario, while most of the processes were well-defined, patch deployment and build management were two areas where the processes were not robust.

The build was not fully automated and there were no workflows with respect to actions to be taken on build failure, no detailed build logs, and so on. Build was tied to one particular machine and was not easily replicable. Patch or hotfixes deployment were also somewhat *ad hoc*.

But since they were identified early on, mitigation strategies, including the setup of supplementary release engineering in the target location, were undertaken. Some investment was made on automating builds on build servers to coincide with the transfer.

Patch deployment was harder to correct since it involved nonstandard branching, and a lack of an appropriate delivery vehicle. Branching recommendations were made post V5.2 release and a new patch delivery process and a download site were defined.

In our case study, post transfer the Bangalore team is expected to do project management, triaging of defects, requests for enhancements, and development. The China team is expected to do the SVT for the product. Product management will remain in Santa Clara.

2.3.2 Technical infrastructure

Part two of this book takes up, in more detail, the various disciplines of the life cycle of a product and showcases some of our solutions for the challenges posed. At this phase of the transition, the domain experts should estimate strengths and weaknesses of the tools. Part of the assessment should also include an estimate of how well the tools that support a discipline interact with the rest of the life cycle. A GDD solution is only as strong as the weakest tool in the life cycle.

Certain questions worth asking are:

- Does the software configuration management (SCM) solution scale well?
- Is the requirement management software effective? Verbal communications and loosely defined requirement management lead to wrong solutions more often in GDD than in single site collocated development environments.
- Does your build management software let you deploy builds independent of location? Does it have scheduling/load balancing capability, and provides concise and clear logs?
- Is there a good project management tool that will let the project manager assess resource deployment, status of various teams in various locations, and so on? Does it meet the reporting requirements?
- Does the defect management tool have capability to handle multiple sites?
- Are there any security concerns? For example, is the site an untrusted site, and do you have to control access to specific portions of the code or defects?

Apart from the development tools, another area to look at is the hardware setup and the network bandwidth:

- Is there any specific need for replicas? If yes, what is the ideal frequency of replication?
- Is there any need for servers to be maintained elsewhere? For example, some companies may choose to have a centralized architecture with data centers for build or test farms isolated in a different location. In such cases, are there right processes and practices to effectively manage them?
- Is the network bandwidth conducive to the development tools? Would technologies such as Citrix or Windows Terminal services be of help? Will there be any latency or firewall issues among the various development sites?
- Is there any specific licensing issues/third-party tool deployment to be resolved?
- Do you have a reasonable estimate of the IT support costs? Are there appropriate requirements for primary workstations/secondary workstations, build machines, test machines, servers, storage and backup? Have you planned with the particular geographies procurement lead time in mind?
- Can existing resources in the target site be used for the short term to jump start the transition? This would also help catch early glitches in migration. Loaned assets are another option to jump start the transition.
- Is there a possibility of transferring the assets currently used? Evaluate the costs involved, timelines, approvals, customs procedures, and other logistics and see if it is feasible.

Expected results

At the end of this assessment, a proposal for the key development tools that need to be deployed or configured should be ready. An understanding of where the servers will be located and the administration and maintenance involved with them should be present.

Case study

One of the strengths for this transition was that many tools that were used were GDD capable. As stated earlier, build management was weak from the tooling perspective, but was addressed effectively with the upgrade to Build Forge. More vital tools were ClearCase and

ClearQuest. In Part 2, "Running the show" on page 57, some of the specific tooling issues and solutions will be elaborated.

For ITSO Inc. Cash Console, one of the first things John did was work with the ClearCase administrator and set up SCM for both the India and China teams. When the change management system and source code became available, the target teams can come up to speed much faster.

Licenses were procured for the tools required and an assessment of the servers were made as well. When machine requirements were being listed, the operations manager in the target location realized the hardware were mostly older configurations and recommended industry standards as appropriate.

2.3.3 Skills assessment and hiring

One of the most difficult aspects of setting up a new team in a new geographical location or adding more products to an existing site's responsibility is hiring the right people. The success of the GDD model in the end depends on the human resources. While tools and processes are much more concrete, understanding the skill set required and finding matching resources can be a challenging task.

A natural starting point would be to study the current team's size, expertise, and experience levels. Based on what we are hoping to achieve after the transfer, we can get an understanding of whether we are ramping down the project or ramping up or maintaining status quo. Whatever the case may be, it is not a simple number math.

In some emerging markets, for example, finding engineers with many years of development experience with a particular tool may prove difficult. It may simply become prohibitive to have a similar team in terms of years of experience. In such cases, with the help of the source team, a list of skills and experiences that one ought to look for has to be prepared. One of the frustrations of the source teams is improper hiring in terms of experience.

The target teams could come up with the minimum requirement based on the availability of the resources and what could be called as a common denominator. For example, it may well be that the product was maintained by five engineers with an average experience of ten years. But is it needed? Can this be done with proper training by engineers with an average experience of five years? On the other hand, it does not make sense to hire five college graduates to do the job of the source team. The source team clearly knows the complexity of the issues that they face and definitely want a team that is worthy of facing the challenges. Both sides must have a discussion to decide on skill set requirements.

Expected results

Availability of the initial assessment of immediate hiring needs and projection during transfer with buffer.

Case study

The core site team had fifteen members with an experience range of 10 to 22 years of experience. This was a difficult configuration to achieve in an emerging market like India. However, by identifying common denominators, the team hired four leads with comparable skill sets and hired junior members with four to six years who were trained during the course of the transition.

For testing, there were six members with automation, and coding skills with an experience range of five to ten years. The China team already had three testing engineers with similar skills and experience levels. Getting ten years experience was difficult, however; the three senior members with domain knowledge and process knowledge with comparable skills compensated for the relative skill set mismatch.

The appropriate plans were made and followed aggressively.

An elaborate hiring plan, similar to Figure 2-1, with the skill set required, expected time of joining, expected time of productivity, and so on, was formed.

1	Developer	3+	Perm / Cont	Core Java, JSP, WebSphere Portal Server					
6	Tester	2+	Perm	Functional Testing, Test case writing, Manual Testing, RFT	Test Automation				
1	TL	15+	Perm	Java / J2EE, JSP, Javascript, Portal Server, WebSphere Application Server, Struts, Good hands-on experience, Linux / UNIX	Leadership qualities Excellent communication / presentation				
4	Sr Dev	10+	Perm	Java / J2EE, JSP, Javascript, Portal Server, Struts, Hands-on, UNIX / Linux	Good communication				
8	Developer	4+	Perm / Cont	Java/ J2EE, JSP, Struts, WebSphere Application Server, Portal Server (Admin + Portlet Dev)					

Figure 2-1   Sample hiring plan

2.3.4 Schedule the project

After a clear assessment on processes, tools, and people requirements are made, the project leader has a better understanding of the time required for transition. Further refinement on the schedule can be made after considering the following points:

► Releases to be done during transfer

   As the target team ramps up, they can start contributing to the release. For a short while, there are extra resources to tackle the release. However, the source team can also be engaged in training activities. Depending on the robustness of the process, tools, and the familiarity of the engineers, this may have proportional impact on the schedule.

► Impact on other deliverables, such as defects, patches and so on, and commitments made to customers

Often, hotfixes, patches, and so on fall below the radar and might not get captured. A transfer is a difficult situation when there is possible confusion on whose responsibility is with what. An adequate buffer has to be added to make sure such customer commitments are met.

► Impact of competition

It is also worthwhile to look at where the product is with respect to competition and how a time consuming transfer will affect the revenue. A transfer is an unlikely incubator for innovative ideas. Post transfer, because of a change of players, there is the potential for creativity, but it is unlikely during transfer. A team lead must plan the schedule so there is enough releases and features committed and be delivered during the interim phase.

Expected results

The results consist of:

► A project plan with a target date of when the transition will be completed
► The timeline for the releases that will be done during and immediately after the transition

Case study

An initial plan of transition spanned four months. The ITSO Inc. Cash Console V5.2 release was planned to be released in the second quarter by June 15. The transition spanned January to April with work done in the maintenance release by both teams. The next major release of ITSO Inc. Cash Console shopper was planned for December 15. The Santa Clara team was to slowly move away from their involvement in Cash Console. Figure 2-2 summarizes the initial plan.

Jan 1 - Jan 21	Planning
Jan 1 – Mar 7	Hiring/training new members Infrastructure setup, Clearcase/Clearquest
Jan 15 – Apr 1	Initial training Code reading Clear case/Clear quest training
Apr 1 – Apr 30	Onsite training
May 1 – May 30	India center fixing bugs China center running tests

Figure 2-2   High-level plan

2.4 Implementation phase

When the initial plan and schedule is in place, the actual transfer of knowledge and assets can be started.

2.4.1 Assets transfer

With the help of the assessment that was done and the GDD model workflow defined, processes and assets transfer can be initiated. Domain experts, such as IT specialists, SCM administrators, and network specialists, must be involved in setting up appropriate access, replicas, and so on.

More in depth study of each discipline is discussed in Part 2, "Running the show" on page 57.

The general guideline is to make sure that the assets setup/transfer precedes the knowledge transfer. It can be frustrating to both sides to have to not be able to apply the knowledge gained because of environmental issues. In our experience, one of the first things that is done, for example, is for the target team to have access to the source code or test cases as appropriate. Similarly, access to the change management system early on gives the target team a feel for the kind of problems or enhancement requests that are logged.

2.4.2 Knowledge transfer

Knowledge transfer, the crux of any work transition, is the most difficult in terms of measuring and tracking. The level of success is apparent only after the transfer, perhaps even after the release, and thus must be planned and executed carefully.

Artifacts

There is often a lack of documents that explain various aspects connected to the project. In mature projects, such artifacts are dated, and in new projects, such documents are incomplete and fluid. A GDD transition in some ways forces the team to document as much as possible, since it is not always viable to talk through things with remote teams.

Easily accessible, preferably indexed, and searchable resources, such as architecture models, functional specifications, functional tests, and so on, must be prepared and updated by the source team. Project transfer effectiveness is directly proportional to the maturity of the processes and documentation available.

Some product teams have mastered this in the form of a new hire wiki or document that is updated by every new hire. It would essentially give the list of things that have to be learned by the new hire. This would be a good starting point for setting up knowledge transfer to the new GDD location.

There are also concepts, such as teamrooms, where project plans, status, architecture diagrams, and test plans are maintained. They could also be CM controlled. These artifacts have to be organized in a standard way for the project and the new users should receive some sort of instruction on what they will find and where they will find it. Another place to get project information would be from Project Console (PJC), where the project members can see "published" artifacts as well as a project dashboard.

Training

Without effective knowledge transfer, the target team is left to flounder and reinvent the wheel. So, in many ways, the goal of the transition is to ensure that the target team is well trained to face the upcoming challenges.

Most of the successful transitions that we have been part of have had a phased approach towards training.

- ► User level training

    This could be considered a prerequisite before the teams engage. In this phase, the target team learns the product as though it were a customer. This gives the team a perspective on usage models and helps them understand why a problem was solved in a specific way. When they are familiar with the user level knowledge, the team could start perusing the related artifacts, such as the design document, specifications, and so on.

- ► Development environment training

    In the second phase, the target team begins to get trained on the environment and tools that are being used. For example, if the engineers are not familiar with the particular development environment or if the testing engineers are not familiar with a particular automation tool, they would have to understand the basics first. It would also help the trainers focus on the core transfer. In a GDD environment, sometimes there is almost a day's worth of delay between a question and an answer. It causes a lot of frustration on both sides when the focus is lost.

- ► Core job training

    At this point, the target team is ready to receive the transfer of the core job responsibility. Depending on the discipline being transferred, we advise making this iterative with measurable goals. This is when the team gets a deeper understanding of the processes and the product. This phase needs to be measured as much as possible to understand the improvement made by the target team. It shows how well the target team is ramping up. Another measurement would be the percentage of the source team's time spent on the product development activities versus training. The development activity would have to taper off.

    Core job training also should include informal tips and tricks that developers use. The biggest liability of the target team is their lack of historical knowledge and why a certain decision was made when it was made. This could cause issues later on if the target team decides to explore something that has already been tried and abandoned. The trainees should take good notes on cheat sheets and debugging diaries of how a particular problem was solved. It is worth planning for storing of the knowledge transferred during this phase in a tangible form.

    This is also the point when there should not be any hesitancy to ask questions. The source team should encourage and be prepared for a lot of questions. They should also be forthcoming in sharing anecdotes related to decisions, abandoned ideas, and so on.

Onsite visits

Onsite visits by a few core members of the team have consistently paid off in our experience. Potential issues, such as delays in getting answers, no overlap of time zones during the intense collaborative periods, and lack of rapport can be avoided by a well planned visit. This helps the target team develop trust and build a relationship with their counterparts. The benefit of meeting face-to-face allows the team members to work better as a virtual team in the future. If the initial relationship is established in person, it is much easier to maintain virtually.

Also, most teams have front loaded the visits, that is, arranged for the visit to be during the intense collaboration point of core job training, kickoff, and so on. If the right chords are struck at this point, the rest of the transfer plays out without discordance.

The few members who undergo the intense onsite visits are senior members of the target team and are expected to act as liaisons for the rest of the team. They are also expected to train the new members of the target team. The folks visiting are senior experienced engineers that possess collaboration skills.

The visitors should consciously and extensively network during the onsite visit to keep the communication channel open.

After the team ramps up, it pays to have the senior members of the source team embedded at the target site for a few months/years in order to provide a level of continuity, and to facilitate ongoing transfer of training, best practices, and so on. Another approach would be to make sure they stay on as mentors to the members of the target team.

Delivery

In many typical transfers, one release is done together with the source team ramping down and the target team ramping up. At an agreed upon point, the target team slowly moves from being trainees to contributory members.

Due to quick growth and the pressures of ramping up, an impact on the product is hard to achieve in the first release. It is better not to commit any major feature for this release. The target team is expected to execute the core job actions in increasing complexity. The crucial point is to make sure senior architect level engineers do not get moved off the project in the initial part itself and stay on until the completion of a successful release.

Metrics

We strongly advise defining some metrics to track the progress of the transfer. The metrics depend on the discipline that is being transferred. The more quantitative the measures are, the better pulse that can be kept on the success of the transition. Based on the discipline the component defined, many iterative goals can be set.

Expected results

At least one release with the help of the core team is successfully done.

All stakeholder engagements are initiated and external stakeholders understand the ownership transition.

Case study

The knowledge transfer was done in phases. As each new hire joined the team, older members helped them get up to speed and the Bangalore team prepared for the onsite visit.

► During the offsite period, the Bangalore team underwent customer level training. They had the code set up and were able to review the documents available and look at the code. They documented whatever was understood. Some of the new members were not familiar with the Eclipse development environment and so they went through training for that as well. Similarly, the China team went through the test cases and automation tools.

► When it came to the onsite period, the team was well prepared and thus was able to use the time effectively in clarifying expert level doubts. This also made things easy for the trainers; they spent time on discussing the pitfalls and problem areas.

Figure 2-3 shows the training schedule for the development team. After intense technical sessions and process overviews, the target team went through the shadowing phase. They worked closely with the engineers from the source team trying to understand the various fixes and the reasoning behind some of the decisions. In the reverse shadowing, the target team took the initiative in coming up with the solutions that were reviewed and discussed with the members of the source team.

ID	Task Name	Days	Start	End	Status
	Knowledge Transfer				
1	Prepare list of KT documents to be made.	1			Done
2	Prepare KT documents.	2			Done
3	**Onsite visit**	20			
3.1	Team introduction and overview of Cash Console.	2			
3.2	Design Overview.	1			
3.3	Sharing code, setting up environment and trying stand-alone conversion	1			
3.4	Package overview and how to do local build.	1			
3.5	Other component overview.	1			
3.6	Support Process.	2			
3.7	Release information/code streams in Clearcase.	2			
3.8	Unit testing process.	1			
3.10	Defect fixing and build process.	1			
4	Getting IDs/Access to DB/Important URLs/Other Contacts.	1			
5	New line items process.	1			
	Shadowing				
13	Walk through old bugs.	2			
16	Assign dummy bugs and review fixes.	3			
17	Assign dummy bugs and review fixes.				
	Reverse shadowing				
18	Assign real bugs and review fixes.				

Figure 2-3   Training schedule for development

Similarly, Figure 2-4 shows the training schedule for the SVT team. Apart from knowledge transfer of test artifacts and in-depth sessions on the product, the SVT team had sessions on some of the initiatives, such as automation efforts.

Task & Responsible Engineer SVT – Testing transition to China 01/04/2007	Start Date	End Date	Start Time	End Time
Intro with Dev **(John)** QE Transition	01/04/2007		9am	Noon
Paul High Level Plan overview and processes followed by us Test artifacts Metrics	02/04/07	03/04/07	Noon	5pm
Brian Credit card component Cash component Other configurations	04/04/2007	04/04/2007	8am	Noon
Susan Test cases overview	05/04/2007	05/04/2007	1pm	5pm
Vinod Automation efforts Automation tools	06/04/2007	06/04/2007	8am	Noon
Elena **Processes**	09/04/2007	09/04/2007	9am	1pm
Yao and Chuck Wrap up	10/04/2007	10/04/2007	2pm	3pm
Meet with Dave. Meet with Tech Support. Meet with Brian 1X1. Meet with Bob.	Yao will schedule this meeting. Yao will schedule this meeting. Yao will schedule this meeting. Yao will schedule this meeting.			

Figure 2-4   Training schedule for the China team

► After the technical sessions, during the onsite visit, the China team was first asked to come up with solutions for low priority defects that were reviewed by source team members.

► Then they took ownership of high priority defects that were reviewed by source team members.

► Then they started working on features that went through normal review process.

Some of the metrics that were used for tracking were:

► Number of bugs resolved/Number of bugs reopened
► Number of SVT test cases run
► Number of bugs found
► Lines of code written

2.5 Execution phase

When the combined release is done, the target team should start looking at their deliverables, and should start planning for the next release. This would be the release done independent of the source site and is in essence signaling the official end of the transition.

Some points for the target team to remember are:

► Ensure standards and make sure they do not conflict with existing standards.

► Improve or enhance the product. By this time, we expect that the engineers have a clear understanding of the strengths and weaknesses of the product. They would be able to contribute like any other engineering resource.

► Improve the process and fix flaws.

► Reach out to the source team for advice.

The source team should also effectively redirect other stakeholders to the target team.

Expected results

Release completed with high quality on time delivery, independent of the source team, including effective interaction with external stakeholders.

Case study

After this transfer, the Bangalore team took over the maintenance releases of ITSO Inc. Cash Console. They were able to decide on enhancement requests, fix bugs, and release patch versions.

The China team was able to improve on the functional verification testing (FVT) and was able to consistently execute the tests for subsequent releases. This transition was considered to be such a success that the China team also took over the FVT for the new release.

2.6 Risk factors

The generic GDD challenges discussed in Chapter 1, "Introduction to Global Development and Delivery" on page 3 are applicable here as well. However, with respect to transferring a responsibility or setting up a new GDD center, there are a few other crucial factors.

2.6.1 Adequate sponsorship

While a decision to go towards geographically distributed development is made at the executive level, if the need for it is not percolated through out the organization, and if there is not buy-in at various levels, the project will suffer extensively. Some of the questions that the leader should ask are:

► Is there a plan for the current developers? In our sample scenario, the current developers were moving on to do new releases. This is almost an ideal situation, and there was an added incentive for the developers to make sure the transition happened. In reality, though, sometimes there may be work force reduction in the source location. This would mean there is no incentive from the source team's perspective for the transfer to succeed. In ITSO Inc., the testing team in Santa Clara had a work force reduction and due to this action, not all artifacts and knowledge transfer went according to plan. The China team had to self-learn and reconstruct the knowledge base based on the various documents. An unwilling source or a lack of source for knowledge transfer and an incomplete understanding of the product architecture will derail the schedule and might cause long-term issues.

- ► Is it clear to the management team that the success of the transfer is their business goal for that review period? Is there accountability in all management levels for the success of the setup?

- ► Are there any pre-conceived notions about the target locations? One of the leads in ITSO Inc. in Santa Clara had, in a previous company, attempted a similar GDD initial setup that had failed miserably. It was difficult for the individual to be optimistic about the transfer. Jay and John worked with that individual in slowly rebuilding trust.

2.6.2 Hiring

Hiring is another major challenge, especially when the target location is an emerging development center in countries such as China or India. Making sure the right skill set is acquired is only one part of it. There is also the worry of attrition. While attrition by itself is a cost, attrition during transition is a compounded cost and may offset any cost benefits. For example, if one of the senior members who had traveled onsite and was supposed to act as a liaison to new members leaves, the knowledge transfer efforts goes back to the starting point. There is also the sense of urgency, since there are some hardstops for the source team to move on. The project leader's time is spent substantially in scouting, interviewing, hiring and training.

We look at some of the people issues and best practices to control attrition in Part 3, "Connecting the dots" on page 179. Here we want to emphasize that it makes sense to plan some buffers in locations where turnover is a major risk.

2.6.3 Priorities

It is important to make sure the target teams are aware of the priorities. Since transition causes a disruption in the continuity, the leaders have to make sure the target sites are aware of the priorities and long term goals of the company.

It is likely the immediate product deliverables are well planned but sometimes certain commitments, such as one-offs or a defect backlog that were made may not have been communicated to the target sites. Care should be taken to convey any and all such customer commitments.

It pays to understand the impact of competition. Transition delays a major release and if the company is in the middle of a crucial release, it is extremely important to have a clear understanding of the impact of a delay and a mitigation strategy.

2.7 Conclusion of work transfer

We saw in this chapter the characteristics unique to work transition and some of the best practices, heuristics, and techniques one could follow to make an effective transition. Investing time and resources up front in this precursor to setting up successful GDD centers pays back substantially as the GDD model in the organization matures.

Each of the disciplines brings its own challenges, which we address in Part 2, "Running the show" on page 57, in greater detail.

GDD process guidance

A process that fosters the development and communication through established best practices is critical in any development situation, especially when team members are geographically distributed.

This chapter discusses the need for a unified process for Global Development and Delivery (GDD) and how IBM Rational Unified Process (RUP) can be used for distributed development.

3.1 Unified process for GDD

Introducing a GDD model into your IT strategy poses substantial risks, namely, the uncertainty surrounding a project team's ability to communicate accurately, precisely, and unambiguously.

Teams doing distributed development across geographies face many challenges, such as:

► Communication difficulty in an environment in which team members may use different languages. People are unable to communicate in real time due to distance and time zone barriers.

► Conflicting in-house processes, knowledge, and work transfer issues and issues involving the ownership of project artifacts.

Common processes, tools, and reporting can address these challenges. The cornerstone of process design is the establishment of a core framework. This framework provides a foundation on which to build a comprehensive and effective distributed team. A process with an extensible framework, which can be customized for specific organizations or projects, is termed a *unified process*.

A unified process helps distributed teams in the following ways:

► Establish a highly repeatable procedure, a set of software development best practices, and standard methods of execution.

► A well-designed process helps users at all locations clearly understand their designated roles within the development life cycle, which can have far-reaching benefits, such as:

 – Productivity increases as rework and duplication diminish

 – Work transfers go more smoothly as everyone involved understands their role in the process

► A unified process provides a common vocabulary and clear definitions of responsibilities that unite dispersed teams promoting a common vision and culture.

► When the process is established, tools can be used to introduce automation for each discipline or an aspect of discipline.

3.2 IBM Rational Unified Process

IBM provides the Rational Unified Process (RUP) framework to address the need for a *unified process*. RUP is a software development process framework based on proven best practices. RUP helps to establish highly repeatable processes for the development and delivery life cycle and standard ways of execution that provide a common vocabulary and clear definition of responsibilities. Before going into details of how RUP can be used for GDD, let us take a look at some of the RUP concepts. If you are familiar with RUP, then you can skip 3.2.1, "RUP concepts" on page 45.

3.2.1 RUP concepts

RUP is based on a set of building blocks, or content elements, describing what is to be produced, the necessary skills required, and the step-by-step explanation describing how specific development and delivery goals are achieved.

The main building blocks, or content elements, are the following:

► Roles (who): A role defines a set of related skills, competencies, and responsibilities.

► Work products (what): A work product represents something resulting from a task, including all the documents and models produced while working through the process.

► Tasks (how): A task describes a unit of work assigned to a role that provides a meaningful result.

Within each iteration, the tasks are categorized into nine disciplines:

► Engineering disciplines

  – Business modeling
  – Requirements
  – Analysis and design
  – Implementation
  – Test
  – Deployment

► Supporting disciplines

  – Configuration and change management
  – Project management
  – Environment

RUP promotes iterative development and organizes the development into four phases (inception, elaboration, construction, and transition), each consisting of one or more executable iterations of the software or system at that stage of development.

Figure 3-1 illustrates the overall architecture of the RUP, which has two dimensions:

► The horizontal axis represents time and shows the life cycle aspects of the process as it unfolds.

► The vertical axis represents disciplines that logically group activities by nature.

The graph shows the static structure of the process framework through a set of disciplines that define roles, artifacts, and activities. Additionally, developing software in an iterative manner indicates the dynamic nature of RUP. To understand the dynamic nature of RUP, consider the implementation discipline. In early iterations, you spend more time on requirements; in later iterations, you spend more time on implementation.

You can find more details about RUP at:

`http://www.ibm.com/software/awdtools/rup/`

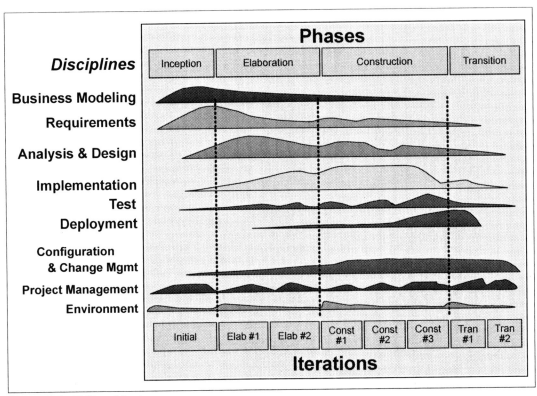

Figure 3-1   RUP architecture

3.2.2 Tailoring RUP for GDD

The RUP framework constitutes guidance on a rich set of engineering principles. It is applicable to projects of different size and complexity, as well as for different development environments and domains. This means that no single project or organization benefits from using all of RUP. Applying all of RUP likely results in an inefficient project environment, where teams struggle to keep focused on the important tasks and to find the right set of information. Thus, we recommend that RUP be tailored to provide appropriate and customized guidance on how to develop and deliver systems relevant to the specific needs of the particular distributed teams.

Process tailoring can happen at two levels:

► At the *organizational level*, where process engineers modify, improve, or configure a common process to be used organization-wide. Organization-level tailoring takes into consideration such issues as the application domain, reuse practices, and core technologies mastered by the company. One organization can have more than one organization-wide process, each adapted to a different type of development. For example, an organization can have different process for collocated development and GDD development.

► At the *project level*, where process engineers modify, improve, or configure a common process to be used by a specific project. When an organization-wide process exists, project-level tailoring is where the organization-wide process is further refined for a given project. Project-level tailoring takes into consideration the size of the project, the reuse of company assets, the type of development life cycle (new product development and product maintenance), and so on. In case of GDD, the process also needs to take into account the geographies involved in the project and their responsibilities in various RUP disciplines.

No matter what level of tailoring you choose, tailoring the RUP generally involves four key steps (though some steps are optional depending on the tailoring level):

1. Develop the method elements.

   This includes developing additional "process know-how" and refining existing content, in areas where the coverage in the RUP process framework is deemed insufficient for the project. You can extend the RUP method framework by adding roles, tasks, and work products, or you can add project-specific guidance to the existing RUP framework. If your project is being performed in various geographies, then you can use the RUP plug-in for GDD as a starting point and refine it according to your project needs. Details about the RUP plug-in for GDD are mentioned in 3.4, "RUP plug-in for GDD" on page 50.

2. Configure the method content.

   This includes deciding what content to include and what content to exclude, as well as providing appropriate views into that content (for example, views based on role or specific domains). Configuring the method content is a matter of right sizing the process to match the needs of a specific organization or individual project. Configuring a process involves selecting the method content (work products, tasks, roles, and so on) that is to be included in the process. Selecting the right set of method content for a given project is not a trivial task. To be effective, the process needs to be relevant and right-sized along different dimensions, like project size (resources and calendar time), formality, technological platform, and domain, just to mention a few.

   For a GDD effort, identify the life cycle model you should use and select the appropriate process configurations. The RUP plug-in for GDD provides two different configurations to cater to the needs of different development life cycles for new product development and product maintenance.

   Careful consideration of the process configuration at the beginning stages of the project significantly benefit the development teams as the project progresses. Also, if you are using certain disciplines only, identify which disciplines will be used and where. Will all or only some of the RUP for GDD disciplines be used? What team or teams will be responsible for which disciplines? This information should be an essential part of your deployed process configuration.

3. Develop the process for the configuration.

   This includes selecting a type of development life cycle (for example, waterfall versus iterative) and defining a process that is fine-tuned to fit the exact needs of the organization or project. For this part of the tailoring work, the process engineer should collaborate closely with the project manager, since the chosen life cycle model lays the groundwork for the project planning process. Depending on the nature of the project, there might be a need to adjust the RUP life cycle to better match the specific needs. For example, an iterative life cycle process can be broken down into phases and iterations. We recommend an iterative life cycle approach to mitigate the risk involved in doing global development and delivery.

   In addition to selecting the overall life cycle model, it is also important to decide how to perform the workflows associated with each of the disciplines that are included in the tailoring effort, as well as to decide when, during that project life cycle, to introduce each part of the disciplines' workflow. Deciding how to perform the workflow involves deciding what activities to perform and in what order. Deciding when to perform each part of the workflow involves deciding where in the life cycle (for example, what phase) to introduce the selected activities. Such workflows are crucial for effective communication among distributed teams.

Some additional information that you may want to specify at this time is the timing and formality requirements of the work products at various points in the life cycle, for example:

- In what phases is a work product created or updated?
- What is the required formality of the work product
- How does distributed team members collaborate to produce or work on work products?
- Does a work product need a sign-off by the customer?
- Who should review the work product?

4. Make the process available.

This includes publishing the configuration (and its process) as a process Web site, or exporting the process to a project planning tool. After the initial tailoring work is done, the resulting process needs to be made available to the project team in a consumable format. This is crucial because it helps in establishing the unified process across distribution teams. One possibility is to make the process available through a Web site that is deployed on a Web server to avoid any overhead associated with updates to the process during the project life cycle.

In a GDD environment, access to the process Web site may need to conform to more demanding performance requirements than in a collocated environment, such as 24x7 availability. Some of the considerations that are important to the use of the process in a distributed environment are as follows:

- Physical network requirements for distribution of the configured process

- Hardware requirements for process deployment

- Process configuration and maintenance approach

- Requirements for acceptable performance and how they will be measured, Service Level Agreements

- Requirements for usability and how they will be verified

3.3 IBM Rational solution for process management

IBM Rational Method Composer is a process customization and publishing tool that enables process engineers to accelerate delivery of customized development and delivery processes. Rational Method Composer provides a set of predefined RUP configurations for specific project contexts. Prior to creating a new configuration, consider using one of the predefined configurations in Rational Method Composer as a starting point. Select and copy the predefined configuration that is closest to the characteristics of your project, and tailor it further by selecting and deselecting method packages, as appropriate. For example, if you are planning for global development and delivery, then you can select the RUP plug-in for GDD, which is based on RUP, and provides variations (contributions, extensions, or replacements) for GDD. More details about the RUP plug-in for GDD are given in 3.4, "RUP plug-in for GDD" on page 50.

Rational Method Composer[1] provides many features for effective customization of method content. Some of the key Rational Method Composer features are as follows:

► Allows creating processes with breakdown structure editors and workflow diagrams through use of multi-presentation process editors. The breakdown structure editor supports different process views: work-breakdown view, work product usage view, and

---

[1] The Rational Method Composer tool platform, which includes RUP, is based on a process model. This process model is derived from a schema that is defined in the UMA, which in turn is based on SPEM 2.0. SPEM 2.0 Final Adopted Specification can be found at http://www.omg.org/cgi-bin/doc?ptc/07-03-03.

team allocation view. Rational Method Composer automatically synchronizes all presentations with process changes.

- ► Is independent of RUP. Although the recent version of RUP is maintained and shipped with Rational Method Composer, Rational Method Composer is a general purpose process engineering tool that provides support for many alternative life cycle models. For example, waterfall, incremental, or iterative models can be created with the same overlapping method content.

- ► Provides a synchronization mechanism that allows changes to method elements to be automatically updated in related process elements. For example, if a name of a method content element is changed, the new name is displayed in processes that use that method element. This feature helps in propagating process changes made at the organizational level to the processes at the project level or to the customized process for various geographies involved in GDD.

- ► Improved reuse and extensibility capabilities through variability elements, such as contributes, replaces, and extends.

- ► Supports reusable dynamically linked process patterns of best practices for rapid process assembly through drag-and-drop.

In addition to customizing the content to be included in a configuration, you can also define views into the content, which can be used to suppress unwanted method elements for given teams within the project, for example, views based on roles (developers, for example, do not necessarily want to see the same details as the project manager). It is also helpful in defining different views for different geographies.

Method configurations are not only used for creating processes, but are also used for publication (That is, a configuration defines which elements are published in HTML and which are not). When a configuration is published, the resulting Web site only contains the selected elements and the views are presented as separate instances (or tabs) of the tree browser. Figure 3-2 shows the sample published content of the RUP plug-in for GDD.

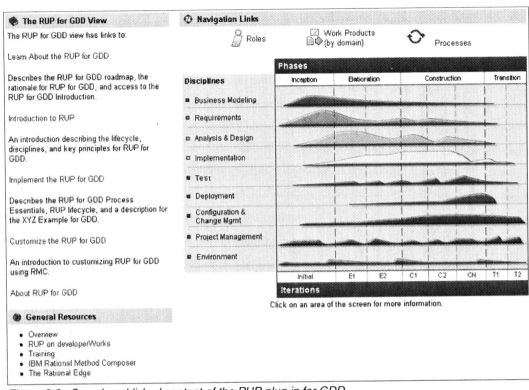

Figure 3-2   Sample published content of the RUP plug-in for GDD

While process is the cornerstone to success of any project, you must integrate your process into the day-to-day operations of your team. Rational Method Composer provides integration with such tools as Rational Portfolio Manager, where processes can be used to define and execute project plans. More details about Rational Method Composer and Rational Portfolio Manager integration can be found at:

```
http://www.ibm.com/developerworks/ibm/library/ar-rmcrpm/index.html
```

3.4 RUP plug-in for GDD

Let us discuss the RUP for GDD process architecture by addressing the plug-in architecture, method content packaging, process elements, and method configurations and views.

Plug-in architecture

The RUP for GDD process is based on the RUP process and the RUP for maintenance process. The RUP plug-in for GDD supports GDD for both new projects as well as for maintenance projects. Let us describe some of the key architectural aspects of the RUP plug-in for GDD.

The RUP for GDD process is based on one plug-in, called rup_gdd, in the default Rational Method Composer library. This rup_gdd plug-in references the rup and the rup_maintenance plug-ins (Figure 3-3).

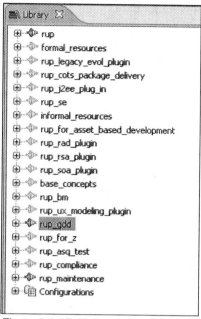

Figure 3-3   RUP plug-in for GDD

Using both the rup and rup_maintenance plug-ins means that the rup_gdd plug-in can accommodate both scenarios in GDD environments in which projects either are started from the beginning or are maintenance projects.

Method content packaging

Method content in Rational Method Composer is primarily expressed using work products, roles, tasks, and guidance. Guidance, such as checklists, examples, or roadmaps, can also be defined to provide exemplary walkthroughs of a process.

Let us look into the details of the rup_gdd plug-in by examining the method content packaging architecture of the plug-in. The rup_gdd plug-in consists of three high level packages: *Disciplines, Distributed Development Preparation*, and *General Guidance* (Figure 3-4). The *Disciplines* package groups method content for the GDD process based primarily on each of the RUP disciplines: Architecture, build and deployment, configuration and defect management, environment, project management, requirements, and test. The *General Guidance* package groups the tool mentor content and the ITSO Inc. example. Finally, the *Distributed Development Preparation* package contains the method content in the form of tasks and guidance that make up the capability pattern for enabling the preparation for GDD implementation.

The rationale for this method content package structure is based on support for key process authoring scenarios in which a team is interested in the entire life cycle, one or several aspects of the life cycle, or only the example/tool mentors. In the first scenario, all of the method content packages would be selected, providing a comprehensive process for geographically distributed development. In the second scenario, only one or several of the specific disciplines with the Discipline package would be selected, depending on the particular area(s) of interest (fore example, requirements, configuration management, build management, and so on). In the last scenario, the example (either the ITSO Inc. example or the tool mentors for GDD or both) is primary area of interest in which case a process configuration containing just the general guidance package would be selected.

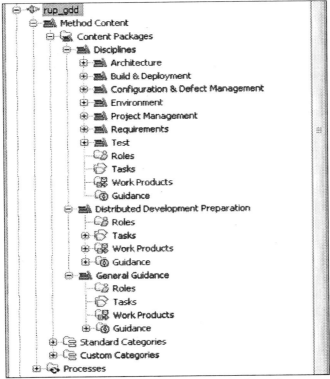

Figure 3-4   RUP for GDD Method Content Package Structure

Process elements

The main process element is the activity that can be nested to define breakdown structures as well as relate them to each other to define a flow of work. Activities also contain descriptors that reference method content. Activities are used to define processes, and Rational Method Composer supports two main kinds: *delivery processes* and *capability patterns*. Delivery processes represent a complete and integrated process template for performing one specific type of project. They describe a complete end-to-end project life cycle and are used as a reference for running projects with similar characteristics. Capability patterns are processes that express and communicate process knowledge for a key area of interest, such as a discipline or a best practice. They are also used as building blocks to assemble delivery processes or larger capability patterns. This ensures optimal reuse and application of their key best practices in process authoring activities in Rational Method Composer.

The RUP for GDD process is based on the RUP classic delivery process. It adds a capability pattern, called *Preparing for Distributed Development*, which is integrated into the Inception phase of the RUP delivery process. In addition, RUP for GDD is also based on the RUP maintenance delivery process for GDD projects that are based on maintenance life cycle. The *Preparing for Distributed Development* capability pattern is integrated into the inception/elaboration phase of the RUP maintenance delivery process.

Method configurations and views

The RUP for GDD process is based on a configuration that incorporates views for RUP for GDD and RUP for GDD maintenance projects. Each view is a part of the same RUP for GDD method configuration (Figure 3-5).

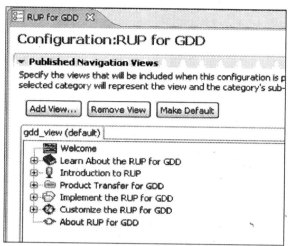

Figure 3-5   RUP for GDD method configuration

There are two views in this configuration: *GDD_View* (the default view) and *GDD maintenance*. Depending on your GDD needs, you may use one or both of these views for your GDD effort.

Note: The RUP plug-in for GDD offering will be available soon at:

```
http://www-128.ibm.com/developerworks/rational/downloads/06/rmc_plugin7_1/
```

3.5 Case study

ITSO Inc. is global leader in solutions for the retail sector, such as their ITSO Inc. Retail Cash Console. Recently, ITSO Inc. undertook an initiative to reduce its own costs, improve customer satisfaction and accelerate the delivery of new releases by aligning its geographically distributed team around a unified best practices based methodology and a unified set of development tools.

A year ago, the ITSO Inc. development organization was located at corporate headquarters in Santa Clara, U.S. When the company added development sites in India, China, and Ireland, the new, geographically distributed team lacked a common development and delivery methodology. Each site was using different tools and following different processes and each had a different culture. ITSO Inc. wanted an industry standard process and a shared set of tools to get alignment across the organization and their goal was to improve their process in order to reduce costs, increase efficiency, accelerate development, and improve quality. To achieve these goals, ITSO Inc. decided to adopt RUP, which is a proven method framework that delivers best practices and guidance for system development and delivery. As RUP is based on best proven practices, it was easier for all the development sites to adopt a new methodology without having to start from scratch. ITSO Inc. is using IBM Rational Method Composer for tailoring RUP to the company's specific needs while maintaining consistency across the team. Pam, a process engineer, has the responsibility of customizing the RUP process for GDD according to the needs of ITSO Inc. Using Rational Method Composer, Pam configured the existing RUP process by simplifying and modifying it wherever it was appropriate to the needs of ITSO Inc. Pam created published content of customized RUP methodology from Rational Method Composer. This unified process will be adopted by all GDD projects done by ITSO Inc.

Now, ITSO Inc. is planning to develop a new product, ITSO Inc. Supply Chain, which will be developed in Santa Clara and India and tested in China and Dublin. John, who is project manager for ITSO Inc. Supply Chain, used Rational Method Composer to tailor the enterprise customized RUP methodology according to his project needs. The process John defined in Rational Method Composer acts as the baseline project plan. This project plan can be imported in IBM Rational Portfolio Manager to define the actual project plan.

Figure 3-6 on page 55 illustrates the architecture of the RUP configured for GDD in ITSO Inc., where the vertical axis for disciplines is subdivided in various geographies involved in the corresponding discipline.

During global development and delivery, various geographies might get involved at various phases in the development life cycle. For example, the U.S. and Bangalore teams are doing development and some amount of testing. Thus, Figure 3-6 on page 55 shows the U.S. and Bangalore are involved in all phases for Business Modeling, Requirements, Analysis & Design, and Implementation. China and Ireland are doing various testing and come in to the picture for the Construction and Transitions phases.

The graph shows how the emphasis varies over time for various geographies. For example, in early iterations, the U.S. team has more emphasis on Analysis & Design. After finalizing the overall architecture, component ownership is divided between the U.S. and Bangalore. This results in equal emphasis on the U.S. team and the Bangalore team on Analysis and Design.

In order to establish a unified process across distributed teams, published content is made available to the teams in various geographies through the company's intranet. This unified process provides a common methodology that benefits distributed teams by facilitating team communication. It also helps ITSO Inc. to unify distributed teams in the U.S., India, and China, and an outsource provider in Dublin with common definitions and workflows so team members understand their responsibility and their relationship to other team members.

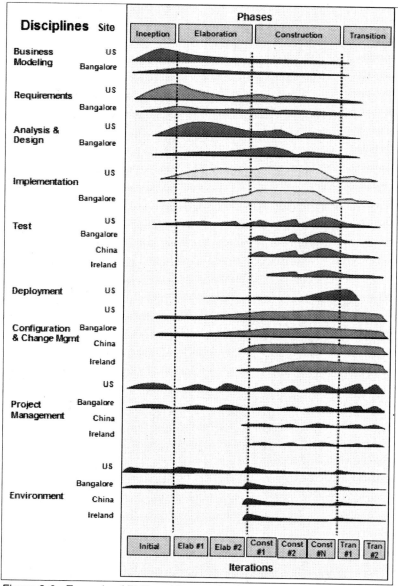

Figure 3-6 Example of RUP architecture for GDD

3.6 Conclusion

In this chapter, we discussed how a unified process helps in addressing some of the GDD challenges unique to a development process. RUP provides a framework for establishing a unified process among various geographies. In many cases, we recommend tailoring RUP to provide appropriate and customized guidance on how to develop and deliver systems relevant to the specific needs of particular distributed teams. The RUP plug-in for GDD offering can be used as a starting point for GDD process and refined according to your project needs.

Part 2

Running the show

This part can be considered as the main part of this book. Five key topics are covered in this part:

- ► Requirements management and software design in distributed development
- ► Maintenance projects in a GDD setting
- ► Software configuration management in distributed projects
- ► Typical issues that distribution teams face with build and deployment
- ► Test management

Requirements analysis and design

This chapter describes requirements management and software design in a geographically distributed team environment. In an environment where the stakeholders are dispersed all around the world, it is essential to have a governed software development process. Such a process must have sufficient traceability between user requirements and the final delivered software.

This chapter is divided into two parts. The first part, 4.1, "Managing user requirements" on page 60, discusses management of requirements. The second part, 4.2, "Designing software" on page 67, discusses software design.

Requirements gathering is important in new product development, as well as in developing enhancements for an existing product. In both cases, the software development process starts with requirements collection and analysis. If you are interested in doing distributed development in either of these scenarios, then this chapter is for you.

If you or your team is mostly involved in maintenance and defect fixing of an existing product, then your distributed development process also involves triaging and estimation at its inception. Therefore, refer to Chapter 5, "Change management and reporting" on page 83, for such scenarios.

4.1 Managing user requirements

Understanding real-world problems, and recording usage models associated with these problems are the first steps for defining requirements. These requirements form the basis of system design, development, testing, and delivery of software.

The distributed nature of software development in GDD introduces new complexities in the requirements management stage, which are discussed in the next subsection. To handle such complexities, a distributed team needs a tool that not only captures requirements, but also promotes better communication and collaboration across all locations.

4.1.1 Key challenges in requirements management

This section discusses key challenges in requirements management for a distributed team, and the characteristics of an effective requirements management system.

Sharing project knowledge

Poorly defined or poorly shared requirements are often the primary cause for project failure in environments. Collocated teams can share and analyze requirements through informal exchange of ideas and face-to-face discussions, but this is not as viable a process for distributed teams. Often distributed teams face language and cultural differences that may make communication of requirements a difficult task.

One way to bridge the geographical distance is for distributed teams to have discussions using Web conferencing, where the participants can share in real time the issue lists and the requirements. This enables the user and the development team to jointly define and validate requirements even when they are located at different geographies.

For distributed development, an effective requirements management system needs to have the following characteristics:

► Requirements should be stored in a central repository that provides easy access to users, both local and remote.

► Requirements should be organized in a way that makes it easy to distribute design and development responsibilities across teams.

► Requirements should be documented with the associated risk, priority, and difficulty. The development team should be able to query the requirement management system based on these parameters, so they can prioritize design and development tasks.

► The requirements management system should provide a context for the requirements through usage documents and diagrams. This helps team members understand requirements better, as they relate to usage scenarios and application workflow. This is important in a distributed team with members having diverse language and cultural backgrounds.

Change management

Requirements change, and it is necessary that the development team understands the impact a change has on the system and on other requirements. Automatic tracking of requirement changes is important in distributed teams, otherwise developers in remote sites may end up working on obsolete requirements.

For a distributed team, a requirements management system needs to manage changes automatically:

- Distributed team members are provided with the latest requirements information at all times. Changes in requirements should send alerts to the team members immediately.
- Requirement changes should be tracked.
- If a change in a requirement impacts other requirements, then such impacts should be immediately visible to the team, however dispersed they may be geographically.

Traceability

Traceability is a key factor in ascertaining that a requirement makes it into design and implementation, and then eventually gets tested. For distributed teams, traceability needs to be automated, so that no requirement gets missed or goes un-tested.

A distributed requirements management system should have the following characteristics:

- High level requirements should be associated with detailed software requirements.
- Detailed software requirements should be associated with use cases.
- Requirements should also be linked with the test system.

Managing collaboration

A software development team needs to collaborate on the requirements. A distributed team should choose a requirements management tool that helps them collaborate effectively, in spite of the team not being co-located.

- The distributed team should be able to record requirement related discussions, and associate them with the corresponding requirements.
- Program management should be able to track requirements. It is important for program managers to keep track of which features make it to a particular release, which ones get deferred, which ones are rejected, and so on.
- The testing team should be able to understand and track requirements as well. Each requirement that makes it to a release needs to be validated and tested in the product.
- All stakeholders should be able to view requirements easily, without elaborate tooling.

4.1.2 IBM Rational solutions for requirements management

A requirements management solution, such as IBM Rational RequisitePro, uses documents to capture and communicate requirements, providing context and order for usage scenarios. These captured requirements are then dynamically linked to a database to provide organizing and tracking information. As requirements are modified, RequisitePro enables increased understanding of the effects of change by linking requirements. This linking enables informed impact analysis decisions for scope management and resource allocation.

The following subsections discuss how RequisitePro helps you manage your requirements in an organized, fashion, manage requirement changes, and impose traceability on requirements.

Easy and efficient storage of requirements

In RequisitePro, requirements can be created and updated directly in Microsoft Word, which is a familiar environment for most people. Requirements can therefore be as verbose as the business analyst wants them to be, and this improves communication across distributed teams. RequisitePro also lets the user specify user-defined document templates across all documents, which helps ensure that requirements produced by geographically dispersed teams have a similar look and feel.

Each requirement type in RequisitePro has a unique set of attributes associated with it (such as priority, status, and risk). These attributes can be used to keep various stakeholders updated on the requirement states at all times.

RequisitePro also lets the user organize requirements into various categories, which helps in distributing functionality across teams. Figure 4-1 shows an example of defining requirements in RequisitePro.

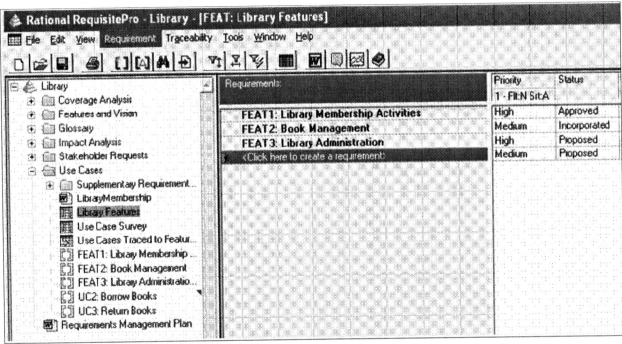

Figure 4-1   Defining requirements via RequisitePro

Sharing requirements

Figure 4-2 illustrates various ways in which RequisitePro helps in sharing requirements. Easy sharing of requirements is one of the features that makes RequisitePro the requirements management tool of choice in distributed teams.

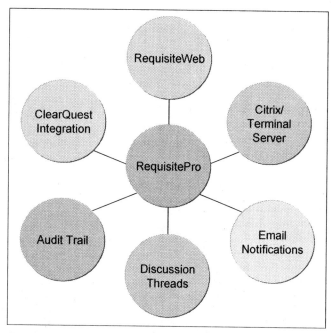

Figure 4-2   Sharing requirements via RequisitePro

Sharing through the Web interface

RequisitePro provides RequisiteWeb, a Web interface through which distributed users can access the requirements. Anyone with Web access can view or edit requirements, attributes, and traceability links. They can also create and edit requirements documents and engage in discussion groups. This works well in distributed teams. Analysts can add or modify requirements, and users can view it in real time.

RequisitePro should be installed where primary users, such as business analysts, are located. Remote users should be provided access through RequisiteWeb (Figure 4-3).

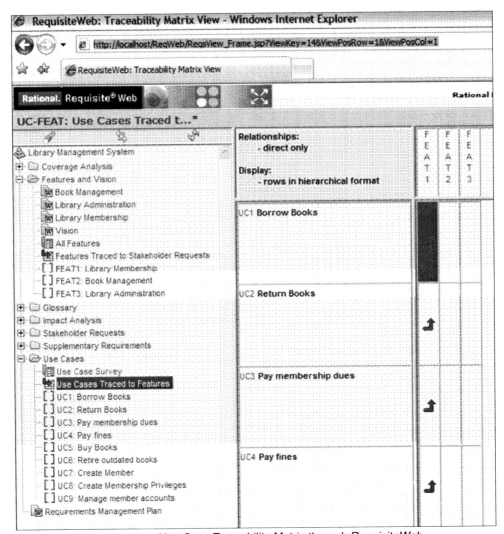

Figure 4-3   Feature versus Use Case Traceability Matrix through RequisiteWeb

Citrix/Windows Terminal Server support

RequisitePro also supports Citrix/Windows Terminal Server technology. For a reasonably small distributed team, this option is useful in providing all users with the full features of native RequisitePro. For larger teams, select members who require the capabilities of the native RequisitePro interface also benefit from using this technology.

Sharing through ClearQuest integration

Finally, RequisitePro requirements can also be shared through its integration with IBM Rational ClearQuest. Through this integration, RequisitePro requirements can be associated with ClearQuest records. This integration is especially helpful in maintenance scenarios, where user requirements are often tracked through enhancement requests or defects.

Collaborative requirements management

RequsitePro lets distributed teams manage requirements in a collaborative fashion through e-mails and discussions threads.

Change notification through e-mail

RequisitePro offers the ability to get notified of changes for requirements through e-mail. If a requirement changes, the analyst changing the requirement can set up e-mail notifications for all stakeholders. These notifications help in a distributed development where there are few face-to-face meetings. This way the various stakeholders can always be sure they are accessing the latest requirements. Ideally, change notification should be set up after requirements have stabilized, to prevent overwhelming emails.

Discussion threads

Stakeholders can also set up discussion threads on requirements. The discussions remain recorded along with the requirement, and this promotes a much better understanding of the whys and hows for the requirement. It also helps in reaching decisions faster; otherwise, in a distributed environment, discussions tend to get repetitive.

Change management

RequisitePro automatically keeps track of all changes to requirements, including who made the change, when and why it was made, and what the change was. This information not only helps stakeholders in understanding a requirement, but also helps in the scoping of the project, since it helps explain why specific features are included and how a decision was reached on the requirement. The requirements' revision histories record the rationale behind project decisions.

Requirements' traceability and coverage analysis

RequisitePro offers several ways of tracking requirements. Requirements can be linked to other requirements, design, defects, and test cases. This helps in collaboration and traceability, by tracking user requirements and determining whether they have been incorporated in the software being developed, something that is often hard to do in a distributed development environment.

Traceability with detailed requirements

RequisitePro allows the user to easily set up and track relationships between requirements to verify whether high-level requirements are associated with detailed software requirements. Querying these relationships provides coverage analysis for requirements.

Traceability with the defect tracking system

RequisitePro can be integrated with ClearQuest so that every requirement can correspond to a Request For Enhancement (RFE) in ClearQuest. ClearQuest can be used in tracking and estimation, making it easy to track requirements, their completion status, their effort estimates, and so on (Figure 4-4). An electronic signature of requirements can be supported via this integration, which provides an additional security measure.

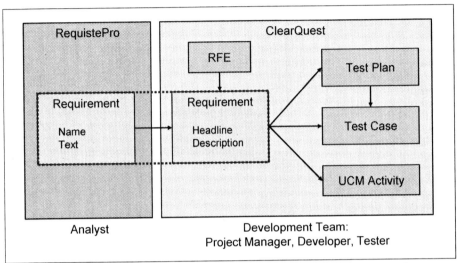

Figure 4-4   Integrating RequisitePro with ClearQuest

Requirements and test traceability

RequisitePro can be integrated with IBM Rational ClearQuest-TestManager. For the testing team, access to the latest requirements is critical to ensure complete and thorough testing. Testers need to ensure that they are building test cases to validate each requirement stored in RequisitePro. Testers also need to know when requirements change so they can understand the impact of changed requirements on the associated test cases. The RequisitePro-ClearQuest Test Manager integration helps in impact analysis by identifying what requirements have changed and what test cases are affected by such changes.

Figure 4-5 shows the RequisitePro integration with the Test Management System (ClearQuest and ClearQuest Test Manager).

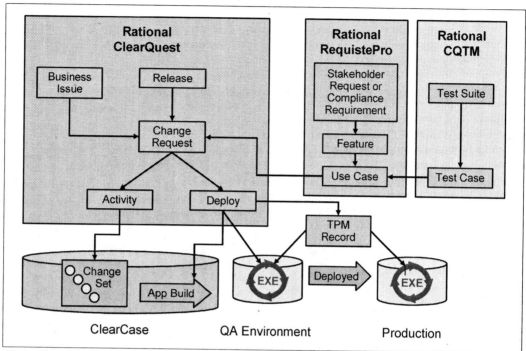

Figure 4-5   RequisitePro integration with the Test Management System (ClearQuest and ClearQuest Test Manager)

Traceability with design

RequisitePro can be integrated with the IBM Rational Software Architect/Rational Software Modeler family of modeling tools. This allows requirements to be linked with use cases and traced all the way through the design.

Controlled access to requirements information

RequisitePro ensures the integrity of requirements because requirements can be created or edited only by users who have permission privileges. Security can be established at various levels, from groups of requirements to individual attributes and even specific attribute values. RequisitePro also provides limited Lightweight Directory Access Protocol (LDAP) support for user authentication.

4.2 Designing software

As requirements are developed and communicated, architects and designers translate these requirements into a design for the software. Developers then work on the high level design to produce detailed design and finally the implementation for the software.

4.2.1 Design philosophies

In this section, we give a brief introduction to model driven architecture and development, which is what we recommend for any software design. The next section focuses on design challenges in distributed teams and builds on these design principles to show how the challenges can be mitigated.

Model driven software design and development

In model driven software development, models play a pivotal role. The building of the software is organized around a set of models by imposing a series of transformations between models.

A tool that supports model driven development helps increase the productivity of the developers, reduces ramp up time for new developers, and improves the understanding of the system.

The Unified Modeling Language

The Unified Modeling Language (UML) has become the software development industry's standard notation for software architecture and design. With UML, software professionals can visually model their analysis and design activities in a uniform and consistent manner. This helps cross-cultural teams by giving them a common method with which to communicate and document a project's architecture and design.

4.2.2 Key challenges in software design

This section discusses the key challenges in software design in a distributed development environment, and the characteristics of a software design process that would work for distributed teams.

Communicating software design across distributed teams

Diversity of languages, cultures, and time zones make it difficult for distributed teams to come to a common understanding of the application functionality and the software design. Unless each member of the team envisions the same workflow, cultural and language differences may cause misinterpretation of project goals.

Often, if the design has not been communicated effectively across teams, developers may also make incorrect assumptions about components being developed in other locations, and such discrepancies surface only during product integration, when they are expensive to fix.

A good design process needs to follow model driven development:

► To effectively communicate software design across geographies, it is essential that a good design tool helps distributed teams build a visual form of the application to be developed - from usage models to data models to application models. Visual modeling becomes important in bridging the geographical gap.

► An effective design tool should also help architects validate the design created by a distributed team.

Distributing ownership of software design

In a distributed environment, parts of the system need to be designed and developed in parallel by different distributed teams. Unless the ownership of design has been thought out carefully, members from different geographies may end up working on the same or on dependent modules at the same time, often leading to frequent and non-trivial model merges.

An effective model architecture relies heavily on good decomposition of the model. After a model is decomposed into components, components can be handed off to individual teams for further design and development. Model decomposition becomes easier to do as the design progresses from abstract to concrete models, so at least a stable high level design should exist before it is decomposed into distributable components. The principles of model decomposition are the same as that in object-oriented development:

► It should try to isolate business functions.

► It should group any items that must remain together.

► If the decomposition contains too many granular items, those items should be grouped into UML packages.

► At the start of each development iteration, the design focus should be on stabilization of common items.

The distribution of responsibilities should ideally be such that co-located teams own inter-dependent modules as much as possible. That way the team members can communicate informally each time they make changes that may affect others. If that is not possible, then there should be frequent synchronizations. Otherwise the design may go completely out of sync.

Handling concurrent design changes

Handling concurrent design changes, which sometimes conflict, is a common problem in distributed team environments, where team interactions are generally much less than in co-located teams.

One way of handling this would be model partitioning, which prevents different users from working on the same portion of the model at the same time and reduces the frequency and complexity of file merges between team members. Different members of a team can then work on their own partitions, and the partitions can be merged back when necessary.

Model partitioning versus model decomposition: Model partitioning is different from model decomposition. Partitioning merely partitions the physical model file into many files. Decomposition is logical and should be considered for distribution of responsibilities across distributed teams.

Synchronizing design and implementation

During product/feature development, a team of architects working on the high-level design may provide design models to the teams working on the implementation. The implementation team converts design into a detailed set of design models and the programming language implementation. Iterations of these representations occur as errors are corrected either in design or in code. Unless a conscious decision is taken to sync models with source code, the abstract model and the implementation model can quickly go out of step. In a distributed team, where face-to-face interactions are usually limited, this can be disruptive to product development.

Similarly, once a product is transitioned, the new team fixes bugs and makes enhancements to an existing application, often making changes in the design. Models can quickly go out of sync with the changed applications. In a distributed environment, where models are the primary source of understanding across teams, this can cause havoc.

Model driven development prescribes different ways in which models can be kept in sync with sources.

One such way is to have roundtrip engineering (RTE), which offers a bi-directional exchange between the abstract model describing the system architecture and the code. Designers and developers can seamlessly travel from implementation models to abstract models and vice versa in this case.

Another way is to provide code visualization in an appropriate modeling notation. As developers create an application, they often want to visualize each others' code through some graphical notation that aids their understanding of the code's structure or behavior. This visual rendering is a direct representation of the code, sometimes called a *code model*.

Traceability with requirements

In distributed software development, we recommend that the design tool helps provide sufficient traceability between requirements and design. Otherwise it is possible to miss some requirements in the design stage and subsequently to deliver software that does not meet all of the user requirements.

Therefore, it is important to have a link between the use cases and their specifications and then between the use cases and the class diagrams. That way, traceability is established from the requirements to the design. This helps to ensure that:

- ► All user requirements are being handled in design.
- ► If a requirement changes, it helps identify which of the design artifacts will change.
- ► If the design changes, it helps identify which requirements may get affected.

Lack of design guidelines

Software designed across the globe may lack uniformity and consistency in design, resulting in poor quality.

The architect should establish design guidelines for the development team to follow. During design, models need to be automatically validated against the established guidelines. This ensures uniformity and consistency in design, even when it is done by team members spread across the globe.

4.2.3 IBM Rational solutions for designing software

IBM Rational has a family of software tools that cater to model driven development:

- ► Rational Software Architect provides modeling and application development capabilities, including Web development.
- ► Rational Systems Developer provides modeling capabilities for systems development users.
- ► Rational Software Modeler is a subset of Rational Software Architect and Rational Systems Developer and provides modeling capabilities.

Depending on business needs, users can choose one tool over the other.

In the following sub-sections, we discuss modeling with Rational Software Architect. However, the modeling capabilities of these tools are quite similar in nature.

Visual modeling with Rational Software Architect

IBM Rational Software Architect is a UML model-driven design and development tool for creating well-architected applications and services.

Rational Software Architect enables the user to create appropriate models to facilitate all development activities and stages in the life cycle, and provides tools to transform models into more detailed or more abstract models to move development work forward. In a distributed environment, this improves collaboration and communication between teams by providing easier translations between analysis and design, and design and code.

Rational Software Architect offers separate perspectives for the analyst/designer and for the developer. It provides an integrated development and modeling environment, and enables the user to browse analysis, design, and source code models all in the same environment, thereby helping in collaboration.

Figure 4-6 shows a window from Rational Software Architect.

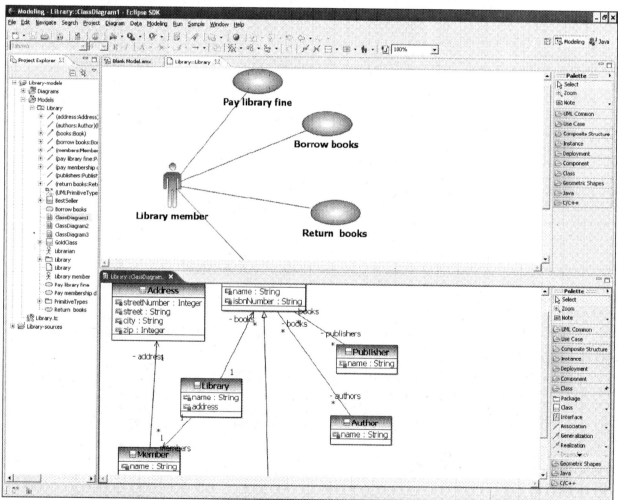

Figure 4-6   Use Case and Class Diagrams in Rational Software Architect

Partitioning models

Rational Software Architect lets the user partition a single model file into several partitions, which is useful for concurrent design in a team environment.

Model compare and merge

Rational Software Architect lets the user compare model files and merge them. This, combined with Rational Software Architect's integration with configuration management tools, is especially helpful in a team environment if different users are working on the same model. Two users may have checked out the same model and may have made concurrent changes to it. At check in, they can compare their workspace models with the one in the repository, and merge the two if necessary.

Publishing models

Rational Software Architect can process model information for viewing outside the tool. It lets users publish models on the Web, as a series of linked HTML pages. It also lets users publish reports about models. Both of these are useful in distributed teams for sharing the design. This allows the team to have limited Rational Software Architect licenses for design and modeling purposes, while the rest of the team still has viewing access to the models.

Integration with software configuration management tools

Rational Software Architect is integrated with such software configuration management (SCM) tools as IBM Rational ClearCase and CVS. So modeling artifacts can be easily shared between stakeholders across the globe. Changes are controlled and auditable.

From design to code and back again

Rational Software Architect provides model transformations. Model transformations enable the user to transform from models at one level of abstraction to another level of abstraction, for example, from analysis to design models, or from design models to source code. Architects in a distributed team can make use of this feature to generate an initial set of sources from the design model, thereby making sure that the developers start with the correct set of source files at the beginning of the implementation cycle.

When developers start on implementation, architects can continue to apply incremental design changes to the existing models and then transform the model on top of the existing sources, ensuring that the newly generated sources contain the newly added model changes, as well as preserve existing source code. This keeps the entire team on the same page as far as design and implementation go.

Rational Software Architect also provides a way in which a UML model can be generated by reverse transformation of the existing source code. The new model can be compared with the original model to validate changes, and take changes back to the original model if necessary. Architects can use this feature to validate implementations by remote developers.

Code visualization

Rational Software Architect provides visualization of existing source code, both Java™ and C++. Users can drag and drop source files onto the diagramming surface, and view language specific constructs as UML elements. Visualization in Rational Software Architect helps collaboration and communication by helping with the understanding of existing code. So if the design for the existing code is either missing or out-of-date or non-existent, visualization helps a lot in getting new teams up to speed. This is especially helpful in project transitions.

When a project is in a sustenance mode, it often needs enhancements. Rational Software Architect allows mixed mode modeling, in which users can design a model that has UML elements as well as visualized code elements. In case the original design is not available to the product sustenance team, team members can start designing with the visualized source code and then make enhancements to the model. In distributed teams, this mixed mode modeling is also a great way to get the design validated from the original stakeholders if required. It also gives an architect the confidence that a remote development team is not designing enhancements in a vacuum.

Traceability in design and implementation

Rational Software Architect provides an integration with RequisitePro through which requirements in RequisitePro can be linked with use cases in Rational Software Architect. Rational Software Architect also provides traceability from use cases to high level design, and from the design model to the source code. This way, users can have traceability all the way from requirements to source code.

Model validation

Rational Software Architect supports model validation based on constraints defined by a user. The architect can therefore define constraints for the design. Designers then have to comply with the constraints, or model validation will throw errors. This is a good way to achieve compliance in design for distributed teams.

4.3 A case study for requirements management and design

In our case study, we look at two different products in the ITSO Inc. portfolio: the ITSO Inc. Retail Cash Console and the ITSO Inc. Supply Chain Manager. Retail Cash Console will be transitioned to ITSO Inc.'s India division.

The Customer Profiler component will be developed out of ITSO Inc.'s India division. Supply Chain Manager will be a joint development effort between the Santa Clara and India offices.

The following sections take you through:

► The various configuration options that RequisitePro has to offer ITSO Inc.

► RequisitePro's integrations with other IBM Rational products, from effective links to design, defect tracking, and testing tools

► How the Indian team in ITSO Inc. used Rational Software Architect for product design and development

► How the India team in ITSO Inc. used Rational Software Architect for product transitioning

4.3.1 Configuring RequisitePro and RequisiteWeb

RequisitePro offers several configurations for a distributed team. The best configuration for a team depends on the team infrastructure. Generally, the RequisitePro server should be hosted locally to the team's central intelligence, or core users. Core users for RequisitePro are the business analysts and the systems analysts.

RequisitePro server location

In case of ITSO Inc., most of the business analysts and system analysts are based in Santa Clara. The host server for RequisitePro is therefore located in Santa Clara.

Katie and the other business analysts from the Santa Clara office are therefore using the native interface of RequisitePro, with all its capabilities.

Determining access levels for the team

The next step is to determine access levels for the rest of the team. These are some of the questions that need to be asked. Which members of the team need to access project requirements? Will they be updating requirements, or will they simply need to review requirements and be notified of changes? After an organization maps out its requirement usage model, it is easier to evaluate how to deploy the requirements management tool.

ITSO Inc. requirements management has the following types of users:

► Program/project managers want to review requirements for tracking purposes, and may need to update priorities, statuses, and risks associated with requirements.

► Architects need to study requirements for desiging the product, and would like to establish links between requirements and high level design artifacts.

► Designers and developers want to review requirements for understanding the system they are designing or developing.

► Testers want to study requirements to design test cases.

► Test architects want to establish links between requirements and test cases.

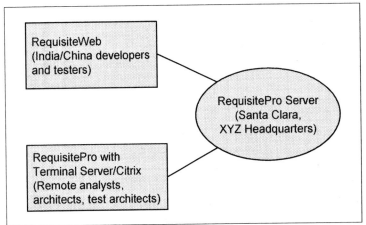

Figure 4-7   RequisitePro and RequisiteWeb configurations for ITSO Inc.

For program/project managers, developers, and testers, access to RequisitePro's Web Client is usually sufficient. The ITSO Inc. developers and program/project managers based in Santa Clara can access the requirements through RequisitePro. The India developers and project managers, and the testers in Beijing can access the same artifacts through RequisiteWeb.

Remote business and system analysts, such as Reena in Bangalore, who require the full capabilities of a native RequisitePro interface, use hosted RequisitePro environments on a Citrix/Windows Terminal Server. Arun, who is an architect in Bangalore, and Zhi, who is a test architect based out of Beijing, use this hosted environment as well, in order to be able to establish cross product links between RequisitePro and design tools like Rational Software Architect or test management tools such as Rational ClearQuest TestManager.

Configuring RequisitePro and RequisiteWeb are the first steps in creating a requirements management system. The next few sections describe how team ITSO Inc. is making use of RequisitePro and its integration with various life cycle products to create, manage, and control their requirements.

4.3.2 Managing requirements

ITSO Inc. records all customer requirements in RequisitePro. Requirements are collected through face-to-face meetings with prospective and current customers, trade shows, Web conferences, joint requirement studies with the customer, and so on.

Business analysts then analyze and collate the requirements and record them in the requirements database.

In our case study, we concentrate on how ITSO Inc. manages requirements for a new component of the ITSO Inc. retail manager, called the Supply Chain Manager. The design and development of this component will be done jointly by the Bangalore and the Santa Clara teams of ITSO Inc.

Requirements for ITSO Inc. Supply Chain Manager

At the beginning of the development cycle for ITSO Inc. Supply Chain Manager, Katie, a business analyst in Santa Clara, creates a new project in RequisitePro called ITSO Inc. Supply Chain Manager. She then creates several use cases in RequisitePro, and assigns them priorities. She creates detailed use case documents using Microsoft Word and links the Word documents with the requirements that she has created.

Katie created the following requirements for the Supply Chain Manager. We look at these requirements for our case study.

1. Do real-time inventory tracking by integration with an RFID system, and inform suppliers when the supplied products are running low.

2. Keep track of the consumption patterns of products.

3. Track supplier performance.

4. Integrate with Cash Console to answer customer queries about product availability.

5. Integrate with Cash Console to get new product requirements.

Collaborating with the teams

Katie starts a discussion thread with Debbie, the program manager from the Santa Clara site, and the two project managers responsible for new development: John from Santa Clara and Jay from Bangalore. Katie uses the discussion thread feature in RequisitePro to keep track of all discussions pertaining to a requirement. This links the requirement under discussion and the associated discussions. See Figure 4-8 for more details.

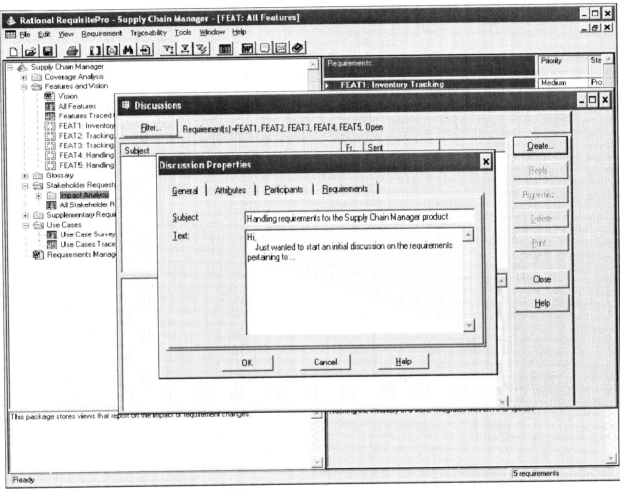

Figure 4-8   Starting a discussion on RequisitePro

Katie grants Debbie complete access control privileges.

Debbie, John, and Jay now plan on the work division between Santa Clara and Bangalore. It is decided that Requirements 1, 2, and 3 listed in "Requirements for ITSO Inc. Supply Chain Manager" on page 75 will be designed and developed by Santa Clara, while requirements 4 and 5 will be handled in Bangalore.

John and Jay are granted complete access control privileges for the requirements for which they are responsible. Architects, designers, and testers at all sites are given read privileges to all the requirements.

In addition, Debbie adds two architects, Arun from Bangalore, and Tom from Santa Clara, to the e-mail notification list for the requirements for which their teams are responsible. This is so that they are aware of any changes in the requirements that their teams design or develop. Debbie also adds the test architects from the Santa Clara and the Beijing locations to the e-mail notification list. This way, if requirements change, the test architects can modify the associated test cases. See Figure 4-9 for more information.

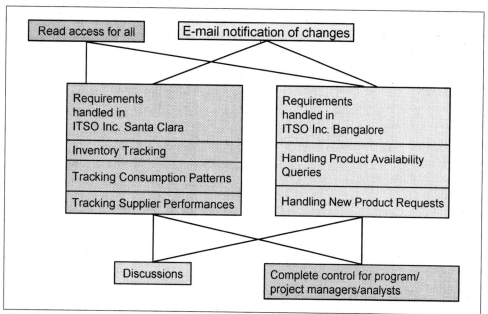

Figure 4-9   Collaborating via RequisitePro

Linking with test cases

The test architects, Cheng from Santa Clara and Zhi from Beijing, create a test suite in ClearQuest Test Manager. Then they make use of the RequisitePro/ClearQuest Test Manager integration to create and associate test cases with each requirement. When the test cases are defined and executed, each failed test case is recorded and tracked. This makes it easy for Debbie to keep track of the status of the requirements that are scheduled for implementation/delivery. See Figure 4-10 for more information.

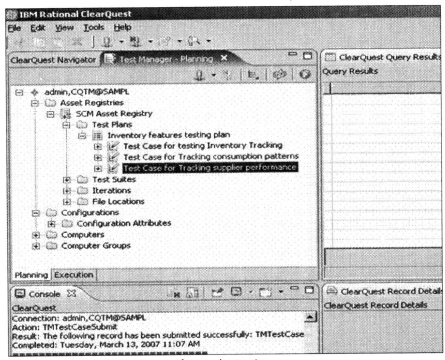

Figure 4-10   Creating test cases for requirements

Communicating requirement changes

After discussions with users, Katie realizes that a lot of the retail stores would like to use consumption pattern tracking to predict how much to order when a store is running low on an item. She enhances requirement 2 in the list above in RequisitePro, so that the requirement now becomes: Tracking consumption patterns and predicting reorders.

Katie also adds a new use case called Predicting Reorders to this feature.

Debbie (the program manager) and John and Jay get notified that a requirement has changed, as do Tom, the architect responsible for this requirement, and Zhi, the test architect responsible for testing the requirement.

Tom adds a new use case in Rational Software Architect, his design tool, corresponding to the new use case in RequisitePro. This use case is now linked to analysis and design classes and eventually will be implemented.

Zhi adds a new test case corresponding to the new use case. The tester responsible for testing the requirement makes sure that the new use case is tested.

4.3.3 Designing Supply Chain Manager using Rational Software Architect

After the requirements are captured in RequisitePro, the architects in Santa Clara and Bangalore start the high level design process. For the purpose of this discussion, we look at the requirement of Handling Product Availability Queries.

Linking use cases with requirements

The design process starts with Jay creating a use case diagram for this requirement and setting up a link between the uses cases representation in Rational Software Architect and their specifications in RequisitePro. This link helps ensure that each requirement that Katie documented is associated with the use cases in Rational Software Architect. See Figure 4-11 for more information.

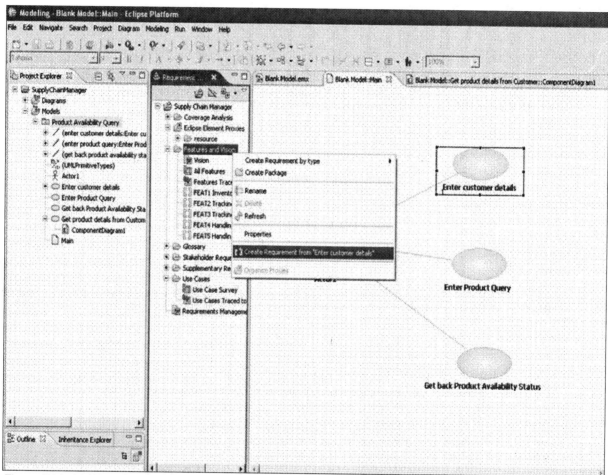

Figure 4-11   Linking Rational Software Architect use cases with requirements on RequisitePro

Creating analysis and design models

Next, Arun (one of the Bangalore architects) and the senior developers in the team create analysis models for the use cases, followed by a high-level design model, as shown in Figure 4-12.

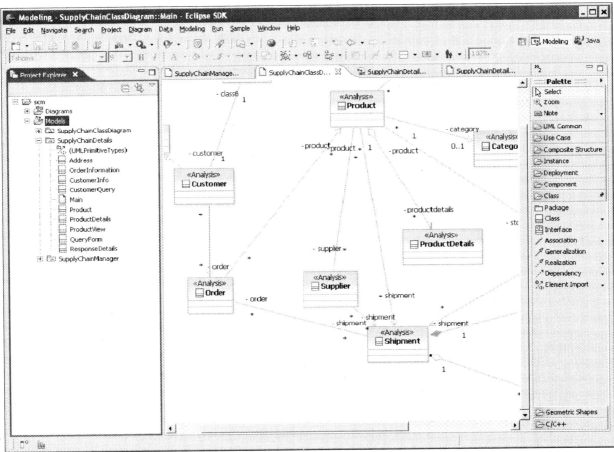

Figure 4-12   Analysis model in Rational Software Architect

Arun partitions the high-level models to allow concurrent access for the senior developers in Gurgaon and Bangalore. At the end of the day, developers who are working on the models are expected to merge the models, so that the two teams do not go out of sync.

Seeding the source project

When the design is stable, Arun runs a UML to Java Transform to generate the initial source code and hand the sources over to the development teams in Bangalore and Gurgaon for implementation.

The development teams implements the generated classes and checks in the source code. Rational Software Architect is integrated with SCM systems like CVS and ClearCase to allow them to do so.

Arun periodically checks the source code and runs the Java to UML transformation, comparing the generated UML model with the UML model, to see if there are any deviations. Occasionally, he also merges back such changes into the original model. Rational Software Architect helps keep the model in sync with the code that is being implemented.

Publishing models

Arun publishes the analysis models using the model publish feature of Rational Software Architect, and send the generated HTML pages to the test team in Beijing. The test team does not have Rational Software Architect licenses, but can still view the models to understand the high level design. This helps the test team come up with more effective test cases.

4.3.4 Transitioning Cash Console using Rational Software Architect

As discussed in Chapter 2, "Work transfer to subsite" on page 25, ITSO Inc.'s Cash Console product is being transitioned to Bangalore from Santa Clara.

One of the primary responsibilities that the Bangalore team has is to understand the source code to be able to maintain it, and enhance it, if required.

Cash Console is an older product, one of the first to be developed and showcased by ITSO Inc. It started with an initial design model, but as ITSO Inc. interacted with more and more users, many features got added, modified, and deleted. Unfortunately, not much effort was spent in making sure that the design remained in sync with the implementation.

The Bangalore team now faces the challenge of understanding the existing design. They can use the several features provided by Rational Software Architect to do the following:

- ► They can simply drag and drop the existing classes onto the diagramming surface. This would "visualize" the sources into a UML diagram. Rational Software Architect provides visualization for source code in Java, C++, or C#. See Figure 4-13 for more information.

- ► They can use the "Show Related Elements" feature in Rational Software Architect to see elements related to an existing class.

- ► They can browse classes in topic diagrams as well, to understand relationships between existing classes.

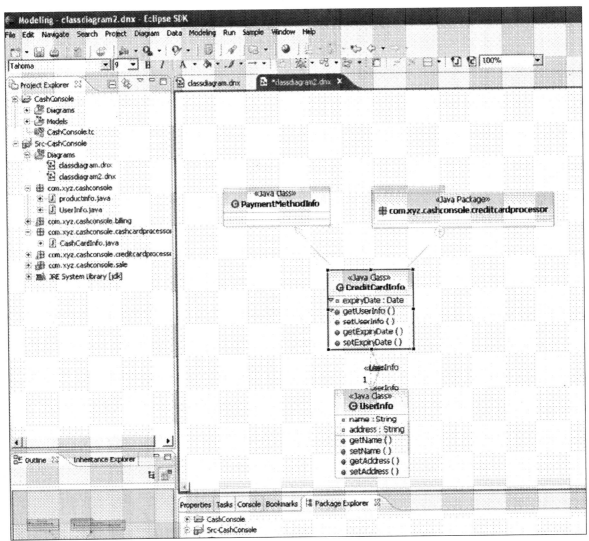

Figure 4-13   Visualizing CashConsole

The Bangalore team can also extend, edit, and modify the visualized code. When they need to make feature enhancements, they use the mixed modeling capabilities provided by Rational Software Architect, to design using the existing visualized classes as well as new UML classes.

The Bangalore team shares their models with the Santa Clara team for design validations.

The code visualization and mixed mode modeling capabilities of Rational Software Architect make transitioning easier and help bring the Bangalore team up to speed so that they can take ownership of the Cash Console product.

Change management and reporting

This chapter explains how to do efficient change management and planning to fix defects or features in time, with optimum utilization of resources in geographically dispersed teams. This chapter has two case studies that are important in geographically distributed change management, with examples on how to solve them using Rational tools. It also shows the various reporting formats and tools that help create efficient reports and charts.

5.1 Change management

Changes are inherent in any software product. No software product is bug-free. As customers use the products, they find defects in the product. Defects and feature requests are often filed within the organization. *Change management* is the process in which you manage changes in the artifacts, for example changes in source code, that are involved in any development life cycle. It involves the process in which a change request (CR) is received, prioritized, assigned, worked upon, and closed.

In maintenance projects, CRs, such as defects, escalations, or enhancement requests, are the triggers for any feature change. They are filed either from within the organization, such as defects filed by the internal testing team, or externally by customers. CRs are triaged based on priority determination, and ultimately ownership is assigned. Estimations are done to determine the time and resources required for resolution. When these steps are complete, execution begins to address the CR.

To manage changes, organizations use change management tools. In the following section, we briefly discuss the features that any quality change management system should have. In addition, we focus on two of the many aspects of change management for geographically distributed teams, namely triage and security. This section also showcases how Rational ClearQuest can help you overcome some of these change management challenges. For Rational ClearQuest terminologies, refer to Appendix A, "Mapping and terminology of the IBM Rational product set" on page 211.

5.1.1 Prerequisites of a change management system

In this section, we discuss what the basic requirements of any quality change management system are and how they can be used in geographically distributed teams.

A consolidated database and fast access to data

The most important aspect of any change tracking tool is its ability to store and retrieve information in a consolidated format. This is even more important in organizations that are geographically dispersed. Deploying a consolidated database means having a fast, real-time repository of CRs that can be looked upon and worked on by dispersed teams. It also makes project monitoring easier across the board.

In an ideal world, such a single database approach is not easy to implement because it introduces latency due to network inefficiency between geographies. You might think that the problem of latency can be solved by having a consolidated database and Web clients to access it. However, the challenge lies in handling scalability issues, especially when you have a hundred or more users who are trying to access the database simultaneously from dispersed locations. A centralized database demands network high availability, acceptable bandwidth, and latency levels. The other challenge is catering to the ever changing nature of a CR record, which can be quite complicated and configurable.

> **Note:** Rational ClearQuest provides a Web client that can be used to access databases over low bandwidth networks.

The problem of latency has been partially solved by the concept of replication. Rational ClearQuest uses a data replication model in its multisite configuration. In replication, each geographical region has a copy of the database, and the databases are synchronized at regularly and configurable scheduled intervals. This gives the user a virtual single consolidated database to work with. Figure 5-1 shows a typical multisite architecture.

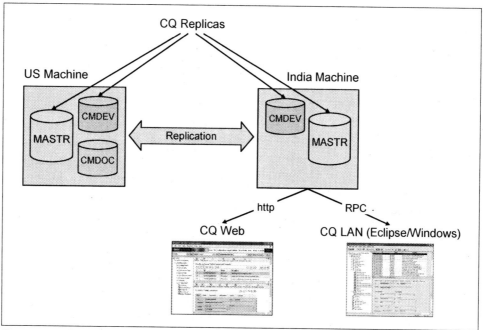

Figure 5-1   ClearQuest multisite and clients

Figure 5-1 shows how replication works in ClearQuest. ClearQuest has two databases types:

▶ Master (MASTR), which contains the schema information
▶ User Database (CMDEV), which contains the data part of the records

Both of these databases are replicated in a multisite environment. ClearQuest native clients, such as Eclipse and Windows clients, work in a LAN environment. The CQWeb client is ideal to remotely access records in a wide area network (WAN) environment and works on HTTP.

In a ClearQuest multisite environment, tracking changes and preventing data corruption are accomplished with an exclusive-right-to-modify scheme called *mastership*. Mastership determines when a user of a replica is allowed to modify data. For example, when record R1 is mastered in the U.S. replica, only users local to the U.S. replica can modify R1. Users local to any other replica find R1 as a read-only record and are unable to modify it. They can only modify the record if mastership of the record is transferred to them.

The concept of mastership was introduced to avoid conflicts between two or more replicas. For example, if there was no concept of mastership, a record might be modified at two different replicas and would cause a conflict during replication. Often users of a different replica use the CQWeb client to modify a record that is not mastered in their own replica. For example, a user in India can modify a record mastered in the U.S. using the CQWeb client.

Note: The CQWeb client can be used to connect to a different replica.

Traceability of change requests in a software life cycle
The other important feature a change management system should support is the traceability of a CR across various stages in a software development life cycle.

The flow of defects and CRs and its relation to other activities in a software life cycle is shown in Figure 5-2.

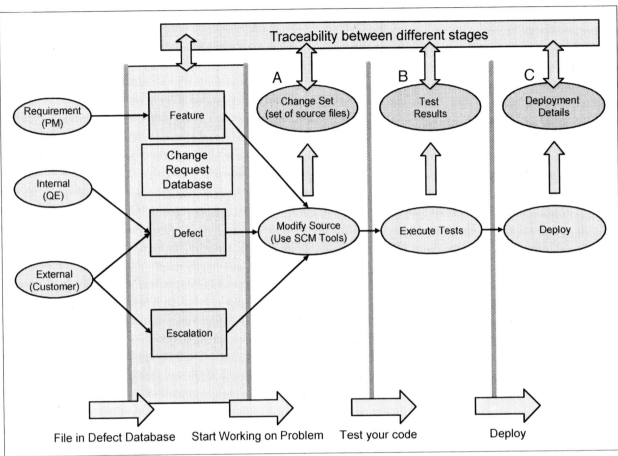

Figure 5-2   Traceability of a CR in a software development life cycle

Figure 5-2 shows the different stages that a product goes through. A CR database ties together all the activities in different stages. It is important to keep the traceability between various stages because you can trace a test case to a requirement and a requirement to the source code. The traceability information can be stored in one single repository, which is the CR database. The important artifacts that form the components in a trace can be the source change set (a list of source files changed to address the CR), test results, and deployment details. This means that you can trace a requirement or a CR to a set of source files and to a set of test cases that test the CR. These components are shown in the ovals marked A, B, and C in Figure 5-2 and are crucial pieces of information to maintain traceability.

Having a traceable solution is crucial for geographically distributed teams, since each of the stages in a software life cycle might be managed by different geographical teams. We recommend that you keep all the traceability, references, and artifacts in one single change management system.

Rational ClearQuest provides integration with software configuration management (SCM) tools such as ClearCase and other third-party SCM solutions. This feature enables you to view change sets inside a CR record. You can read more about ClearCase and ClearQuest Integration in 6.6, "ClearQuest integration" on page 141. ClearQuest Test Manager provides mechanisms to create test plans, execute test cases, and record the test results inside ClearQuest. For more information about Test Manager integration, see Chapter 8, "Test management" on page 167. ClearQuest comes with many ready-to-use schema packages, such as BuildTracking and DeploymentTracking, which help track build and deployment activities. Thus Rational ClearQuest supports traceability across the SCM, testing, build, and deployment disciplines.

Security

Security is another important aspect of change management in geographically distributed teams. Sometimes work is outsourced to a different lab where the trust level is low and therefore enforcement of certain access restrictions is desired. A change management system that enables you to manage groups and provide access restrictions to records helps to implement a more secure system. Organizations in geographically distributed teams often have granular security requirements. We can classify security needs in a matrix as shown in Figure 5-3.

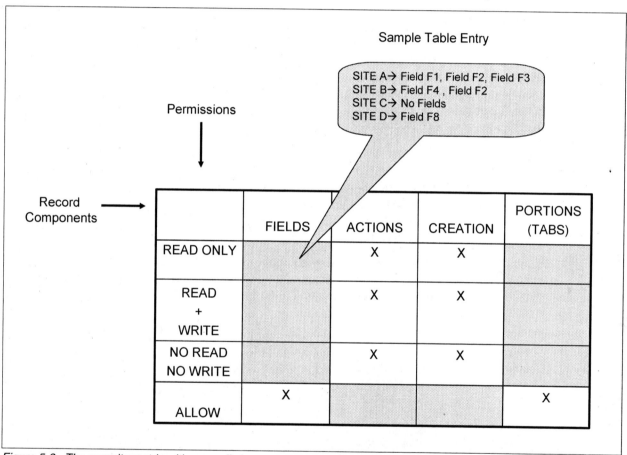

Figure 5-3   The security matrix with one cell shown as an example

In Figure 5-3, the shaded boxes should have a valid list of distributed sites or groups, indicating which privileges each group has. For example, in the box at the intersection of the "Fields" column and the "Read only" row, we specify a set of groups that have only read only permissions to certain fields. In the box, we specify both the groups and sites and the fields to which each group has permission for read only. An entry example is shown in the call-out. This way, we can uniquely define the security requirements of an organization. You must determine whether your CR tracking tool helps you implement the security matrix that you define.

ClearQuest can be customized to implement the security matrix. We examine such a case study in 5.1.2, "A case study on security" on page 90.

High availability

In distributed teams, high availability of a centralized repository for change management is important. In geographically distributed teams, if the server or network connection in one site goes down, other sites should still have access to data.

The concept of replicas in Rational ClearQuest helps organizations take advantage of this kind of high availability. For example, if you use ClearQuest multisite, you have replicas at each of the geographical sites. These replicas act as a backup for data. Even if one replica is down or destroyed, the other replicas still hold the information even if the link is not working.

Communication and governance

Change management systems used by geographically distributed teams should facilitate the process for distributed teams to stay connected with each other and with the work in progress. Change management systems should integrate with mailing systems to send notifications to the required people.

Rational ClearQuest has an e-mail notification feature that automatically sends mail to the required people whenever a change happens in the system. This way everyone can be aware of what is happening. Another means of communication enables a person to place comments in the Notes section of every record. This allows everyone to keep track of all conversations that happen about a particular CR.

Compliance and auditability are important aspects of governance and should be part of any change management system. Compliance involves making sure that company rules and regulations are followed. Often change management workflows involve signoffs from various people. In distributed teams, these people might be located in different geographies. Rational ClearQuest comes with such features as e-signature, which helps ensure that people can perform certain actions only after they sign in with a username and password.

Auditability involves keeping track of all the changes that have occurred. Organizations want to keep information in regard to who did what and when in any change management system. Rational ClearQuest helps keep auditability using the Audit Trail package.

A configurable and flexible change management infrastructure

Any quality change management system must be customizable and provide several ready-to-use solutions to help accelerate implementation and deployment of the system. Today's software processes are continually changing, and geographically distributed teams continue to grow and are required to collaborate more effectively. To meet these changing business needs, change management systems must have the flexibility to be customized.

Consider the example of increasing the state of a defect. The state of a defect signifies the stage it is in. For example, a defect can have states such as Submitted, Assigned, Active, and Closed. This means that the defect moves from one state to another as the software life cycle progresses. If a defect goes through these four states, and you want to add another state (for example, Open) to meet an organizational need, you should have the ability to do so and deploy it in a short span of time. Rational ClearQuest gives you this ability by offering several ready-to-use schemas that help you address your needs faster.

Organizations might want to add new workflows, new integrations with other tools (for example, data sharing between two tools), or new kinds of records (for example, the ability to manage risk). All these are possible only if your change management system allows customizations.

In the following example, we show you how the particular needs of geographical teams are addressed using the ability of ClearQuest to customize schemas. To understand more about the ClearQuest schema, see Appendix A, "Mapping and terminology of the IBM Rational product set" on page 211.

Let us take the example of the scenario in this book where the testers are located in China and the developers are located in India. Every ClearQuest record has a mastership associated with it. This is true whenever there is a multisite implementation of ClearQuest. A record can be mastered in only one replica at any particular time. When a record is mastered in, for example, China, it cannot be modified by any user in India by connecting to the India replica. (You can use the CQWeb client to connect to the China replica and make the change). Users belong to a particular replica.

Let us take a scenario where triaging of defects happens in Santa Clara. Defects can be worked on in any lab. However, verification of defects only happens in China. Since the testers are in the China lab, whenever a defect is resolved by a developer, their work starts. This means that any defect in the resolved state is owned by the China lab. Therefore, we can group the various states of the defect according to the geographical regions shown in Figure 5-4.

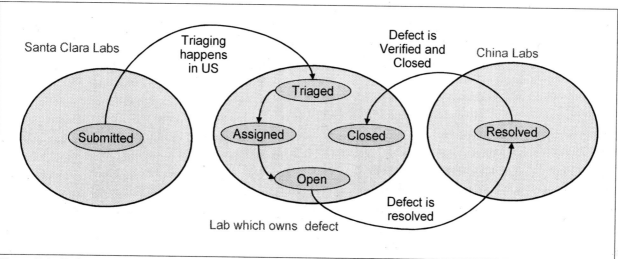

Figure 5-4   Defect states across geographies

For the sake of simplicity, in the model in Figure 5-4, we have only own a couple of states and the normal flow (see arrows).

Let us look at the implementation of the requirements. ClearQuest allows you to produce this schema with one of its powerful features called *hooks*. In ClearQuest, you can add hooks that get fired whenever the user does a particular action. Hooks are pieces of code that you can write in a scripting language such as Visual Basic® or Perl. They are embedded in the schema, when someone is designing it. ClearQuest API methods called from the hooks allow you to have read and write access to most of the contextual information in a ClearQuest record. For example, you can write a hook that populates a field in a record with a certain value whenever a particular action is applied on the record. Hooks are also useful to do integrations with other tools, to move data to and from ClearQuest to other systems, and vice versa.

To implement the scenario we described previously, we write a base validation hook for a defect where we make the mastership change. A base validation hook is called every time a change happens to the defect record. The way a base validation hook is created is shown in Figure 5-5. This is done inside ClearQuest Designer.

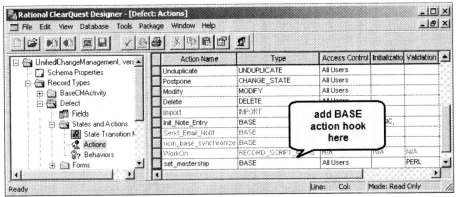

Figure 5-5 ClearQuest multisite: Automating a state-based change of mastership

The Perl script hook to do this is shown in Example 5-1. In this example, we try to see the state of the record and accordingly set the ratl_mastership field of the record. The ratl_mastership field determines in which replica a record is mastered.

Example 5-1 ClearQuest multisite: A state-based mastership hook

```
sub Defect_Validation {
my($actionname, $actiontype) = @_;
my $result;
    $sessionObj = $entity->GetSession();
    $state     = $entity->GetFieldValue("State")->GetValue();
    $owner     = $entity->GetFieldValue("Owner")->GetValue();
    $site      = $entity->GetFieldValue("ratl_mastership")->GetValue();
    # check state value
    if ($state eq "Submitted") {
        #set mastership to Santa Clara
        $$entity->SetFieldValue("ratl_mastership", "SANTA_CLARA");
    }elsif ($state eq "Resolved")
        #set mastership to China
        $$entity->SetFieldValue("ratl_mastership", "CHINA");
    }elsif ($state eq "Assigned" | "Opened" | "Triaged" | "Closed") {
        #get mastership of the current record owner
        my $userObj        = $sessionObj->GetEntity("users",$owner);
        my $userMastership =
            $userObj->GetFieldValue("ratl_mastership")->GetValue();
        #set mastership of record to match current owner
        $entity->SetFieldValue("ratl_mastership",$userMastership);
    }
return $result;
```

5.1.2 A case study on security

Let us take an example of a scenario from ITSO Inc. where the company might want to implement a secure mechanism of dealing with groups where work is outsourced. In this example, Dublin Lab is an outsourced partner to ITSO Inc. that does translation.

Currently, work is assigned to Dublin Lab in the form of defects, which contain the file that needs translation. When the job is complete, the translated file is returned to the core site. A simple mailing mechanism would be sufficient here, but ITSO Inc. wants to integrate the efforts of Dublin Lab in their existing Defect Tracking database and keep track of their work for auditability reasons. ITSO Inc. wants to make sure all the teams in the different geographies use the same Defect Tracking database, even if they are contractors who are in an untrusted network.

The other important requirement for this process is that the Dublin Lab should not have visibility of all the defects in the organization, but just the defects that are assigned to them. Even in the defects assigned to them, ITSO Inc. does not want Dublin Lab to modify certain fields of the Defect Record and do certain actions. The only actions that are allowed are to "Open" a defect (meaning someone has started working on it) and then to "Resolve" it (meaning the person finished the work). Moreover, the U.S. Lab does not want to show the History Tab for any defect to the Dublin Lab users. In the following section, we show you how Rational ClearQuest can help you implement such a workflow using the Security Context feature of ClearQuest.

Implementing the case study using Rational ClearQuest

IBM Rational ClearQuest can help you implement this case study. In this example, we show how you can alter the defect schema supplied with ClearQuest to achieve security needs. We use certain features of ClearQuest such as security context, Tab hiding, and the feature to allow actions for a set of users to implement the case study.

What is security context

Security context is a feature in ClearQuest that helps address the security needs of ClearQuest records. It helps in hiding certain records for a particular set of users. You can use it to hide a set of records, or you can customize it such that you hide the records only when they attain a particular state. We use this security context feature to implement this scenario.

Figure 5-6 shows what a security context is in ClearQuest and how to design a secure system with using the security context.

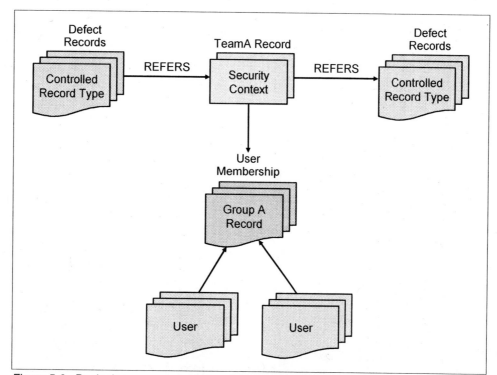

Figure 5-6   Designing a secure system using security context in ClearQuest

Figure 5-6 shows the elements that are used to design your security system. Each defect record in a security system references one or many security context records. Any record can be made a security context record. For example, you have a record type called "TeamA". If you make it a security context, then you have to tell which user groups can access that record. In this case, this record is TeamA, which signify all the members belonging to TeamA. Whenever the TeamA record becomes a security context, ClearQuest asks you to add user groups to TeamA. The user group signifies the users belonging to TeamA. A defect can point to multiple security contexts (such as TeamA and TeamB). In that case, people who belong to both teams can view and modify the records.

Creating user groups in ClearQuest

To implement the security case study, first you must create the user groups, before you decide on which user group has what permissions. A *user group* is a name that signifies a set of users. Whenever you create a group, you must add users to it.

We create two user groups: one for the Dublin users (called Dublin) and the other group for the rest of the team, which is the U.S. team (called US). There is also a group called Everyone, but we do not use it in this schema. Assume for the sake of simplicity that Dublin has just three members, sam, jon, and tom. We use the ClearQuest User Administration Tool to create the user groups. Figure 5-7 shows how the Administration Tool looks after the groups are created.

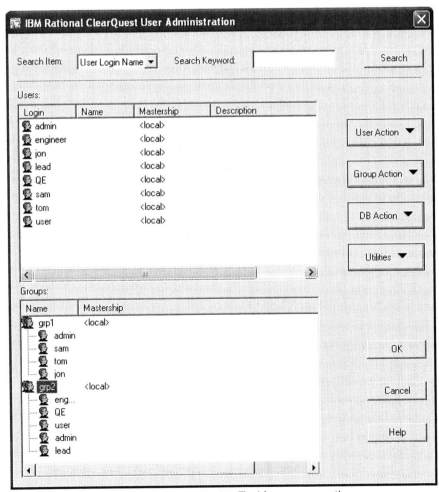

Figure 5-7   ClearQuest User Administration Tool for group creation

Changes in the ClearQuest schema

In this scenario, we have two teams: one for the Dublin team and one for the rest of the company. Therefore we need two security context record instances of a particular record that will be our security context record. In this case, we create a stateless record called "Team". (A field in the Defect record needs to refer to this security context record.) We create a field called "team" for this, as shown in Figure 5-8. The field "team" can have two values, as explained in the following sections.

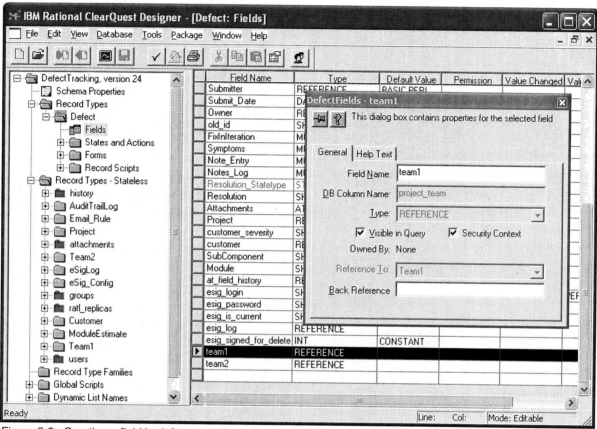

Figure 5-8   Creating a field in defect record which refers to a security context

In Figure 5-8, the Security Context option is selected, which indicates that if the field "team" has a valid value, then members who belong only to that value (that is Team) can access the records.

Next we restrict some of the Actions such as Submit and Assign to Dublin users (that is the Dublin group). We use the Designer feature on Actions to do this. Figure 5-9 shows how you can allow the Action "Assign" only to users in the U.S.

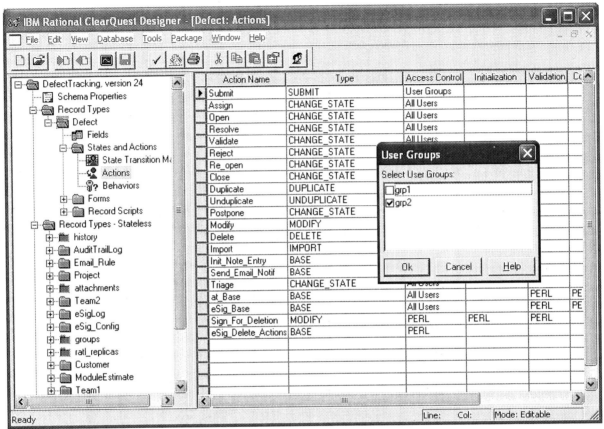

Figure 5-9   Restricting Assign Action to the US group only

Other features are the ability to disallow modification of certain fields in the Defect Form and the ability to hide certain Tabs in ClearQuest. For example, in this scenario, if we do not want the Dublin users to view the History pane of a defect record, we open the Tab Properties of the History tab in the Forms view in Designer as shown in Figure 5-10. We select the U.S. group to enable only members of the U.S. group to view the History tab.

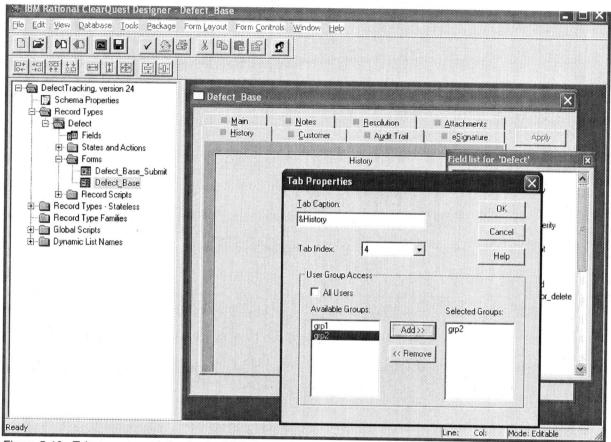

Figure 5-10   Tab access restriction for the History tab

When these steps are complete, you are ready to deploy your schema.

ClearQuest client side record creation

The next step is to create instances of Record Type "Team" in ClearQuest and set the group permissions in them. We need two instances of record type Team. One instance is for only U.S. users, and the other instance is for users in both the U.S. and Dublin. In this case, we need two instances. If you have more groups where you want to enforce restrictions, you need more than two such instances.

The administrator does this by submitting a new record, one for the U.S. group and one for everyone. The "Ratl_security" tab in Team record is automatically created by ClearQuest whenever a record is used as a security context. It is important for the administrator to complete this Tab with the appropriate user group associated with this security context.

Figure 5-11 shows how the administrator adds both the "Dublin" and "US" groups in the Ratl_security tab of the record instance named "Everyone". When a record refers to security context record "US", only US group members can see it, not the Dublin users. If the defect record refers to "Everyone", then both Dublin and US members can see the records.

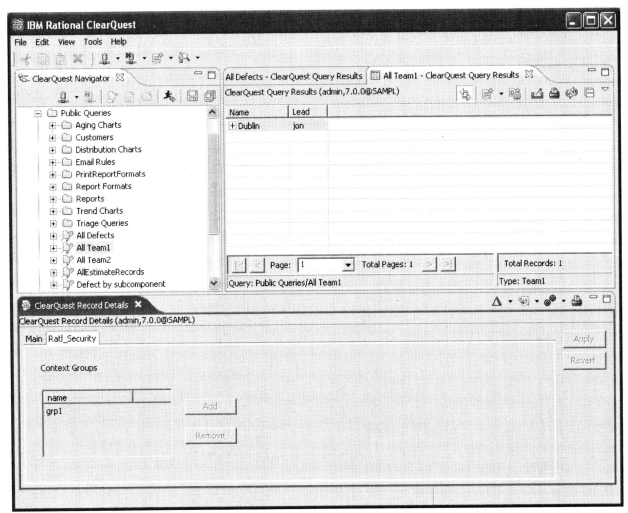

Figure 5-11   Associating the correct groups in a security context record

ClearQuest client usage by users

Now when a user from the core group in the U.S. logs into ClearQuest and views records, the user sees all the records including the ones that are meant for the Dublin users. However when someone from Dublin logs in, the user sees only the records that are assigned to the Dublin lab. Moreover the Dublin users are not allowed to perform certain actions, such as Assign. Figure 5-12 shows the view for a user in the U.S.

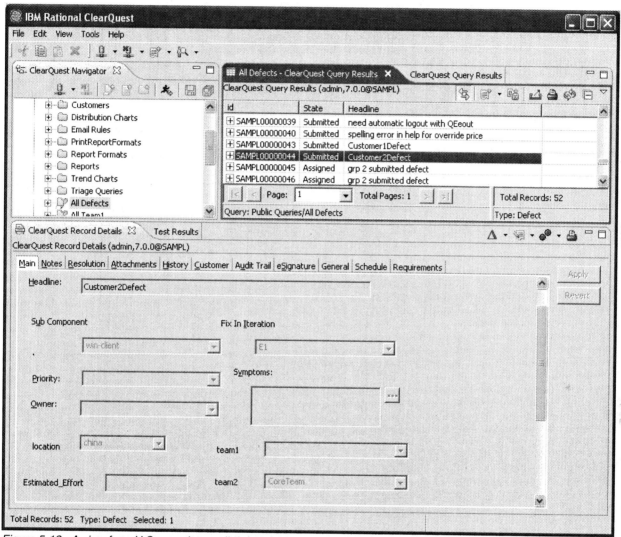

Figure 5-12   A view for a U.S. user (sees all defects) with the History tab visible

Figure 5-13 shows the view for a user in Dublin.

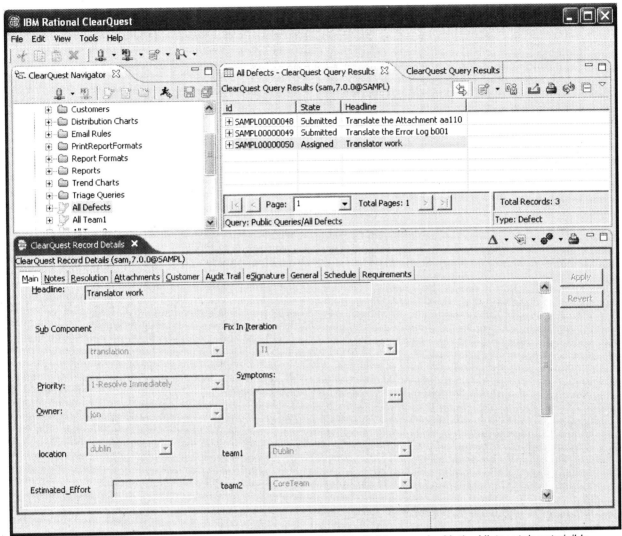

Figure 5-13   A view for a Dublin user (sees only defects assigned to Dublin group) with the History tab not visible

The field called "team" either has the vale "US" or "Everyone". For records that need to be seen by the Dublin users, team has the value of "Everyone". For records that do not need to be seen by the Dublin users, the value is "US".

Therefore, it is important that the "team" gets properly filled. One approach is to use a hook to populate it. For example, whenever the defect is assigned to a Dublin user, we can assign this field to "Everyone" using a hook at assignment. Again whenever a defect is resolved, we can clear the "team" field and assign it back to "US". The system can be so designed that we do not need to show this field (namely "team") in the form, and it can be internally managed by hooks. This makes it seamless to users who are both in the U.S. and in Dublin.

5.1.3 A case study on triage

Triaging is the process of looking at the submitted CRs, prioritizing them, and deciding whether the defects can be fixed in the current iteration and if not in which iteration. Sometimes it might not be submitted CRs but a backlog of CRs that your organization has. Triaging is a challenging process especially in projects that have a high inflow of defects. Without proper triaging, CRs can pile up, and deciding which CR to fix might become a daunting task for the project manager. Regular triaging is a must to ensure proper inflow and outflow of CRs. This section shows how you can effectively triage CRs by using a proper triage process on a regular basis.

Why a proper triage process is important for geographically distributed teams

In change management, triaging is an important aspect. With different teams across geographies, it becomes even more important. There is a huge inflow of CRs from various sources, and you might have limited set of resources to fix them. Therefore, it becomes important to understand the priority of a defect and decide who and by when to fix it.

Whenever you have geographically distributed teams, it is important to involve all the key stake holders while making such a decision. A proper workflow or process is needed to achieve this. Geographical teams with an informal change management process often fail to deliver in time or deliver unimportant components. One of the main reasons for this is a lack of communication and cumulative decision making at the beginning of the project. A proper triage process avoids such lack of communication and helps make projects successful.

Triaging process

In this section, we discuss triaging across geographies.

Triage participants and meetings

The group of people who do triage are often called the Change Control Board (CCB). The CCB not just is responsible for triaging, but also for deciding if fixes for CRs should be delivered for a particular release. Typical members in this triage group are:

- Technical leads
- Project managers
- Technical customer support lead
- Triage coordinator (can be the CCB lead)

All of these participants can be geographically distributed. For a single product, there are multiple components. Each component has a lead and a project manager, and sometimes one person handles both of these responsibilities. The role of the technical lead is to get a feel for the complexity of a defect fix and the number of days needed to fix it. The role of the project manager is to look at the work from a broader perspective and make a commitment.

Triaging involves technical support, since support spends quite some time with customers and knows their problems and pain. They are important contributors in triage meetings because they help the team prioritize the CRs and set deadlines. What looks like an appealing feature to a technical lead may not make much business value to a customer. A customer support person helps keep with reality.

There has to be a meeting moderator, who coordinates the show. That person is a project manager. This role can rotate among project managers. However, it has been determined that better results have come if this is a full-time job, specifically for products that have a high inflow of CRs. The job then becomes not just of a meeting coordinator, but of one who makes sure that the backlog of CRs are low. This person can also track whether other project managers are meeting their commitments. Triage coordination can be a role that existing project managers can take for extended periods of six months to a year.

Triage meetings should be held at least twice a month. However, if the inflow of CRs for a particular product is high (say greater than 15 a week), triage meetings should be held every week. Meeting timings should be arranged so that it is convenient to all participants in various geographies.

The triage workflow

Figure 5-14 shows the workflow for a typical triage process.

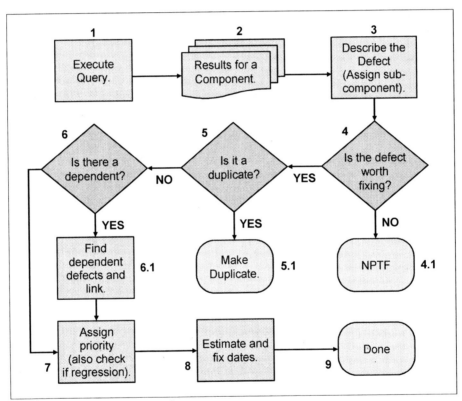

Figure 5-14   The triaging workflow

The steps are self explanatory. In this workflow, certain steps are challenges in a GDD environment:

► Step 4: Deciding on No plan To Fix (NPTF)

In this step, the team checks if the CR is worth fixing. Some CRs might not be critical from a customer's point of view. For example, a customer CR was filed two years ago, the customer no longer has ties to the organization, and no such problem will be encountered in the future. This is an ideal situation for NPTF. Whenever a CR is closed to NPTF, proper reasoning should be entered in the CR tracking database. Remember that often it is not possible to fix all CRs for various reasons such as development resource, testing resource, and time to market. Therefore it is important to make decisions so that important and critical CRs are handled first. Such a decision should be made with all stakeholders from the various geographies to contribute to the final decision.

► Step 7

An important step is to assign priority. Going by the same principles of an NPTF, it is important to prioritize CRs properly. The primary reason is that because resources and time are limited, working on CRs that are high priority makes sense to the business.

An important aspect in this step is to check if the CR is a *regression*. A regression is a CR that was introduced because of changes made to fix another CR. A regression is found by the internal testing team. Give a regression a high priority and start working on it immediately. It is also good practice to link CRs and their regressions in the CR tracking database. so you can look later to see whether you introduced a lot of defects while fixing a CR.

In the next section, you see how Rational ClearQuest can help you create and follow such a workflow for a team that is geographically distributed.

Triaging using Rational ClearQuest

In this section, we show an example of how you can use Rational ClearQuest to implement the triage workflow mentioned in the previous section. The advantage of using ClearQuest in this scenario is the fact that it is inherently distributed and all teams can access it, even if they are geographically distributed. Here we assume that we have a geographically distributed team of technical leads and project managers and customer support personnel who are using ClearQuest at their respective sites.

State diagram design in ClearQuest

Rational ClearQuest is a CR tracking tool where you can design your own schema. To learn more about a schema, refer to Appendix A, "Mapping and terminology of the IBM Rational product set" on page 211. Here we show how you can add one more state to the existing defect tracking schema that is shipped with ClearQuest to achieve a triage workflow.

Figure 5-15 shows the different states that a defect has and how you can move from one state to another. We introduce a new state called "Triaged", which you can apply if your organization needs to do triaging on CRs. Even without the state called "Triaged", you can still do triaging with the basic defect tracking schema that is shipped with ClearQuest. Addition of a new state makes the process more streamlined, thereby ensuring that your organization follows triaging rigidly.

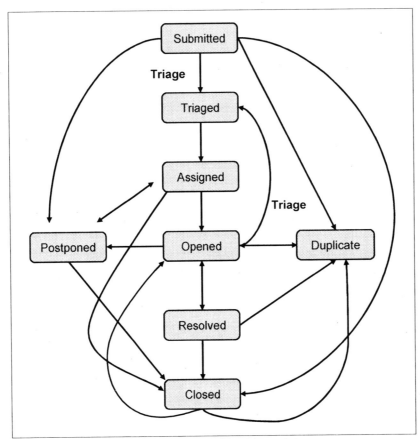

Figure 5-15   Diagram of a defect state with a triage state

In Figure 5-15, the "Triaged" state can be attained either from a "Submitted" state or an "Opened" state. This means that we not only allow triaging of submitted defects but also of defects that were triaged earlier but were never fixed and caused a back log.

To move to the "Triaged" state, you have to apply the "Triage" action. For brevity's sake, we have not mentioned all the actions in the diagram. When someone applies the triage action, certain fields must be filled:

► Sub-Component (to which subcomponent of the product does this defect belong)
► Priority (as discussed in "Step 7" on page 101, it is important to assign priority)
► Owner (the project manager owning the subcomponent)
► Fix In iteration (the time frame in which the defect should be fixed)

In ClearQuest designer, there is a way to specify which fields need to be mandatory when moving to a particular state. We use that feature to perform the previously described action.

Triaging in ClearQuest client

After the ClearQuest schema is designed, it can be deployed and triage teams can use it. In the triage meetings, the meeting coordinator executes the "Submitted Defects for Product P" Query, which is a Public Query. We are considering the case where we triage only submitted defects; the same process can be applied when you want to triage "Open" defects. In the case of "Open" defects, a different query can be used. For example, it can be a Dynamic Query, which asks if the user wants defects that have been "Open" from a specific time T. T can be input by the user. Dynamic Query is a feature in ClearQuest where the parameters of the query can be given when the query is executed. Note that all these steps can be done at the respective geographical sites of the project managers, as they have access to the same ClearQuest repository.

Figure 5-16 shows a window from the ClearQuest client, when someone wants to triage a defect. In this example, the defect getting triaged is "SAMPL00000032".

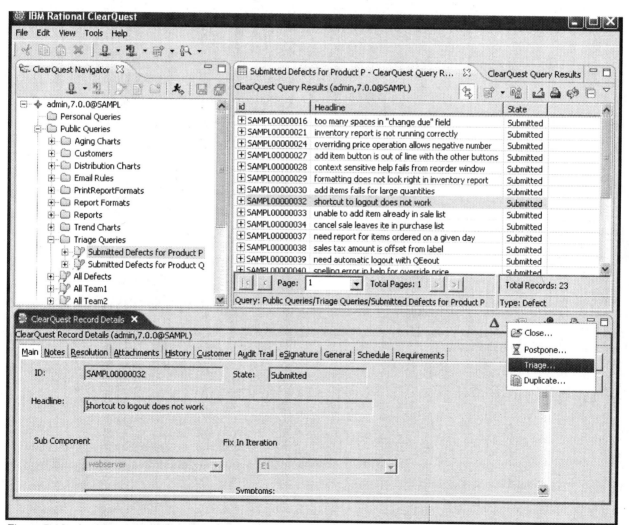

Figure 5-16   Applying the Triage action

After clicking Triage, the user completes the mandatory fields that are described in "State diagram design in ClearQuest" on page 102. The form looks like the one shown in Figure 5-17. The *Sub Component, *Fix Ir Iteration, *Priority, and *Owner fields are mandatory fields to take the defect to a triaged state.

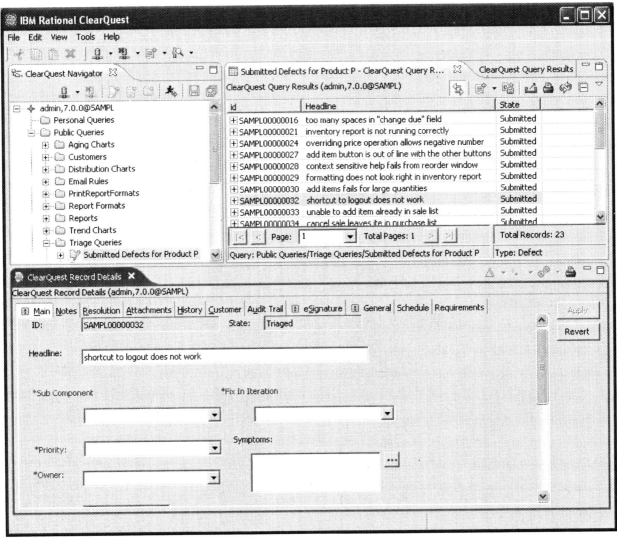

Figure 5-17   Mandatory fields for triaging

5.2 Reporting

Reporting is a means by which you present your status or findings. Good reporting is about displaying the right data so that you can make the right decisions to achieve your objectives. Good reporting also means how intelligently you can present data in less space and with simplicity, so that it is faster to read and interpret.

In geographically distributed teams, reporting is a means by which important decisions are made about the strategy and future of a company. Whether you are a CEO sitting in New York and wanting to view how projects are going on in Bangalore or a project manager in China wanting to view whether all the test cases passed in the Boston machine, everyone loves to view status or results in colorful diagrams giving you maximum information in a limited space.

In the following sections, we discuss some of the useful reports. We discuss some of the important reporting features of tools like Rational Portfolio Manager, ClearQuest, and Project Console.

5.2.1 Project health

Monitoring project health is an important activity for senior management and decision makers. Understanding which projects are doing well and which are draining company resources is important. Having a complete view of project portfolio in comparison with each other is necessary. The view should also let a decision maker drill down in a particular project and find out why it is not doing well.

Rational Portfolio Manager provides good reporting to show the health of projects in one chart called the bubble chart. The projects can be executed geographically distributed, but Rational Portfolio Manager gives you one dashboard for the health of all the projects. Note that this is a unique graph that gives you four degrees of information, namely the X coordinate, the Y coordinate, the size of the bubble, and the color of the bubble. Figure 5-18 is a "Running The Business (RTB) Active Projects" template of bubble charts available in Rational Portfolio Manager.

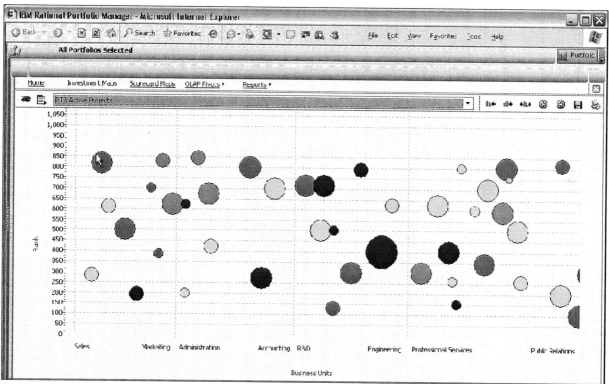

Figure 5-18   Bubble chart in Rational Portfolio Manager

In Figure 5-18, the X axis has the various projects in the organization. The Y axis is a forced ranking of the various projects. The size of the bubble indicates the project cost and the color of the bubble indicates whether a project is running smooth or bad. Red indicates that there is trouble and green indicates everything is great. Other colors indicate that the project is between red and green. You can define the thresholds that determine when a project goes red, and even the parameters that will be considered. For example, in the previous portfolio, we consider Schedule and Budget Variance as important parameters. Other parameters that are considered are customer satisfaction and risks in the project.

The other important aspect of this bubble chart is that you can drill down to the last level of detail. For example, if project bubble A is in red and is huge, a decision maker can click it and look at the parameters that caused it to under perform. Each parameter can then be analyzed to check why things went wrong and what aspects need to be improved. Therefore, we see that such a bubble chart can help decision makers quickly come to a conclusion and make decisions with the help of objective data.

5.2.2 Defect management charts

Defect trends can be of various types. We give you four such examples which can be useful in geographically distributed product development.

Components distribution across geographies

This kind of chart shows the component distribution across geographies. It is useful in understanding the competencies that different geographies have. Figure 5-19 shows the example in Rational ClearQuest. From the figure, we can conclude that Dublin Lab just does Translation.

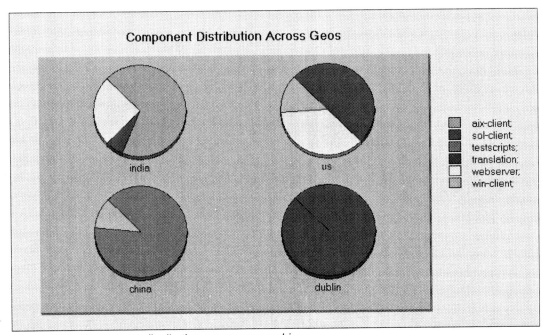

Figure 5-19   Component distribution across geographies

Defect distribution across geographies

This shows that the defect states in the various geographies act more like a status of progress for the different geographies. Figure 5-20 shows how we can create a chart in Rational ClearQuest that gives us information as to how many defects are in the Assigned State, how many are in Submitted, and how many are in Resolved. If a particular geography is having less resolved or assigned defects, it means that geography needs assign defects and start correcting them. In all these examples, we have a field called "location" in the Defect record type. It can be populated automatically depending on the mastership of that record or manually by somebody, or it can be populated depending on who owns the defect (user name/group).

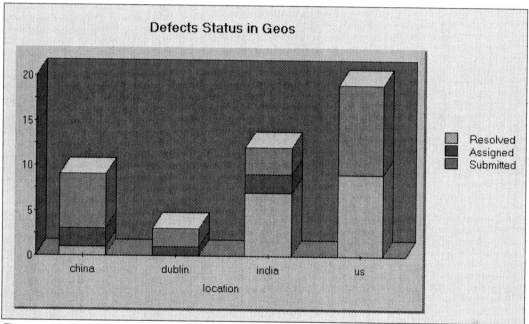

Figure 5-20   Defect status across geographies

Defect resolution rate

This a useful chart where we plot Submitted/Open Defects to Resolved Defects. This is especially useful in new product development. New products start with a high number of submitted defects and a low number of resolved defect. Gradually, the submitted defects decrease and the resolutions increase as the product becomes stable. The point where the two graphs meet indicates that your project has reached stability. Figure 5-21 shows you such a graph in Rational ClearQuest.

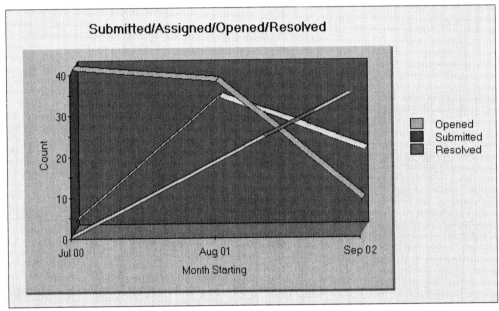

Figure 5-21   Defect resolution rate

Defect density

Defects can be mapped across components, showing which component has more defects. An example can be a simple pie chart. This is useful for you to understand which part of your product is more buggy and concentrate on improving it. Each slice of the pie can show the number of defects per kilo lines of code (KLOC). Rational ClearQuest can help you create this sort of presentation. A simple way is to keep the LOC for a particular component in a record type and update it whenever code changes occur. This can be done by writing a hook in ClearQuest so that it fires whenever a resolution happens in a component; the hook checks the change-set from the SCM tool (if it is a UCM-CQ Integration, the change-set is readily available), checks the lines of code added (by doing an SCM diff), and adds that in the LOC for that component. Currently, there is no such integration that is immediately available. However, you can write ClearQuest hooks to automate this process. Figure 5-22 shows such a chart in ClearQuest that captures the defects per KLOC for each of the components.

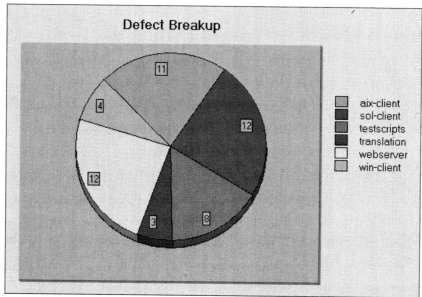

Figure 5-22   Defects in various components per KLOC

5.2.3 Status reporting

Status reporting happens through mail across geographies. We see that every team has their own status formats that they fill and send on a weekly basis. However, status reporting can also be automated, especially if you have a single dashboard for your products. Rational PJC (Project Console) provides such a dashboard. It is Web-based and thereby can be accessed by any geographically dispersed team. It also integrates with Rational ClearQuest and Rational Portfolio Manager to capture their data and display it in a dashboard. Figure 5-23 shows the PJC dashboard that can give you information about the project's status.

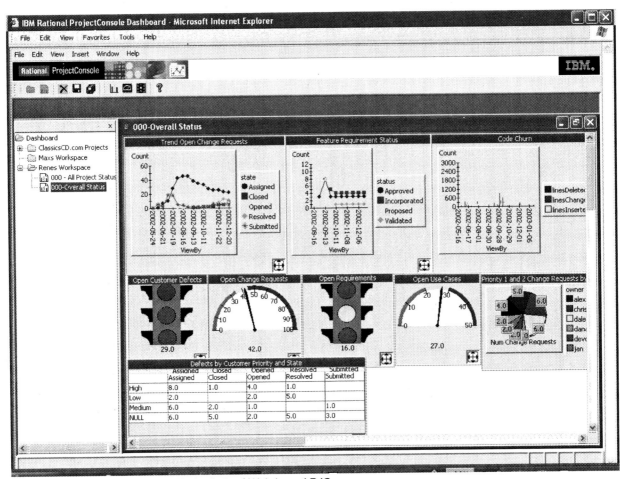

Figure 5-23 Status reporting with the help of Web-based PJC

Another useful and venerable technique is status reporting through e-mails. ClearQuest Web Client V7.0 provides a useful feature called ShortCut. You can create a ShortCut, which is a URL that takes you directly to the ClearQuest page. The user name and password are embedded in the URL. This unique feature enables status reporting through e-mails even more informative and less hassle free (you do not have to log into ClearQuest). In the e-mail, you can embed the URL shortcut, which when clicked by the recipient takes him directly to the Report/Chart showing status details. If the e-mail client is intelligent enough, it can expand the URL within the e-mail, thereby giving you the status picture within the e-mail itself.

A useful status report is the status of your test cases. One might want to view the status of test cases for, for example, whether they passed/failed/gave errors. Components can be owned by various geographical teams and one might one want to view the status of test cases in each of these components. ClearQuest Test manager can help you achieve this objective. ClearQuest Test Manager is a feature in ClearQuest V7.0 that enables you to manage test plans and test cases. You can read more about it in Chapter 8, "Test management" on page 167. There is a feature in ClearQuest Test Manager that helps you create test assets. An asset in this example can be a geographical region that runs a set of tests every night. A nice graph to show you the results of a test run in the various geographical regions is shown in Figure 5-23 on page 110. The graph is taken from the ClearQuest Test Manager tool. Note that this is called a *verdict distribution* in ClearQuest Test Manager. The figure is an example and only shows a couple of test cases. In real scenarios, the number of test cases can be in the order of thousands. The diagram gives you a quick snapshot of the health of various components in different geographies.

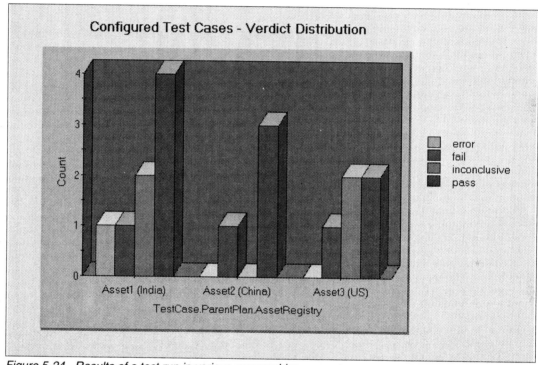

Figure 5-24   Results of a test run in various geographies

5.3 Conclusion

In this chapter, we have shown you the challenges for any change management system in a geographically distributed development environment. We have also shown how Rational ClearQuest can help you solve many of these challenges with its scalable, reliable, and highly customizable framework along with its powerful reporting capabilities. Hopefully this chapter has helped you to understand the powerful features that Rational provides in the area of change management and reporting.

Software configuration management

Software configuration management (SCM) can be thought of as the backbone of a development organization. This chapter describes the SCM implementation challenges geographically distributed teams face and showcases how Rational solutions can help solve some of these challenges.

The chapter also focuses on exposing some of the features that Rational SCM tools provide. In describing the features, we focus on the GDD aspects. For a more elaborate discussion about Rational SCM, see *Software Configuration Management: A Clear Case for IBM Rational ClearCase and ClearQuest UCM*, SG24-6399.

This chapter also presents case studies with relevance to 1.7, "Scenario description" on page 17, that show how Rational SCM tools can help you implement the scenario.

After finishing the planning, the project manager assigns the change requests or work items to individual developers. A developer uses the SCM tools to modify source files or any other artifact in the repository, such as models or documents, to help deliver the work.

6.1 Challenges of SCM in GDD

SCM tools provide mechanisms for version control of your source files. However, version control and having a repository of your files is just one aspect of SCM tools. When geographically distributed teams work together, various other aspects of SCM tools become important. In this section, we address the specific GDD challenges an SCM tool has to address, and in the next section we show how Rational solutions address them.

Single centralized repository for software development artifacts and faster access

It is important to have a centralized view of your repositories across geographies. This means that whenever a change happens in any element in your repository from any part of the world, you should be able to view it immediately. This is one of the biggest challenges any SCM solution has to address. The difficulty in implementing this lies in overcoming the bandwidth and latency that is inherently present between geographies.

Almost all SCM tools provide the centralized repository model and lightweight clients to access them. However most tools provide a pull model where a client pulls in new changes whenever they want. Therefore it is up to the user to obtain the latest changes. When the user wants to view the latest changes, this model is called the *push model*. In the push model, the centralized server pushes any new changes to the respective clients that need it. The clients view elements in their latest state without any intervention.

Ease of deployment across geographies

Deployment of SCM tools often involves planning carefully, defining usage models, and customizing the hardware. SCM tools that can be deployed quickly can help geographically dispersed teams deliver faster. Often SCM deployment involves a large amount of time in planning; getting the configurations right; and setting up builds, deliveries, customization, and so on. In today's fast paced world, people want to get up to speed in the quickest time possible. Therefore an SCM solution that comes with prepackaged configurations and ready-to-use solutions for faster deployment has a tremendous advantage in geographically distributed teams.

Security and availability of assets

Security and availability of assets are an important concern for many organizations in the new age of outsourcing. Often we want to outsource work to a different geographical region where the trust level is low. In the new global development model, you have to share development artifacts with teams in different geographies. In this scenario, you may want to expose certain parts of your repository and give access rights, such as read, write, or read+write permission, to individual groups.

The other aspect is high availability and disaster recovery. What happens if one of your geographical location goes down completely due to a natural disaster? Do you have enough backup in the other regions to help you bring back your system immediately and protect your intellectual assets? These are important questions organizations have to answer when implementing an SCM system.

Process enablement

Often we want to roll out a particular process that developers should follow when changing development artifacts such as source files. For example, developers should link the source file that is changed with the change request on which they are working, they should code review it, or they should do a unit test and a local build in their geography before delivery into the main product. If your SCM tool already comes pre-packaged with these process implementations, it becomes easy for your organization to roll it out to the various geographical centers.

Another aspect is automation. Not everything comes pre-packaged with your SCM tools. An SCM tool may not have considered your organization's unique requirements. It mostly would have been designed to automate processes to solve problems that are generic in nature, for example, a ready-to-use solution like linking a defect to the set of files changed to fix the defect. However it is important that the SCM tool provides enough flexibility to implement the process that you want or to build on top of a solution. For example, whenever someone delivers code, you want comments to be in the source code. An SCM tool should provide the means and mechanisms to allow you to configure the it so that the tool can help you implement your company's processes.

Auditability and traceability

An important aspect of any SCM tool is to keep track of what changes happened to elements in the repository. Version control inherently does that. However, traceability between a defect or a requirement and your source code is also important. In GDD teams, this is important since your organization may have one geography that files a change request, a different geography that fixes it, and a different geography that tests it. Therefore your SCM tool should be well integrated with your change tracking and test tools. It should encompass all geographies to capture this information. Enabling traceability among geographically dispersed teams is a challenge because it requires multiple repositories to connect and communicate across geographies.

Low cost of maintenance, easy upgrade

SCM tools often involve lots of maintenance. In fact, that is why we have SCM administrators and elaborate SCM plans. However, as we talk about faster rollout, we also talk of self healing systems and good administrative tools to manage your SCM processes. Administrative tools that help you find the bottlenecks and the causes of errors faster are crucial in geographically distributed teams. A single Web console to manage the SCM problems and the ability to track the performance and load on the system reduces the headache of many SCM Administrators.

The other important aspect of any SCM solution is easy upgrade and installation. SCM tools often involve an upgrade of both the server and the clients. It is important that any upgrade has little downtime and clients get upgraded easily. An ideal solution would be if the clients get auto-upgraded without the intervention of the user. Whenever a server upgrade happens, clients should automatically get upgraded. Another important aspect is the ability of older clients being able to work seamlessly with a new server and vice-versa.

6.2 Addressing the challenges using Rational solutions

In this section, we show you how Rational SCM solutions help in addressing many of the important challenges that geographically distributed teams pose. First, we look at the various solutions Rational provides in the SCM space. After that, we address the concerns in the order they were discussed in the previous section.

SCM solutions from Rational

The Rational solution to SCM is ClearCase and ClearQuest. We discuss Rational ClearQuest in Chapter 5, "Change management and reporting" on page 83. In this chapter we discuss primarily Rational ClearCase. Rational ClearCase has been around for almost two decades now and is one of the most widely used Rational products. ClearCase clients come in various types, but they are segregated into two types, namely the LAN clients, which are supposed to work on a high bandwidth network, and WAN clients, which you can use to work remotely, for example, by connecting to your company's network by means of a DSL line. The LAN clients are the older ClearCase clients available on various different platforms. The WAN client is called ClearCase Remote Client (CCRC) and the ClearCase Web (CCWeb) client. We discuss more about the WAN clients in 6.4, "CCRC and CCWeb in GDD" on page 123.

Apart from the basic ClearCase product, which is often called Base ClearCase, there is Unified Change Management (UCM), which provides a set of tools and processes that you can use to manage your SCM life cycle better. UCM is a wrapper around ClearCase that provides developers an easy understanding of SCM concepts. In the UCM world, developers find it easy to make modifications and deliver their work. UCM gives your organization pre-packages SCM processes that you can exploit. We look at a real life GDD deployment using UCM in 6.5, "An example of UCM deployment" on page 132.

How do you decide if UCM or Base ClearCase is best for your situation? Figure 6-1 might give you some insight. Note the mention of Rational ClearQuest; ClearQuest is the change management or defect tracking tool from Rational. You can read more about it in 5.1, "Change management" on page 84. Defect Tracking and SCM are tightly coupled and form a process flow in the SCM workflow. In order to fix a defect, a developer starts modifying a set of files. This set is called a *change set* and the work the developer did is called an *activity*. Activity and change sets are important concepts in UCM. UCM integrated with ClearQuest provides you a pre-packaged solution to associate defects with your change set and activity. This helps you enforce an SCM policy in your organization, which in turn helps you achieve traceability and auditability. While the Base ClearCase does not come prepackaged with such an integration, refer to 6.7, "An example of Base ClearCase deployment" on page 144, to see how you can implement a similar process in UCM. However the trade-offs are more, because you need to write scripts to do so.

If you use Base ClearCase and ClearQuest and do not want to migrate to UCM, but want to implement some functionality of UCM, such as associating a change set with a defect, refer to 6.7, "An example of Base ClearCase deployment" on page 144. However if you do not have any SCM tools from Rational and want to cover the entire spectrum of an SCM deployment, then you should look at ClearQuest technology-enabled UCM. ClearQuest technology-enabled UCM can help you to connect a change request in ClearQuest to a change set (set of files changed to fix the change request) in ClearCase. ClearQuest technology-enabled UCM also helps to automate some of your company's processes over change management easily. Some examples of ClearQuest technology-enabled UCM are given in 6.6, "ClearQuest integration" on page 141.

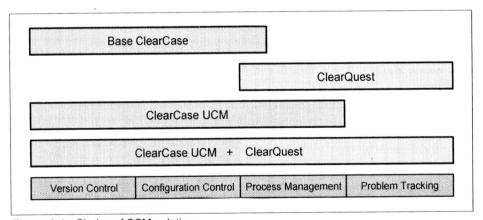

Figure 6-1   Choice of SCM solutions

Some organizations use a combination of both UCM and Base ClearCase depending on the requirements their projects have. In fact, Rational itself has been using a combination of both UCM and Base ClearCase in its different groups.

Now let us look at how ClearCase and UCM enable you to address the GDD challenges we discussed in 6.1, "Challenges of SCM in GDD" on page 114.

Single centralized repository for software development artifacts and faster access

ClearCase has a unique model that consists of both push and pull models. Using a feature called *dynamic views*, changes are reflected immediately to all users within a replica. This way the centralized server can push any new changes to each of the clients that need it. A *replica* is a copy of the repository in a particular geography. Although they represent virtually a singular repository, physically they are not one. The concept of a replica comes in multisite ClearCase, where various replicas exist in different geographies, and they synchronize with each other at regular intervals. Therefore, we see that this push model of dynamic views solves the problem only partially, since you do not see the changes of someone in a different geography immediately. You see them only after the next replication happens. However, the push model works well in ClearCase within a replica.

Multisite configurations can happen in various topologies. Some of the important configurations are shown in Figure 6-2.

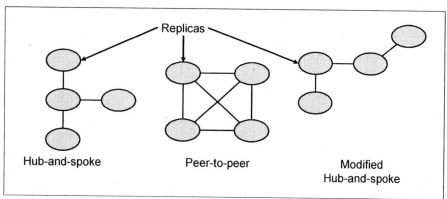

Figure 6-2   Sample multisite replication topologies

Replications can be uni- or bi-directional, depending on the roles of the geographical sites. A site that is doing testing, for example, may be bi-directional for ClearQuest replication, but only uni-directional for ClearCase replication.

Let us describe some of the topologies:

► Hub-and-spoke: Each site replicates with a central server.

  − This method minimizes the work at the remote sites.

  − There is a lag time for remote sites in receiving updates from other remote sites. If we replicate every 15 minutes, the other remote sites do not receive the update for 30 minutes.

  − If the central server goes down, you have to re-route your topology. It is not difficult to re-define a replication pattern, but it does require manual intervention.

► Peer-to-peer: Each site replicates to all the other sites that share its repositories. This method provides the quickest updates between sites, and is the most resilient to network trouble, but causes the highest workload for each server.

► Modified hub-and-spoke: There are several hubs. For example, there may a hub in the U.S., Europe, and Asia, with sites synchronizing to their regional hub.

To implement a pull model, Rational has lightweight clients such as ClearCase Remote Client (CCRC) and CCWeb. These clients work on the pull model and let you pull in changes from a different geography or replica immediately. In this model, CCRC has a Web server at the replica site. Using the CCRC client, you connect to the server and do ClearCase and UCM operations. You may sit at your home behind your organization's firewall and still work with your source files. Therefore, depending on your needs, you should choose multisite, CCRC, or both. Each option has its own benefits, but the combination works better for some organizations. For example, you would choose multisite if you want the powers of dynamic views and faster access within your geography. You would choose CCRC if you want faster deployment of your SCM tools and if the pull model is good enough for you.

Companies use a combination of multisite and CCRC, which gives them optimum efficiency and flexibility. This way, people can access their sources using CCRC when they are at home. They use the normal ClearCase clients when they are at the office (refer to Figure 6-3). Figure 6-3 also has ClearQuest, which can be accessed in a similar way. ClearQuest Web (CQWeb) is currently the only WAN client. CQWeb has LAN clients and can be used to access replicas remotely. Within IBM Rational, we use both CCRC and ClearCase MultiSite® to do our development across geographies.

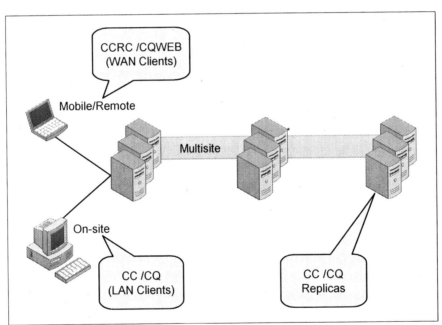

Figure 6-3   ClearCase and ClearQuest multisite along with CCRC and CQWeb

Ease of deployment across geographies

CCRC and CCWeb are easy to deploy, but multisite deployment requires more effort, because it involves the setup of replicas and Versioned Object Bases (VOBs). We discuss more on multisite deployment challenges and how you solve them in 6.3, "ClearCase and ClearQuest multisite setup for GDD" on page 120. However, client installation for ClearCase and ClearQuest is fast and easy.

Safety and security of assets

ClearCase provides for the safety of your code. It is one of the SCM tools that large companies have used for decades without having to worry about losing information. ClearCase is well supported for conventional backup systems like RAID and NAS (for details, refer to Chapter 6, "Planning for ClearCase", of *Software Configuration Management: A Clear Case for IBM Rational ClearCase and ClearQuest UCM*, SG24-6399). If you are using

ClearCase MultiSite, you are also indirectly backing up when you use replicas, so ClearCase MultiSite is giving you a secondary backup and a mechanism for disaster recovery.

Security Issues are of prime concern in product companies and intellectual property rights are important. ClearCase provides mechanisms where you can create groups and give access to code to particular groups. However you have to properly design your system so that the Versioned Object Base (VOB) you want to expose to an external group is singled out. Security is currently available at the VOB level.

Process enablement

SCM solutions like Unified Change Management (UCM) and ClearQuest allow you to enforce a process that software developers must follow in their day to day development activities. For example, using UCM with ClearQuest makes sure that every source file checked out is associated with an activity in UCM, which is again associated with a defect in ClearQuest. This way, you can make sure to keep track of all your development activities.

UCM comes with certain processes that are easy to use. You can also implement your own process on top of it. We show such this type of process enablement in 6.5, "An example of UCM deployment" on page 132. ClearCase also provides triggers that help you to write custom hooks that get fired on any particular event. For example, if you want to make sure that every code change should have a comment in the beginning, you can write a ClearCase trigger to check that. It should get fired whenever someone makes a delivery in UCM or merges in Base ClearCase. It checks all the source files (Change Set) that are being delivered, does a difference check between the source and destination files, and checks if there is a comment preceding the difference. You can even check if a defect ID is mentioned in the comment. Triggers in ClearCase can be written using simple scripts. You can find useful triggers at the following Web site:

http://www-128.ibm.com/developerworks/rational/library/4311.html

Auditability and traceability

Version control is the most basic requirement of any SCM solution. It is the means by which versions of source files or other assets are kept. The primary reason for keeping versions is to make sure that you can discover who did what and when. The other important aspect is the ability for you to roll back to the original changes. Figure 6-4 shows the typical file structure in a product development scenario.

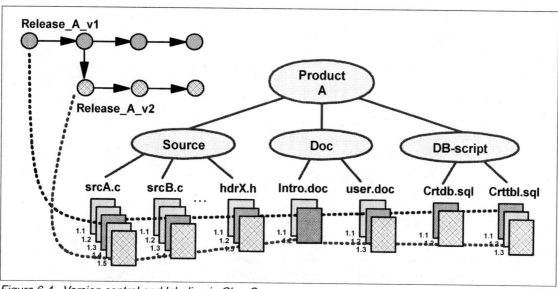

Figure 6-4   Version control and labeling in ClearCase

Notice the dotted lines that delineate a particular version of each file. Release V1 consists of Version 1.2 of user.doc, while Release V2 consists of Version 1.3 of the same file. This way, ClearCase provides you a means by which you can isolate a particular release and revert back to it if required.

The other information ClearCase keeps are the details on how each version was created. The details can be:

► Who created the version?
► When was it created (date and time)?
► Why was it created? Was it a part of some defect fix? If so, which defect fix?

> **Note:** This comes as a part of UCM with ClearQuest integration enabled. In 6.5, "An example of UCM deployment" on page 132, and 6.7, "An example of Base ClearCase deployment" on page 144, we show how you achieve this particular goal.

This way, version control allows you to trace back and help in auditing a particular change.

Associating a defect or a requirement to a set of changed files also introduces the traceability part.

Low cost of maintenance and an easy upgrade

ClearCase clients like CCRC and CCWeb are low maintenance and can be easily upgraded. They are ideal for scenarios where you want to roll out your SCM client application to a group of users in order in a particular geography to enable them to deliver faster.

ClearCase also comes with good set of administrative tools that help you diagnose problems.

6.3 ClearCase and ClearQuest multisite setup for GDD

Setting up a ClearCase and ClearQuest multisite requires careful planning. In this section, we briefly touch upon some of the aspects that you need to be aware of and how you can tackle them. You can find a detailed discussion on this in Chapter 12, "Planning for distributed development using MultiSite", of *Software Configuration Management: A Clear Case for IBM Rational ClearCase and ClearQuest UCM*, SG24-6399. Also refer to the online tutorial for step-by-step multisite configuration on the Web at:

`http://www-128.ibm.com/developerworks/edu/i-dw-r-rmultisite-i.html`

Multisite background

The multisite add-on products provide a mechanism for distributed development in an UCM or ClearCase environment. Multisite implements a replicated repository environment; each site ends up with local repositories, called *replicas*, for local client access. The replicas are synchronized on a regular basis through automated processes. The basic replication process (export → transport → import) is described here and summarized in Figure 6-5:

► Export: The repository is first dumped into an architecture/database independent format called a *packet*. When the replication process is initiated (*replica creation*), the whole repository is exported. Subsequent exports (*replica sync*) create packets with only the incremental changes since the last replication.

► Transport: Packets are shipped to the remote server over whatever connection is available. Although there is a built-in tool available (a *shipping server*), MultiSite is transport independent; it does not care how you get the packets between the sites.

► Import: The packets are imported on the receiving server. During the replica creation process, empty database tables are populated for ClearQuest and new VOBs are created for ClearCase. During synchronization, the repositories are updated. If the shipping server is used, a *receipt handler* can be configured to import sync packets as soon as they are received.

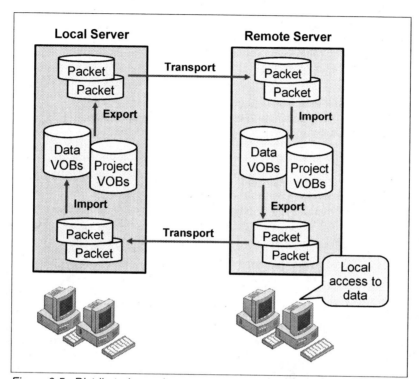

Figure 6-5   Distributed repository management with Multisite

When the replication is complete, each site has local access to both the data and metadata contained in the repositories. The replicas are independent; if one server, or the network, goes down, the other site is not affected. In addition, if a replica at a site is damaged (for example, due to a hardware failure), it can be restored from one of its replicas, current with the last synchronization.

To implement the replication functionality, ClearCase MultiSite adds two more components to our CM environment, a *shipping server* and a *synchronization service*. The synchronization service manages the packet export and import process.

The shipping server, also known as the *store-and-forward server*, is a general, TCP/IP-based, file transfer service that manages the transport of packets among servers. The shipping server can be configured to provide these capabilities:

► Packet size management: Manage export packet size.
► Packet routing: Set up routing topologies.
► Multiple storage classes: Define different transport profiles for different use cases.
► Receipt handler: Run a script on receipt of a sync packet.
► Network failure management: Manage delivery failures.

Multisite setup considerations

Some of the infrastructure requirements that you must consider before setting up MultiSite are:

► Hardware: What additional hardware is required to support this effort?

The shipping server is the utility provided with MultiSite to manage transport of packets between servers. Each VOB server with replicated VOBs includes a shipping server function. On fast, well-behaved networks, the shipping service does not usually add much of a burden to the server, at least while you are only replicating to a couple of sites. However, if your network is slow and you are transmitting large packets (greater than 100 MB), you might consider having a separate shipping server. The replication packets are stored in named shipping bays (directories) on the shipping servers. Shipping bays minimally have to be large enough to hold the largest collection of packets you might have on the server at any one time.

► Software: What software upgrades are needed to support MultiSite?

MultiSite is a *configuration option* for both the ClearCase and ClearQuest installation. MultiSite adds a small footprint to the installation, so it is common to include MultiSite in your standard installation (rather than maintain two installations). MultiSite has no impact on non-replicated repositories. You are likely to upgrade your VOB server and install one or two new small servers to act as shipping servers.

MultiSite is enabled for a repository when its first replica is created. Separate MultiSite licenses are required for both ClearCase and ClearQuest.

► Licensing: What new licenses are required?

If you have a single project VOB for your site, you need as many ClearCase MultiSite licenses as you have ClearCase licenses. If you are buying MultiSite licenses separately, cluster your project VOBs and user databases around a smaller set of projects to minimize the MultiSite licenses required for projects without distributed development.

► Connectivity: What transport methods can be used?

The network connection between the sites is an important player in the MultiSite infrastructure. *Security* and *stability* are the important characteristics of the intranet. Since synchronization happens in the background through incremental updates, *network performance* is not as critical, though you do not want to send additional traffic to a network that is already over-burdened.

Multisite infrastructure can be implemented in a network with or without a firewall. If it is without firewall, you use a normal IP address mechanism to ship packets. If there is a firewall, any method to get files securely through the firewall works. The methods used are Secure File Transport Protocol (SFTP), any third-party transport software such as IBM Tivoli Data Moving Service, which is a part of Tivoli Configuration Manager, or using the ClearCase shipping server itself, which is configured to work through firewalls.

► Automation: How do you automate the synchronization process?

The initial creation and transport of a replica is done manually, probably during off hours. The subsequent synchronization process is automated to run as a fairly continuous background process. It is typical to replicate every 15-30 minutes between sites.

The MultiSite administration commands are done from a command-line interface. To set up automated replication, create or use existing scripts that run from a scheduler. ClearCase includes a scheduler, but any scheduling mechanism is fine. For example, the UNIX® cron scheduler is still commonly used.

► Organization: What resources are required to support CM across multiple sites?

It is important to have a centralized CM Plan, which should be used across all CM teams across the geographies.

Both central and distributed services models work well. Part of the updated CM plan should articulate how the remote site will be supported.

- Central-services model

  In the central-services model, the initiating organization manages the CM infrastructure remotely: purchasing and installing, and maintaining hardware, software, and licenses. The remote site designates a CM lead to serve as the onsite contact.

- Distributed-services model

  In this peer-based model, sites coordinate efforts to ensure that standards are enforced and appropriate, but each site manages their own infrastructure and users. You may end up with a mix of service models, providing CM administration directly for small sites and working in a peer relationship with the larger sites.

If the distributed site is not currently using ClearCase and ClearQuest, at least plan to perform the role of CM mentor while the team comes up to speed. If possible, a site visit at production cutover is useful.

6.4 CCRC and CCWeb in GDD

ClearCase Remote Client (CCRC) and ClearCase Web (CCWeb) are Rational's answer to accessing ClearCase resources over a low bandwidth connection (such as DSL). In this section, we tell you when to use CCRC and CC Web, and discuss some of its features. CCRC and CCWeb are important in GDD since they provide lightweight clients that geographically distributed teams can use to access ClearCase.

ClearQuest Web (CQWeb) is the Web version of the ClearQuest client. CCRC and CCWeb use the same CCRC server, while CQWeb has a different server.

CCRC, CCWeb, or CQWeb are used in the configuration shown in Figure 6-6.

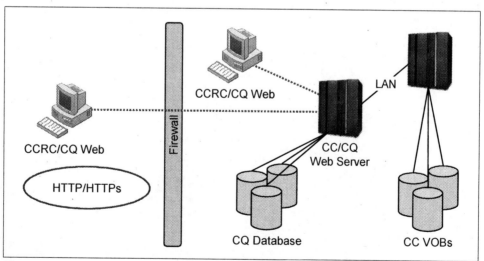

Figure 6-6   CCRC and CQWeb deployment

The advantages of CCRC and CCWeb are:

- A thin, auto upgradable client (addresses the ease of deployment issue)
- Designed for high latency networks
- Requires only a single port to traverse firewalls
- Users are authenticated on the server

You use CCRC, CCWeb, and CQWeb in subsites that are not big (less people logged in simultaneously) and where the network latency is high. Currently these WAN clients tend to slow down when the number of users increase. However if your team size is bigger, consider replicas for both CC and CQ in case you are doing geographically distributed development. You can also consider using CCRC for a small set of users in one geographical region and replicas for regions that have a larger number of users.

In this model, you have a combination of CCRC and multisite. Often this combination works best for teams that have differently sized groups and are doing distributed development across geographies. We show such an example of a combination of CCRC and multisite in our case study in 6.5, "An example of UCM deployment" on page 132. Keep in mind that this example of using WAN clients for smaller groups may change in the future when Rational develops more powerful WAN solutions for both ClearCase and ClearQuest.

6.4.1 CCRC

CCRC allows you to both work on UCM as well as Base ClearCase. A developer can use CCRC to do activities like checking out a file, modifying it, and delivering the changes. The developer can create branches, streams, labels, and baselines, and recommend baselines.

Considerations in CCRC deployment

CCRC creates snapshot views, which are often called Web views, in your machine. This means that whenever you create a view, you specify certain *load rules*. Load rules are specific to a Web view; it tells the client which files or directories to load into your view. Therefore if your load rules encompass lot of files and directories, it might take a long time for the Web view to be created. The time to create the Web view is directly proportional to the size of the view.

Therefore, for teams using CCRC, it is important to have load rules that load only the files you are interested in. However, sometimes that is not good enough, since you might need a set of files to do builds even if you are not modifying those files. A good design of the product build mechanism should take care of enabling module builds that are unit testable. Also, the module builds should be so designed such that they have less dependency on other modules. Figure 6-7 gives an idea. Suppose that the product has five modules, M1 through M5. Site A uses CCRC and works on Module M1 and M2. Site B works on module M3, and Site C works on modules M4 and M5.

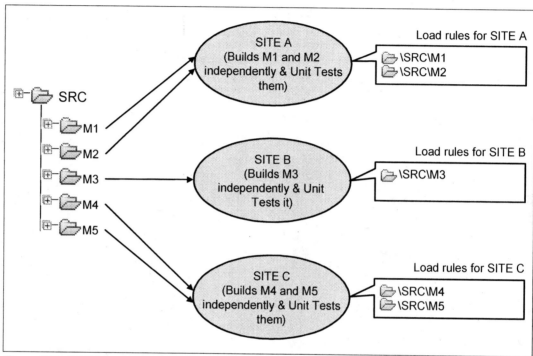

Figure 6-7   CCRC load rules in various geographical sites

It is important to design the product such that individual modules can be built independently and unit tested in each of the sites. Since Site A works only on modules M1 and M2, it does not want to load M3, M4, or M5. Loading them means larger size of Web views and more time while the views are created or updated. Therefore, for Site A users, it is important that they can build and unit test modules M1 and M2 without any dependency problems. However, the core site where integration happens has load rules for all modules and uses ClearCase LAN clients with a dynamic view.

However, in a scenario where code is shared between modules, this model does not apply.

Features in CCRC

You can find a good demo of CCRC online at:

```
http://www-128.ibm.com/developerworks/rational/library/05/0809_CCDemo/
```

The following sections has been created from this online demo; if you have watched the demo, you may only want to lightly peruse this section.

In CCRC, users need to log in to the server. The CCRC server resides within the organization connected to the other ClearCase servers, such as VOB server, Registry server, and so on, by means of a high bandwidth. Figure 6-8 shows you what the log-in dialog in CCRC looks like.

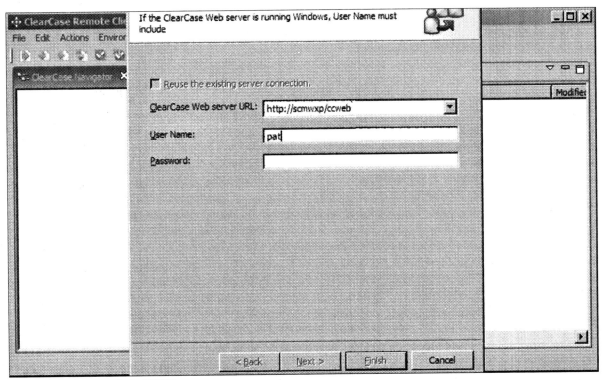

Figure 6-8 Logging in to CCRC server

CCRC supports both UCM as well as Base ClearCase users. In UCM, when logging in for the first time, a user joins a UCM project, creates a development stream, and creates a development and integration view.

The next important step in CCRC is to specify the load rules. Load rules is a configuration specification for a snapshot view. It tells your CCRC client what files/directories/elements to load or pull in from the CCRC server. CCRC views are based on the snapshot technology, as opposed to the dynamic views that we discussed in "Single centralized repository for software development artifacts and faster access" on page 114. In snapshot views, you specify the files that you want to see using load rules. CCRC copies those files/directories into your local machine into your snapshot view.

Figure 6-9 shows how to specify the load rules in CCRC. Notice the broken lines on the folders. This is a good feature in CCRC that shows the folders that are on the server but have not been loaded into the client. You can select a broken folder and load it. CCRC gives you this powerful feature of loading exactly what you want. However, an important consideration, as we discussed in "Considerations in CCRC deployment" on page 124, is to make sure that all dependent folders or modules are loaded by you, since there might be build or runtime dependencies between these folders or modules.

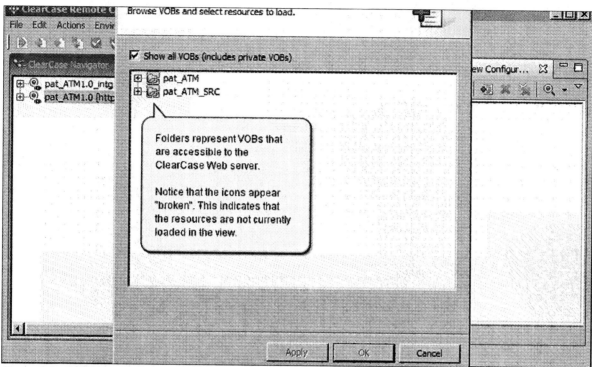

Figure 6-9   Specifying load rules in CCRC

After all these steps are done, a user's workspace looks similar to the one shown in Figure 6-10. Notice that you get all the information about a file.

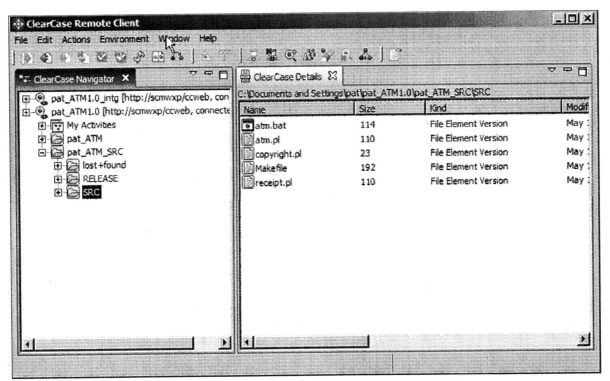

Figure 6-10   CCRC File workspace

The next step for a developer is to check out a file, make changes, and then check in. A developer can right-click a file, check it out, modify it, and then check it in. CCRC provides a powerful feature called Search that allows you to search for all the checked out files, private files (files that are not ClearCase elements), and hijacked files (files that were not checked out but whose write permission was forcibly made true). This feature is useful when you are done with your work and you want to check in your changes.

Figure 6-11 shows what a CCRC Search looks like.

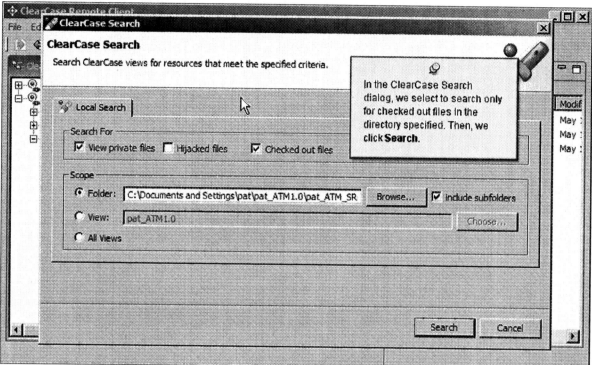

Figure 6-11   CCRC Search window

After a user has checked in the files, an important operation is to update the view with the latest changes and then do a build and test before delivering. CCRC provides mechanisms to do Update and Deliver. If files have merge conflicts, CCRC brings up the usual ClearCase merge manager to help you manually merge files. In addition to this tool, CCRC also provides a version tree viewer for all ClearCase elements.

CCRC also supports views where you can view your UCM Activities or you can create Baselines and recommend them. This is called the Metadata explorer and is shown in Figure 6-12.

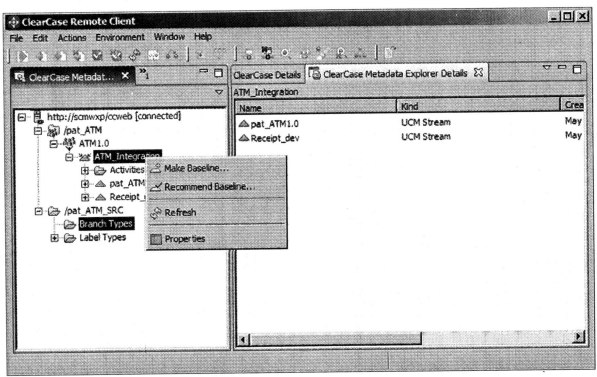

Figure 6-12   CCRC Metadata explorer

We have shown you the features to do UCM development using CCRC. CCRC also provides all the tools to do Base ClearCase development. In Base ClearCase, instead of a deliver operation, you invoke the Merge Manager view, where you specify the source and destination branches.

6.4.2 CCWeb

CCWeb is a lightweight version of ClearCase on a Web client. It does not give you all the functionality that CCRC gives, but is good enough for you to do quick operations like checking out a file, modifying it, and checking it back in. It works both for UCM and Base ClearCase. An ideal scenario for its usage would be, for example, when you are in an airport and you want to modify a document. However, you do not have CCRC installed on your machine. Using CCWeb, you can accomplish that operation with the help of any Web browser. Figure 6-13 shows a view of the CCWeb Client.

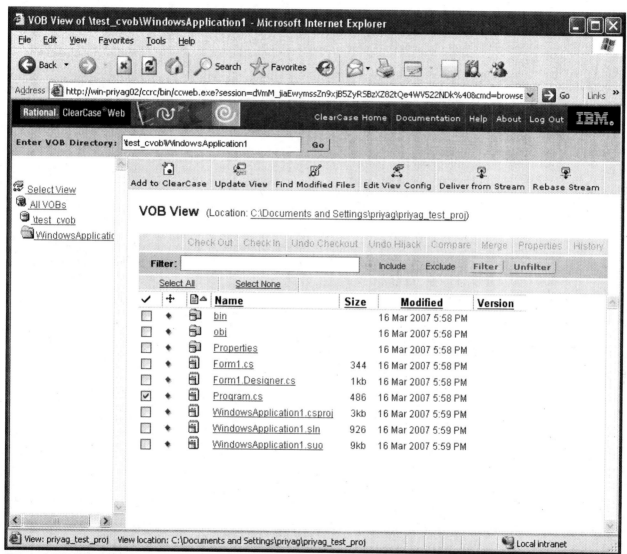

Figure 6-13   The CCWeb Client

6.5 An example of UCM deployment

In this section, we show a real-life scenario where UCM can be implemented along with ClearQuest. It will be helpful to you to identify yourself in this scenario so you can learn some tips and techniques to deploy UCM in a geographically distributed team. The process mentioned in this chapter is taken from a group within Rational that uses UCM in a GDD environment. For UCM terminologies, refer to "UCM terminology" on page 217.

Note: In this section, we show how a geographically distributed team within Rational is currently using UCM. However, we adjusted it for the scenario that we have discussed. Use your discretion in using such a model for your organization, since it may not be the right model for you.

6.5.1 GDD scenario and releases

Consider the scenario mentioned in 1.7, "Scenario description" on page 17. Consider only three locations for the UCM deployment in this section:

- ► Santa Clara (U.S.): With 100 people, they have a ClearCase and ClearQuest Replica.
- ► Bangalore (India): With 100 people, they also have a ClearCase and ClearQuest Replica.
- ► Gurgaon (India): With 20 people, they do not have a Replica and they use the WAN clients.

India Lab owns two components in the ITSO Inc. Retail Manager product, namely the ITSO Inc. Data Entry Console and the Admin Console. Right now, there is a plan to transition the whole of ITSO Inc. Retail Cash Console. Integration and packaging happens in Santa Clara.

Until now, the problem was that both of these components in India were a part of ITSO Inc. Retail Manager. The Retail Manager build was done in the U.S. and there was no local builds. This was leading to a lot of build breaks in the Integration Build.

Both ITSO Inc. Retail Manager and ITSO Inc. Cash Console are part of a Suite that has a Release schedule, as shown in Figure 6-14.

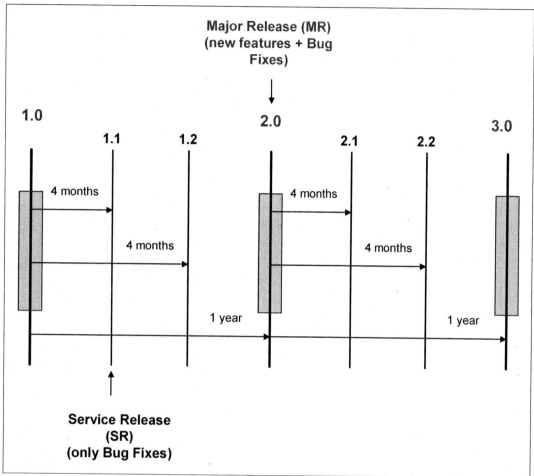

Figure 6-14   Release schedules

Figure 6-14 shows the releases for the products. The yearly release consists of new competitive features and bug fixes. Every year there are two service releases (SR) that happen every four months. These are patches following the major release and consists of only critical bug fixes.

Apart from this, escalations may need to be delivered to individual customers. Customers might be using any version of the product and the company has to support escalations on them. The service-level agreement (SLA) states that any escalation over the last two years needs to be fixed. If it is more than two years, customers are encouraged to migrate to the latest major release version.

6.5.2 UCM workflow

UCM introduces a workflow that ensures seamless development, build testing, and packaging. The typical UCM workflow is shown in Figure 6-15.

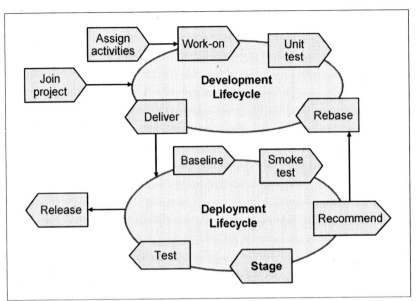

Figure 6-15   UCM workflow

In the following example, we show how we implement this workflow.

6.5.3 Projects, components, and baseline design

In this section, we tell you how you will design your projects, components, and baselines. For terminology definitions, refer to "Base ClearCase terminology" on page 214. The ideal component design in this case is to have a rootless component called Suites, which is comprised of two components, namely retail_mgr and retail_cash_console. Each of these components denotes the products ITSO Inc. Retail Manager and ITSO Inc. Retail Cash Console respectively. Each of these components have sub-components. Retail_mgr has four sub-components, such as data_entry, admin_console, report_console, and retail_server. ITSO Inc. Retail Cash Console has two sub-components, namely credit_card_unit and main_console. We design the whole component in the hierarchy shown in Figure 6-16. In this design, Suites is a rootless composite in UCM terminology. There are many advantages in having such rootless composites, including:

▶ Code may or may not be dependent between two or more children of the composite
▶ More flexibility
▶ New baselines are never code changes in suites

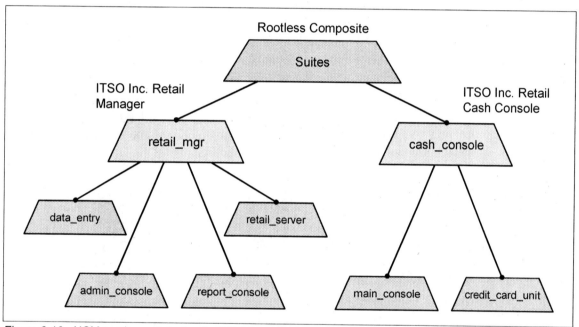

Figure 6-16   UCM component design for ITSO Inc.

There are just two VOBs in the codebase and it has sub-directories as shown here:
▶ \vobs\retail_manager
  - \vobs\retail_manager\data_entry [owned by Bangalore Labs]
  - \vobs\retail_manager\admin_console [owned by Bangalore Labs]
  - \vobs\retail_manager\report_console [owned by Santa Clara]
  - \vobs\retail_manager\retail_server [owned by Santa Clara]
▶ \vobs\cash_console [getting transitioned to Bangalore Labs]
  - \vobs\cash_console\main_console
  - \vobs\cash_console\credit_card_unit

Note that cash_console is now being fully transitioned to India. Previously, the developers in India were not working on the code base for Retail Cash Console. Therefore, the VOBs for Retail Cash Console, which is about 100 GB, was not replicated. This is a good strategy to manage UCM in multisite. You do not replicate all the VOBs. The India developers were using only the VOB \vobs\retail_manager. Also, the UCM component they used for baseline is retail_mgr.

The other requirement in this project is that it has a release cycle as described in 6.5.1, "GDD scenario and releases" on page 132. To support this requirement, we need an SCM process in place that indicates which project to create and how. One of the important criteria in such a decision is the ability to work in parallel on patch fixes on an earlier release, as well as work on new features for the new release. We show how you can do so.

In order to manage the release cycles, a good mechanism is to have separate UCM projects for each of the major and minor releases. Therefore, in this case, you have separate UCM projects for MRs and SRs. The idea is your SR project (say, SR 1.1) and the next MR project (say, MR 2.0) start in parallel. There are two development groups: one working on the SR project that mainly fixes defects and one working on the MR projects that mainly adds features. After SR1.1 is over, the MR project should be updated with the latest changes. A lock-down is done on the MR Streams and an intra-project delivery from SR1.1 to the MR streams is done. This ensures that people working on the features get the latest bug fixes. Also note that an Escalation Stream should be created out of all the Project Integration Streams (both SR and MR). This escalation integration stream should be used to give fast hot fixes to particularly important customers. Escalation streams are open ended, meaning that they are never merged back. However, if you feel your escalation fix is a major bug that might affect the product as a whole, you should deliver contents of an escalation stream to its parent and up to the SR or MR stream.

6.5.4 UCM stream design

The idea in stream design should be that the remote site, namely India, should deliver code so that it does not break the integration and is well tested. To ensure that we design such a stream, as shown in Figure 6-17, we use the Local Integration Stream model. We have found this useful in GDD scenarios where components are shared between geographies. Note that there is another model called the Producer-Consumer model that is applicable whenever you have components belonging to different geographies and there is no sharing. However, that model does not work in this particular scenario.

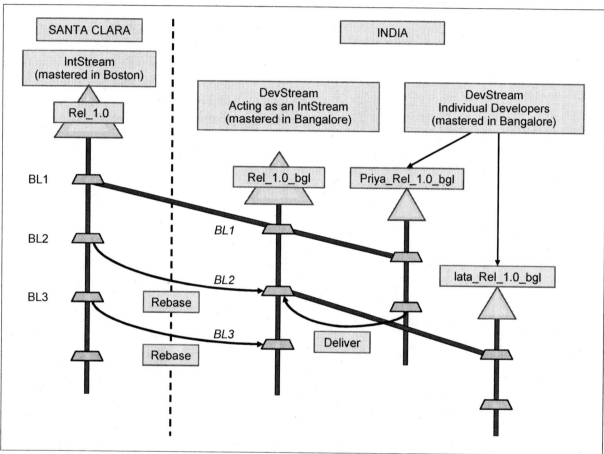

Figure 6-17   Stream structure

The above figure shows a good stream design for remote development. The idea is to have a development stream in Bangalore called "Rel_1.0_bgl". This stream is used as an Integration stream for the developers in Bangalore. It is the stream where nightly builds happen. From this stream, all the developers in Bangalore create their own private development streams. Rebase and Delivery are UCM operations by which you pull or push changes respectively from or to another stream. You select a baseline of the source stream while rebasing (telling UCM which versions to pick up). Similarly you create a new baseline in the target stream when someone delivers changes using the delivery operation.

6.5.5 Automating build and delivery

The developers in Bangalore need to follow the following process whenever they need to work:

► Create a child stream from Rel_1.0_bgl (for example, Priya created Priya_Rel_1.0_bgl) and use the recommended baseline.

► Do the work on that stream.

► Do a Rebase from Rel_1.0_bgl.

► Do a build in their own stream and unit test their fix.

► Deliver to Rel_1.0_bgl. Since both developer stream and Rel_1.0_bgl are mastered in Bangalore, there is no problem with delivery.

Therefore, every day a couple of UCM activities are delivered to Rel_1.0_bgl.

After this task is done, we need to deliver these fixes to the main integration stream. In order to do this, we automate everything instead of a manual delivery. The process we follow is shown in Figure 6-18.

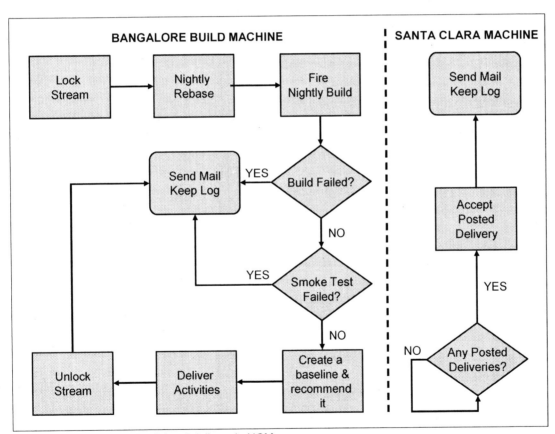

Figure 6-18 Automated build and delivery in UCM

You need a minimum of two machines to do the automation, one in Bangalore and one in Santa Clara. The Bangalore machine is the build and test machine. If you choose, you can also have two machines in Bangalore, one to do builds and one to test. However, in the scenario we discuss, we use one machine with ClearCase installed in it to do everything, because we are just doing the Smoke Test, which is not CPU intensive. If you are planning to run an entire battery of tests, consider using multiple machines.

The idea is to make sure that the build is not broken and that the functionality is fine (by running the tests) before doing a delivery.

The other aspect is that you create a baseline in the integration stream in Bangalore every night, thereby allowing developers in Bangalore to share the work among themselves.

The script that runs in the Santa Clara machine periodically checks to see if there are any posted deliveries. If there are, then it accepts the posted deliveries. This is one activity every night because all individual UCM activities will be merged into one single activity. Since you will be aware of when the build starts in India, you can schedule the script in Santa Clara to start at a particular time and end at a particular time, thereby ensuring that the machine is not consuming CPU cycles all the time.

Now consider the case where you are supporting multiple streams for parallel development. For example, you have Rel_2.0_bgl, Rel_1.1.bgl, and Rel_1.0_bgl_escalation, which contains development activities for Release 2.0, Release 1.1, and escalations in Release 1.0, respectively. In this case, you have to support nightly builds and deliveries in all three streams every night. It is a good idea to have three such machines, assuming that at any point of time your team works parallel on three separate releases. In case you need to work on more streams, you should get more machines. You can also switch streams in each of the machines. Suppose that you know that for a particular week that there will be no delivery from a particular stream. You can change the machine designated for that stream to some other stream that has active development.

Using Build Forge to automate

Build Forge can be used to implement the workflow we described instead of user created scripts. However, you still have to execute the ClearCase commands. Note that Build Forge allows you to run commands one after another, thereby acting like a good scheduler. You can read more about Build Forge and learn how to use it in 7.3.2, "Build management solution using IBM Rational Build Forge" on page 157.

In the case where you do parallel development on multiple streams, Build Forge is really convenient. Using Build Forge, you can schedule build and delivery in different machines for each of the streams. Build Forge allows you to keep environment variables that can be changed whenever needed. In this case, you can have an environment variable $stream for each machine. Whenever you move on to a new release stream, you need to change this environment to automate build and delivery on the new stream. The other advantage of using Build Forge is that it supports GDD. You can schedule the script that checks for posted deliveries as well as the scripts that post the delivery from the same Build Forge console.

Figure 6-19 shows you how to configure Build Forge using a Web interface.

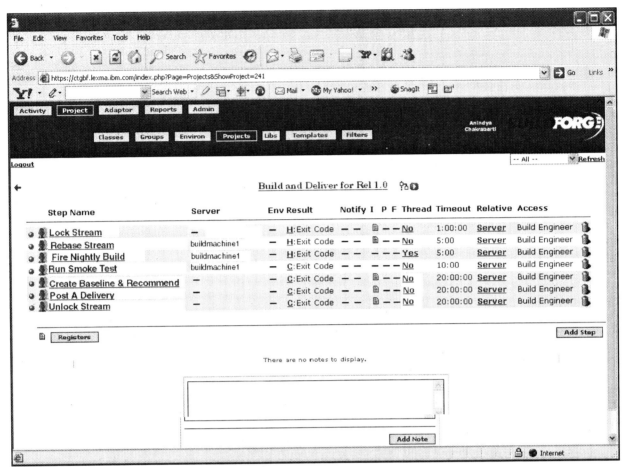

Figure 6-19   Setting Build and Delivery in Build Forge

6.5.6 Advantages of this model

Often we find developers directly create development streams from the integration stream, even if they are in a different replica. This means that in the above example, a developer in India creates a child stream out of Rel_1.0. However, we do not recommend such a mechanism of working in multisited environments. The model we suggest where you have an intermediate development stream has several advantages, including:

► You are able to make sure that check-ins from India do not break build or break test cases.

► The developers in India do not have to do a posted delivery. It is up to the Release Engineer (RE) in India to manage these deliveries. In fact, if you use the automation, you do not need a release engineer for manual delivery. The RE has to set up the automation either using scripts or Build Forge and monitor every night's build and delivery outcomes. If anything is broken (for example, during Rebase, a merge conflict happened), then the RE has to do the delivery manually.

► The other big problem of posted deliveries is that when a developer posts a delivery from a stream, the mastership of the stream changes to that of the target (in this case, the mastership changes to Santa Clara). In such a scenario, a developer cannot work in the stream till the delivery is complete, which might take two to three hours depending on the interval of replication you have set. The model we suggest does not have that problem, as the developer creates a stream out of a development stream, which is mastered in the local replica (in this case, stream Rel_1.0_bgl, which is mastered in Bangalore).

► Developers do not have to spend time logging into the remote replica and accepting the posted delivery.

6.5.7 Using CCRC in this scenario

ClearCase Remote Client addresses the WAN requirements of a ClearCase client. You can read more about CCRC in 6.4.1, "CCRC" on page 124.

This section describes how CCRC can help in the scenario we discussed. In the scenario, we had a small team of 20 developers sitting in Gurgaon. We can use CCRC for this set of developers. CCRC is well suited for such small teams where you do not want to have a multisited replica.

To implement such a model, we designate Bangalore as the CCRC server. Therefore, Gurgaon acts like a subsite or a satellite site. The developers in Gurgaon work the same way as any developer in Bangalore (for example, they all create child streams out of Rel_1.0_bgl for Release 1.0 and all deliver to this stream). The nightly builds and deliveries for the Gurgaon people happen in Bangalore. The only difference is that the Gurgaon developers have to create snapshot views in their machines. It is therefore a good idea to provide these developers machines that have more storage space.

6.6 ClearQuest integration

ClearQuest is well integrated with UCM. Using ClearQuest Integration, you can link up your UCM activity to a defect and vice versa. This way, you can keep track of the change set (list of files you modified) to a defect. It also enforces a particular workflow.

To enable ClearQuest Integration, you have to set it in your UCM Project setup. You can use ClearProjectExplorer, right-click **Project**, select its **Properties**, and select the **ClearQuest** tab. You see a window similar to the example in Figure 6-20.

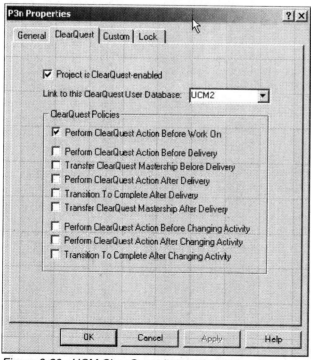

Figure 6-20   UCM ClearQuest integration setup

The different policies state what exactly you want to do. For example, if you choose Transfer ClearQuest Mastership After Delivery, the defect record's mastership is changed to the remote location when a UCM delivery completes. It makes sure that whenever someone delivers from Bangalore, the defect/s mastership associated with the activity gets transferred to Santa Clara. This way, people in Santa Clara can modify the defect. The policy settings give you the flexibility to implement certain process around SCM in GDD environments.

In UCM, whenever you check out a file, you have to associate it with an activity. However, in the case of ClearQuest enabled UCM, you can associate a checkout with an existing defect. If the defect does not exist, you can file a new one, as shown in Figure 6-21.

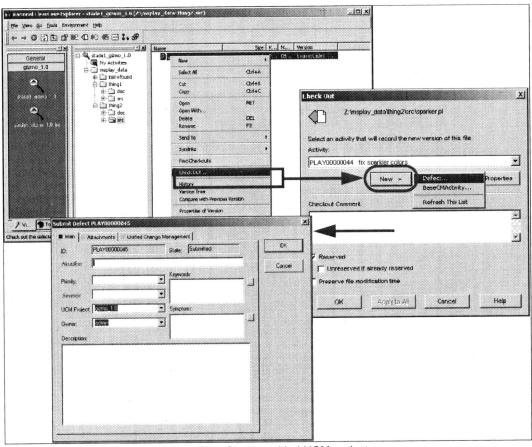

Figure 6-21   Creating an activity in a ClearQuest enabled UCM project

If you want to associate an existing defect, click **Browse**, which opens the Activity Entity Browser window, as shown in Figure 6-22.

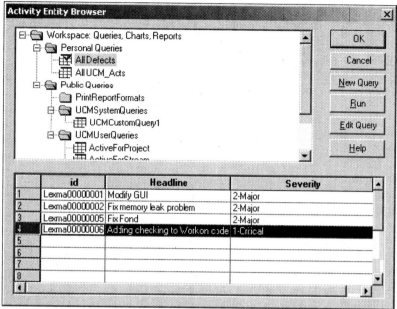

Figure 6-22   ClearQuest entity browser

Here you can select the existing defect you want to associate. You can even create/edit a ClearQuest Query using the entity browser. Using a different query yields you a different result set.

Another important feature of UCM-ClearQuest Integration is the Change Set display in a ClearQuest Defect. The change set is the set of files and their versions you create in order to fix the defect. Figure 6-23 shows a defect with the UCM tab opened, which has the change set information.

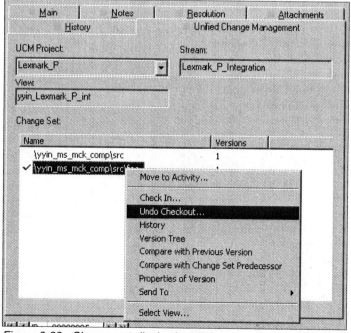

Figure 6-23   Change set display in a defect

Note that you can perform all ClearCase operations on the files shown from within this ClearQuest view. This feature helps you keep track as to what files you changed to fix a particular defect. For example, if your tester finds out that the fix did not solve the problem and in fact created a regression, you as a developer can check what went wrong by looking at the source files with the help of the change set viewer.

6.7 An example of Base ClearCase deployment

This section shows an example of a Base ClearCase deployment. Base ClearCase came before UCM evolved. UCM helped companies implement many of their Process Enforcements and Integration with Defect Tracking. However, even Base ClearCase allows you to enforce processes and integrate with defect tracking, but not with as much ease as in UCM. In this section, we show you how to do so using certain branch strategies and scripts, thereby enabling Base ClearCase to add value to your SCM process from a GDD perspective. The contents of this section are taken from a team within Rational that uses Base ClearCase to do GDD. For any Base ClearCase terminologies, refer to "Base ClearCase terminology" on page 214.

6.7.1 Branching strategies

The branching strategy consists of having a local integration branch in your geographical location. This helps in many ways, especially when you are sharing your work with developers within your own geography. The strategy is simple, and is shown in Figure 6-24.

The idea is to have a branch called \main\india where all developers in India work in their private branches. Using private branches this way prevents users from interfering in each other's work. Whenever a developer finishes the work, the developer does a merge from \main\india to the developer's branch to get the latest updates. After that, the developer does a minimal build and test to check if the changes are compatible with the changes from others and merges back the work into the local integration branch \main\india.

Another important strategy is to rename the private branch to a meaningful name in order to indicate the work done. This concept is similar to an activity in UCM. A meaningful name can be the name of a defect that the developer is developing. This mechanism of renaming branches enforce traceability and auditability.

Note that in this model builds are fired on \main\india and smoke tests are run every night. If they pass these tests, the merging from \main\india → \main is initiated. To perform the merge, the mastership of \main\india is transferred to the U.S. team and then a merge is initiated. All these activities can be automated with the help of scripts.

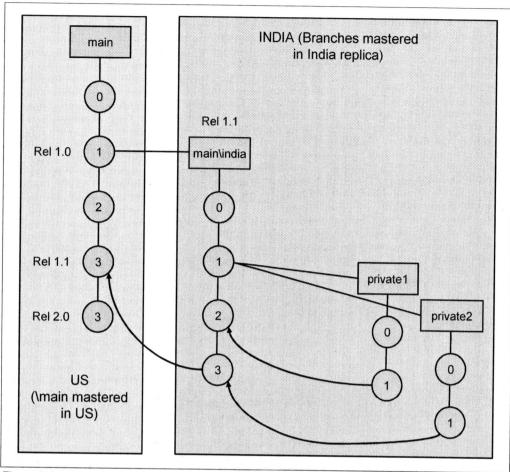

Figure 6-24   Branching in Base ClearCase for GDD

6.7.2 Basic workflow and scripts

In this scenario, we provide the following tools/scripts to the developers. The developer runs them in the order mentioned.

First, the developer creates a view. Then the developer updates the view with the label or time stamp needed from the parent branch. The developer then makes the changes to the code by checking out files, checks them in, and updates the view to resolve any merge conflicts. The developer merges the changes into the parent. Finally, the developer renames the private branch that was worked on to Defect -id in ClearQuest.

Figure 6-25 shows the workflow. Note that an example file's version tree is shown. This particular file does not have an element on the private branch. Therefore, a branch is created when the developer checks out a file.

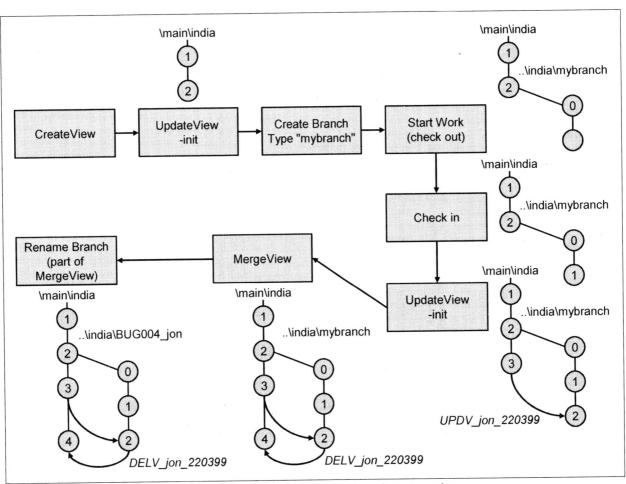

Figure 6-25 *Workflow for a developer (shows the file's version tree in various stages)*

In the next section, we look at the scripts/tools that can be useful in implementing the workflow.

CreateView

The CreateView script creates a view for the user. It is a simple script that creates a Base ClearCase view. Users may not use this script directly. They can use the `cleartool mkview` command.

The CreateView script does a certain level of checking as to whether the global storage location is valid or not, whether the storage is sharable, and whether the view-storage ends with a ".vws". The script can even enforce certain company standards on naming the views.

Figure 6-26 shows how to run the command in UNIX.

```
CreateView -tag achakrab-hp /nfs/u129/achakrab/views/achakrab-hp.vws
```

Figure 6-26 *Running CreateView*

The script can also use certain options:

- ► -host
- ► -hpath
- ► -gpath
- ► -h

Using these options, you can get the same behavior as the `mkview` command. When the view is created, it has a simple configuration specification, as shown in Example 6-1.

Example 6-1 Config spec for a view created by CreateView

```
element * CHEKEDOUT
element * /main/LATEST
```

UpdateView

The UpdateVeiw script has the following options:

- ► -h
- ► -time
- ► -now
- ► -vobs
- ► -m
- ► -init

Figure 6-27 shows the first step that a user runs.

```
UpdateView -init
```

Figure 6-27 First step in UpdateView

This creates the proper configuration specification for him. For a developer sitting in India, the config spec created looks something like the output shown in Example 6-2.

Example 6-2 Config spec in India

```
element * CHECKEDOUT
element * /main/india/mybranch/LATEST
element * /main/india/LATEST -time 12-Jan.10:45 -mkbranch mybranch
element * /main/india/0 -mkbranch mybranch
element * /main/LATEST -time 12-Jan.10:45 -mkbranch india
element * /main/0 -mkbranch india
```

For a developer in Santa Clara, the same command generates a config spec similar to the one shown in Example 6-3.

Example 6-3 Config spec in Santa Clara

```
element * CHECKEDOUT
element * /main/mybranch/LATEST
element * /main/india/LATEST -time 12-Jan.10:45 -mkbranch mybranch
element * /main/0 -mkbranch mybranch
```

Basically, this script should set up the views properly for development depending on what your geography is.

After the developer has run the command, if the branch "mybranch" does not exist, the developer must create a branchtype using the command shown in Figure 6-28.

```
cleartool mkbrtype mybranch
```

Figure 6-28   Creating a branch type

When this is done, the developer can start making modifications to the source files. When the modifications are complete, or in between, the developer might want to get the latest changes in the parent branch. To do this task, the developer runs the command shown in Figure 6-29.

```
UpdateView -now
```

Figure 6-29   Updating a private branch to the latest one

This command updates the "time stamp" in the configuration specification to the current time. It also merges any files that have been modified in the parent branch and as well as in the private branch. It also labels the files merged. The whole thing has the effect of making sure that the developer has everyone's latest changes. This step must be done before the developer plans to deliver the changes to the parent. After completing this step, the developer should run a new build in the view, do some minimal testing, and then deliver.

Note if you want to update the view to a particular time, you use the -time option with the UpdateView command. You use it only in certain rare circumstances where you want the changes until a particular date and not after that. For example, you know that somebody has introduced a regression after a particular date, so you do not want those changes till the regression is fixed.

The -m option can be used with -now option to bring up the ClearCase merge utility. By default, ClearCase automatically merges files if the difference is trivial. However, if there is a conflict (for example, the same lines of code were changed), ClearCase brings up the merge utility. With the -m option, you force ClearCase to bring up the merge utility even in the case of trivial merges.

The -vobs option makes the script work for only a set of VOBs. The VOB set can be defined after following the -vob tag. This makes the command faster, as you tell ClearCase to limit the search within a sub set of VOBs.

The -h is the help option.

We recommend that you keep some internal tags in the configuration specification, for example, a tag to indicate whether the configuration was generated by UpdateView. We also recommend that you use the list of VOBs for that project. Limiting this list to a few VOBs enables the scripts to function only on those VOBs, thereby increasing the performance considerably.

Example 6-4 shows an ideal configuration specification.

Example 6-4   Using tags and default VOBs

```
# ITSO Inc.Org config spec
# Default Vobs: /vobs/retail_manager
element * CHECKEDOUT
element * /main/india/mybranch/LATEST
element * /main/india/LATEST -time 12-Jan.10:45 -mkbranch mybranch
element * /main/india/0 -mkbranch mybranch
element * /main/LATEST -time 12-Jan.10:45 -mkbranch india
element * /main/0 -mkbranch india
```

MergeView

The MergeView utility should be similar to UpdateView. However, one important aspect of MergeView is that it should show the user the list of files and directories that need merging. If the user is happy with the list, the user goes ahead with the merge process. Another important aspect is that MergeView should allow the user to rename the private branch to a meaningful name, like Defect ID. In fact, MergeView can be made powerful enough to talk to ClearQuest and get the list of defects from which to choose. This can be quite easily done using ClearQuest APIs on Windows. Using ClearQuest APIs, you can even update the defect record in ClearQuest with details as to when the merge happened, who did it, and what was the change set. MergeView should also put in labels to the destination branch.

Automated build, test, and nightly merge

What we discussed until now were the scripts and tools to be used by developers. Apart from these tasks, a nightly build should happen on the local integration branch (for example, on \main\india) on a nightly basis. Some smoke tests should be run to check if the product is working fine.

Finally, a merge to the main integration branch (namely \main) should be done on a nightly basis. To do this merge, the mastership of \main\india has to be changed to the U.S. using the cleartool **chmaster** command, and then the merge can be done with the help of the MergeView script.

Build and deployment

This chapter highlights the typical challenges with build management and deployment in a distributed development organization and suggests possible solutions through processes and tools. We focus on how a central build management system provided by Rational Build Forge can help standardize and manage distributed development better.

7.1 Introduction to build and deployment

Build and release activities provide the crucial connection between the development and quality teams and are responsible for on time delivery to the customer. A standardized, comprehensive build and release system is an important factor to meet committed dates and milestones and provide high quality deliverables.

Many nonstandard practices, such as *ad hoc* / on demand builds, out of process inclusion of changes, *ad hoc* patching of QA machines, install testing late in the life cycle, and the problems arising out of such practices, are often muted in a single site development environment. However, when there is theoretically no night for nightly builds, such practices have a major cost in terms of time and quality of the product. In this chapter, we discuss some of the challenges and possible solutions.

7.2 Build challenges in GDD

In organizations where the development life cycles are all done in a single location, build and deployment processes are not mature. Common issues with *ad hoc*, nonstandard build systems multiply when the operating environment becomes distributed. Some of the issues are:

► A of lack of clarity of role and ownership in GDD caused by manual build start and multiple build components

► Complicated build components

► Bottleneck caused by single-point build execution unavailability

► Lack of build failure/completion notifications causing unnecessary delays

► Difficulty in finding new build contents resulting in wasted QA/Dev cycles

► Low awareness level of developers on how to effectively use SCM and build system

► No standby for build machine

► Few product/compiler licenses

► Noninvolvement of build engineer in release planning

► Unknown corporate network service-level agreements (SLAs)

► Unknown state of build servers

► Shared build machines

► Build assets scattered across different machines, with no knowledge of the "correct" version to use

Although there are numerous solutions available on the market that provides ready-to-use basic build and other value added features, most of the deployed systems fail to realize real life scenarios of integrating different styles of build mechanisms, as there are no industry standards for the same. Our experience shared here is focused on how that conventional "Build System" need to adapt and improve to align itself with the changing needs of GDD.

7.2.1 Automating the build system

Often the build engineer's time is wasted on fire fighting and managing nonuniform product release process. The engineer often caters to out-of-bound build requests for immediate deliverables. Clearly this does not scale well when the teams are distributed. It does not make sense to have multiple build engineers in each location or to have the teams blocked on the availability of the next build whenever that happens.

Whenever a change is committed to the source base, irrespective of the location, the build system should automatically detect it and trigger a build. This can be optimized to wait for a minimum number of code changes, high risk changes, urgency of delivery, and so on, or a combination of all. Basically, some kind of automatic logical calculation mechanism should be used to find when a build is needed in addition to scheduled ones.

Depending upon the time zone difference and development life cycle size, the build cycle needs to be optimized to leverage the day to day development and maintenance activities. In order to have the right processes to streamline and govern distributed teams, we need to have the appropriate environment in terms of hardware needs, software requirements, and build execution strategy.

Important: The automation mentioned previously requires a well-planned source code stream locking strategy to eliminate source change during builds, especially when the build time is in the order of hours. Also, this level of automation requires a well laid out process, education to the team about the process, and clear communication between engineers and the release engineer.

7.2.2 Reduction and tuning of build time

Distributed teams are effective in using time zone differences in terms of sharing product sources. However, at the same time, they make the job of the build and release engineer challenging as the idle time (time when team members are just sitting and waiting for build) is reduced to few hours and therefore forces the build and release engineer to modify the build process so that the product build time is reduced to a minimum. For example, considering the scenario provided in 1.7, "Scenario description" on page 17, the Santa Clara Lab commits their changes to SCM by 6 p.m. local time and the Dublin Lab starts their business day at 8 a.m. local time. The time for the product to be built and be ready for testing by the Dublin team is six hours If the same build is needed by the Bangalore Lab, then the build engineer only has 30 minutes.

Perhaps there are builds that are automated and can be triggered by every check-in. But if the build time is, for example, nine or ten hours, then it is unlikely that the teams are going to be able to see each other's latest changes.

The following tips help you understand the build system and parallelize it.

Identifying component coupling

Contrary to procedural programming languages, **make** is more dependency driven than the control flow and therefore leaves enough room for parallel execution of all non-dependent components or targets. Most of the **make** interpreters provide parallel execution of the **make** target commands, for example **gnu gmake** uses the -j flag to read how many targets to make in parallel. As we are talking of parallelism here, we recommend using a multi processor machine as a build machine in order to exploit the real parallelism.

Optimizing computational power and hardware topology

The idea is to have enough computational power in order to execute and build the product in an acceptable time. Build machines can be a server farm of several machines with average memory, CPU, and disk, and a good tool that can control these server farms distributed over geographies. The tool should be able to locate the appropriate build machine from the server farm, start the build, monitor it, and finally publish the same to the users, which might be internal test teams.

> **Note:** By doing this task, we are setting up an environment for making parallel builds possible. Though building in parallel is not a new thing in building systems, this is important for distributed teams, especially working in 24/7 mode where the build time is crucial and should be as minimal as possible. It also helps maintain clean configurations.

Common intermediate objects reuse

As we are talking of multiple users distributed across geographies, that would mean at least one build per user in use at any given time. Also, when it comes to changing freeze dates, builds are done quite often. One important thing to note here is that every user updates a limited set of source files as part of a new feature or a defect fix, but that change requires a rebuild of the entire product or component of the product. This becomes an alarming situation when it comes to products with a huge source base. Basically, the idea is not to build/compile the source files that are unchanged by the current user; instead, use the latest Derived Object (DO) of the referred source file, which might exist somewhere in the network.

7.2.3 Local build availability

Having a centralized build and SCM system might be desirable when the distributed team size is small enough. However, as the team starts growing, the number of changes committed to the SCM also increases, and the probability of errors due to inappropriate code merges increases. Every time a product integration build breaks, it results in the loss of productive man hours, whether it is the build engineer that investigates the failure or the test teams who are waiting for the latest product binaries to perform integration testing.

Therefore, it is a best practice to have the product built locally before any changes are made visible to the product integration build machine. This not only reduces integration build breakage, but also firms up team credibility in terms of the quality of new code delivered into the product. Also, it is a best practice to keep the build request interface the same, whether it is local build or integration build.

7.2.4 Web interface

For a tool to be successful in a geographically distributed environment, it should be accessible and controllable over the network, whether on the Internet or intranet. It is also desirable that when accessing the build system in this distributed client server scenario, the client is always a Web browser; otherwise, it defeats the purpose of easy accessibility. Considering all such points, the following should be the basic Web interface support by the build tool:

► Scheduler interface
► Customization interface
► Controller interface
► Troubleshooting interface
► Summary view/dashboard interface
► Build status and history interface
► Administration interface

7.2.5 Build deployment

Deployment control deals with the synchronized release of applications to the product environment itself, taking into account dissimilarities between the various platforms that a given application must operate on in a target technical environment. For example, ITSO Inc. Retail Manager used by users in New York and Chicago has client interfaces operating on Windows XP, MQSeries® middleware running on IBM System z™, databases implemented under DB2®, and various extended client platform trading integrations through multiple Web servers. Each of these components of the application architecture require a separate release, with coordinated deployment across these disparate platforms.

Therefore, unless there is specialized tool support for deployment, it is difficult and prone to error to deploy product in a recommended environment.

The first level of build/product deployment happens when the product is made available to internal test teams for performing tests. At that level, deployment is not a formal process, and the build can be published by having a FTP site in place. The final deployment can be done easily by scripting if the product can be installed from a command-line interface. A functional test tool like IBM Rational Functional Tester (RFT) can be used if the installation process is GUI intensive, to play back the standard steps.

7.3 IBM Rational solution for build

Until now, we discussed the features and functionalities to look for while selecting a build and deployment tool. Let us now discuss the features that exist in the IBM Rational solution for build system. The products under discussion here are IBM Rational Build Forge, IBM Rational ClearCase, IBM Tivoli Provisioning Manager, and IBM Rational ClearQuest, which provide an adaptive framework for multi-platform, reliable, controlled, and high-performance build system for geographically distributed teams (Figure 7-1).

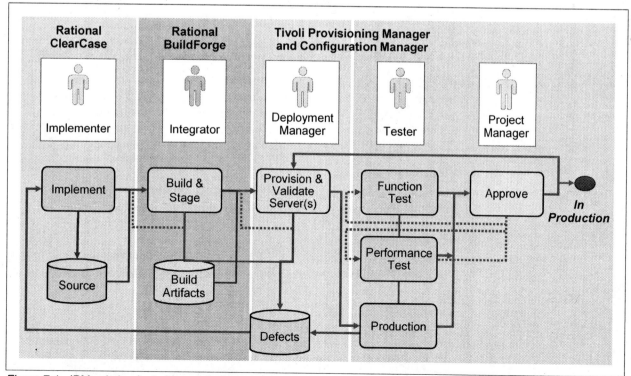

Figure 7-1   IBM solution for build and deployment

7.3.1 Build strategy solution with IBM Rational ClearCase

The Rational solution under recommendation here is IBM Rational ClearCase. ClearCase includes two independent build programs, **clearmake** and **omake**. However, both programs incorporate major ClearCase build-related features, including configuration lookup, derived object sharing, and config record maintenance.

The **omake** program's strength lies primarily in its support for users who require compatibility with other build programs designed for personal computers, including Borland Make, Microsoft NMAKE, Intersolv Polymake, and OPUS Make.

Distributed and parallel build mechanism

ClearCase can perform builds in which multiple processes execute in parallel the build scripts associated with **makefile** targets. The processes executing the build scripts run on a single host. By using more concurrent processes, parallel builds can reduce the overall build time significantly. Instead of one process running one build script at a time, you can have multiple processors working in parallel. For large software systems, this performance improvement can make a critical difference, especially in a GDD environment.

The **clearmake** command schedules and manages target rebuilds as follows:

► It executes the build script for an out-of-date target after it is detected as system build resources allow for it.

► It does not assume that executing a build script for a specific target implies that the target was updated.

Starting a parallel build

To start a parallel build, invoke **clearmake** by using the -J command-line option or set the CCASE_CONC environment variable. For example, to start a build that builds up to five targets concurrently, use any one of the commands shown in Example 7-1.

Example 7-1   Starting parallel builds in ClearCase using clearmake

```
user@host% clearmake -J 5 my_target           [command-line  option]
user@host% setenv CCASE_CONC 5;clearmake my_target    [environment variable]
```

When **clearmake** builds a **makefile** target, there may be side effects that you cannot address in a makefile. For example, one of your build tools may create temporary files that are not guaranteed to have unique names and then delete them at the end of its processing. When you use this tool serially, there are no problems. However, if you invoke it in multiple parallel builds in **clearmake**, the tool may create identical files and cause the builds to interfere with each other.

You can solve this problem by using the .NOTPARALLEL special **makefile** target. To disable parallel building for a makefile, use this target without any arguments, for example:

```
.NOTPARALLEL:
```

To prevent specific targets from being built in parallel with each other, specify them as a set of arguments. Note that parallel builds are prevented only within the set of targets, for example:

```
.NOTPARALLEL: %.a
.NOTPARALLEL: x.c y.c
```

In this example, **clearmake** does not build any .a file in parallel with any other .a file, and x is not built in parallel with y. However, **clearmake** can build .a files in parallel with x, y, or any other file.

Note: clearmake does not pass the -J (parallel build) flag to child make processes involved in a recursive build. But if you explicitly instruct the child make processes to build parallel, and if the idleness in the build host and the bldserver.control files does not prevent it, then the build runs the risk of starting more parallel target builds than you want or than the build server can handle.

To prevent such a situation, use the .NOTPARALLEL special makefile target.

7.3.2 Build management solution using IBM Rational Build Forge

Here are a few points of concern in the GDD environment that can be addressed effectively by deploying IBM Rational Build Forge.

Automatic build start

Instead of a build engineer starting a build manually, Build Forge provides a build scheduler that several users can use without understanding how the actual component is built (Figure 7-2).

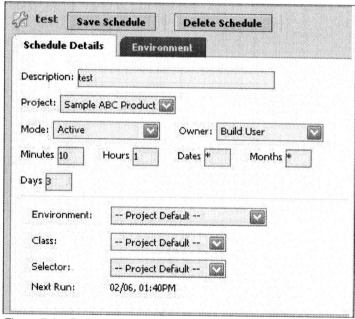

Figure 7-2   Build Forge scheduler

Users can schedule as well as view an existing list of scheduled builds (Figure 7-3).

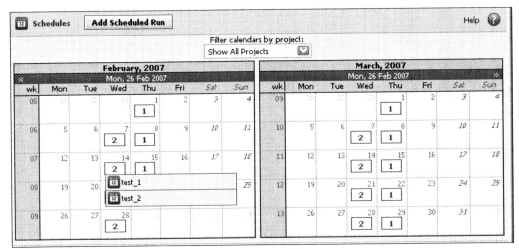

Figure 7-3   Scheduler displaying existing scheduled builds

Simplified build components

Using Build Forge, entire build process can be broken down into steps making it more robust, reusable and modularized (Figure 7-4).

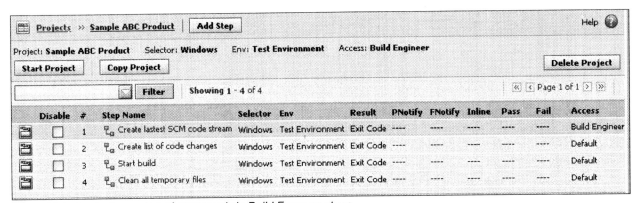

Figure 7-4   Logical grouping of commands in Build Forge as steps

A step can be a single command or a command collection, as shown in Figure 7-5. By grouping the build process into steps, a user can find exact points of failure because Build Forge reports which step failed. Dependency of steps is also handled when configuring steps during the project setup (Figure 7-5).

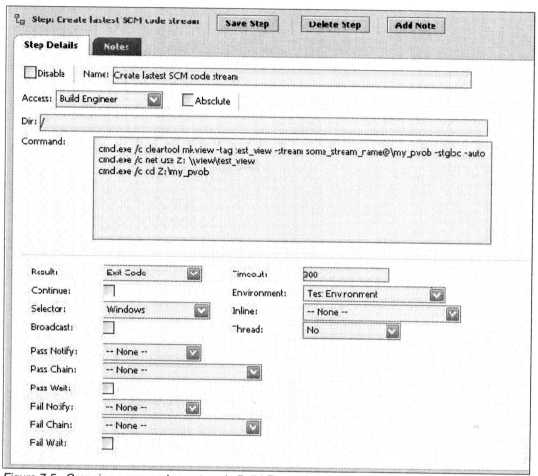

Figure 7-5   Grouping commands as steps in Build Forge

Web-based build control

When all build scheduling and initiation happens through a Web interface, the system becomes a transparent mechanism for a geographically distributed team.

Build failure/completion notifications

Build Forge provides various notification templates, as illustrated in Figure 7-6, which can be customized for products and then can be used for almost any kind of build event (start, pass, fail, and so on).

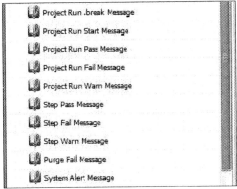

Figure 7-6   Build Forge default build notification templates

Build notification templates can be changed easily to meet specific product or user needs. Figure 7-7 shows how the subject and body of the notification can be configured easily by using a shell variable that is available on build machine. Also, the notification messages have a direct hyperlink to the details report page of the build activity.

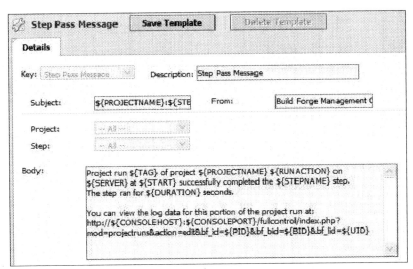

Figure 7-7   Step pass message templates

New build contents publishing

As shown in Figure 7-7, a shell variable can be set to the updated contents of build. The command to find the change set varies for different SCMs.

Awareness of developers for using the SCM and build system

When the IBM Rational Build Forge build system is in place, building any component of the product becomes transparent to the user. To start a build, a user only needs to login to Build Forge and schedule a build or execute the build on demand.

Build machine standby

As seen in Figure 7-8, every entity in the Build Forge architecture is an independent system in itself and therefore can be configured to have a standby for every individual component.

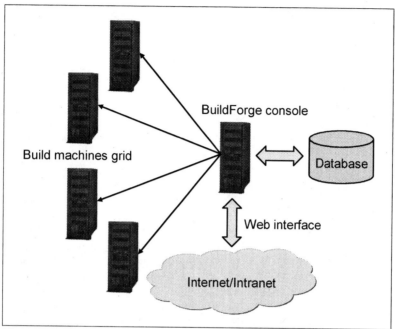

Figure 7-8   Build Forge architecture

The Build Forge project information can be saved into a configuration file and can then be imported to any other machine with the Build Forge engine whenever needed.

Optimized resource utilization across geographies

Different geographies working on the product have different budget constraints, different component ownership, different environments, and different hardware configurations. These factors should be taken into account when scheduling a build by the build system.

Build Forge provides a mechanism called *dynamic server management*, which uses collectors, manifests, and selectors to find and filter build machines as per requirement.

A collector consists of a series of properties that are assigned to any server that uses the collector. However, the specific values of the properties can vary from server to server, because a collector is a set of instructions for collecting data.

Figure 7-9 shows the default set of basic collectors that come predefined with Build Forge.

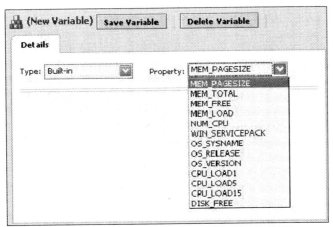

Figure 7-9   Default list of collectors provided by Build Forge

Suppose a particular component requires a **perl** version on a build machine to be 5.8.x or later, **gcc** Version 3.2 or later, at least 5 GB disk space, and at least two processors to be on the build machine. This can be done by creating an appropriate collector for every property, as shown in Figure 7-10, as a combination of default and user defined ones.

Property	Value	Type	Regex
NUM_CPU		Built-in	
DISK_FREE		Built-in	
GCCVersion	gcc --version	Built-in	gcc (GCC) 3\,[^12]\,[0-9]
PerlVersion	perl -version	Built-in	v5\,8\,. built for cygwin

Figure 7-10   Collector definition in Build Forge

After collectors are defined, one or more appropriate selectors needs to be created that define the project requirements for selecting a server to execute.

Server selectors allow you to describe the kind of server that a project or step should use by listing desired properties and values. When you apply a selector to a project or step, the system uses the selector to determine which servers are valid choices for the task, and then selects an available server from the valid ones (Figure 7-11).

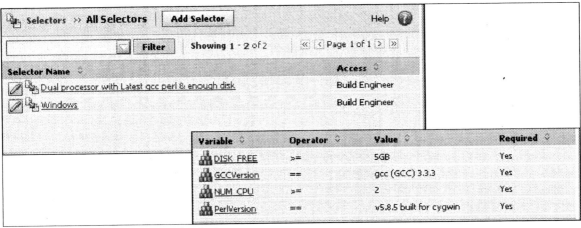

Figure 7-11   Selectors as group of collectors

By doing the previous configuration per the product requirements, you can make sure that you are optimizing use of your available resources and that a project does not execute on the wrong machine.

Automatic build baselining

When a build is over and it passes testing successfully, the source base in ClearCase can be automatically labeled to mark a new recommended baseline so that all new views created for the stream have the latest contents by default.

Automatic build scheduling

The last piece here is the automated build start whenever any fix is delivered to SCM. Considering that the SCM being used is IBM Rational ClearCase, ClearCase provides a mechanism where an action (build) can be triggered whenever there is a delivery on any source code stream or branch. Now starting a build for every delivery does not sound smart. There can be numerous ways to optimize this task, and one method is to trigger builds with CRITICAL_FIX_ whenever the activity delivered starts (for UCM based ClearCase) or any file in change set has an attribute CRITICAL_FIX with value Yes (for base ClearCase).

7.3.3 Product deployment using IBM Tivoli Provisioning Manager

IBM Tivoli Provisioning Manager allows you to create, customize, and quickly use best practice automation packages. Pre-built automation packages provide control and configuration of major vendors' products, while customized automation packages can implement your company's datacenter best practices and procedures. These procedures can then be automated and executed in a consistent, error-free manner. In fact, using these automation packages, Tivoli Provisioning Manager has the ability to provision and deploy a server with the single push of a button.

Some of the features of Tivoli Provisioning Manager (Figure 7-12) are:

► A graphical user interface designed to simplify change execution tasks for the datacenter operator, hardware, software, and network resource discovery, and drift detection to help ensure that desired configurations are maintained.

► Integration with Tivoli Configuration Manager for enterprise-wide software distribution, and image and script management to help leverage the existing company standards and procedures in a consistent and controlled way.

► Provisioning Manager also incorporates solution install, a self-managing autonomic technology that enables the deployment of complex applications to multiple real and virtual servers.

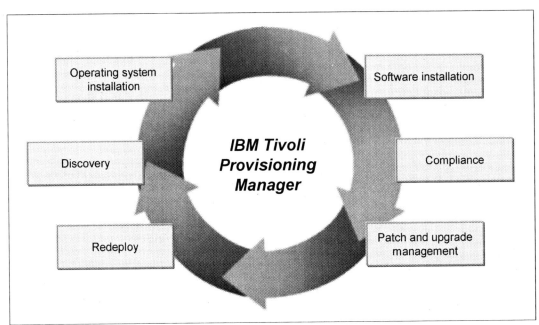

Figure 7-12   Managing system life cycle with Tivoli Provisioning Manager

To learn more about IBM Tivoli Provisioning Manager, refer to:

`http://www-306.ibm.com/software/tivoli/products/prov-mgr/`

7.3.4 Deployment tracking with IBM Rational ClearQuest

Different users will have different processes and strategies for product deployment. IBM Rational ClearQuest can be customized to cater to almost any process. It not only streamlines the process, but it also enforces it.

When the process of deployment is decided, a schema for the deployment needs to be created in ClearQuest. The system is now traceable throughout the development life cycle (Figure 7-13).

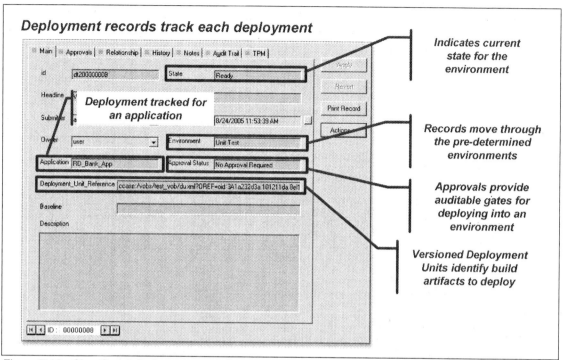

Figure 7-13   ClearQuest deployment record

7.4 Case study

ITSO Inc. Santa Clara is responsible for build deliveries and have a build and release engineer named Sam working full-time on it. Sam and his team have an integration build creator, a local build creator, and a build scheduler (IBM Rational Build Forge) as separate machines. Build Forge is scheduled for daily nightly builds (U.S. time) for local as well as integration builds. The SCM system implemented with IBM Rational ClearCase is in place with the appropriate users' mastership (U.S. and India).

As ITSO Inc. Bangalore also participates in development activities, they have a localized ClearCase SCM repository for the entire product that is synchronized with the Santa Clara replica every 10 minutes. In addition, the Bangalore team has a local build machine (controllable through the Build Forge console at U.S./Web) that picks up the source from the local ClearCase repository and does nightly scheduled builds (India time). After all changes are verified by the Bangalore team in the local component build, changes are pushed to the product packaging build machine in the U.S. and the same is replicated with the ClearCase replica at Beijing for integration testing.

ITSO Inc. Beijing is responsible for testing components developed by Bangalore and system and integration testing of all components, Beijing also has a integration build machine (controllable through the Build Forge console at U.S./Web) so that the team saves time instead of copying large binaries over the network. As the integration build environment is exactly the same as that of the U.S., the team is assured that the builds are identical to U.S. integration builds.

Sam has following job scope:

- ► Maintain the build machines at Santa Clara, Bangalore, and Beijing.
- ► Maintain ClearCase at the Santa Clara, Bangalore, and Beijing replicas.
- ► Maintain the build system console at Santa Clara.
- ► Create new code branches/streams appropriately and add the corresponding product configuration setting so that users can schedule builds on these code branches/streams.

Changes done at Santa Clara are available to India and China in their respective working hours and this saves bandwidth and waiting time for build. Similarly, changes by Bangalore are available to Santa Clara without delay because of the time difference. A similar strategy can be adopted for the time zone difference with YBJ, Dublin.

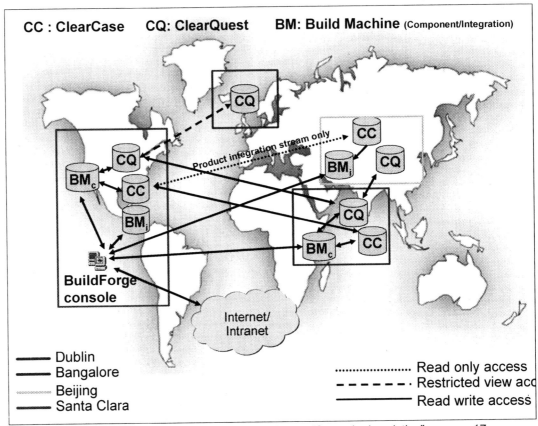

Figure 7-14   Case study of the scenario mentioned in 1.7, "Scenario description" on page 17

Ideally, everything is controllable over the network, but as build machines are distributed over geographies, depending on the product complexity and team size, its a best practice to have build/release engineers at Bangalore as well to leverage time zone differences and have a local point of contact for problem troubleshooting of the local development team.

7.5 Conclusion

In a nutshell, we can say that the important things to take care for build and deployment are automation, build time reduction (by parallelization, object sharing, and so on), and a Web interface, which is the most valuable part, as it make the build and deployment system available to all geographies. IBM has tools such as IBM Rational Build Forge, IBM Tivoli Provisioning Manager, and IBM Rational ClearQuest, which can take care of almost every aspect of the build and deployment domain challenges.

Test management

In the last few years, there has been an emergence of strong, dedicated, and objective testing capabilities or centers of excellence in companies that specialize in outsourcing projects. Perhaps the perception of manageable risk, relative independence, and different skill sets required for testing have all contributed to the increase in the number of testing projects that have been outsourced or have been performed by a remote site.

This chapter discusses typical scenarios and concerns of testing in a GDD environment. We also discuss test tools, testbed, and a test strategy more suitable to a multisite development.

8.1 Introduction to test management

Software quality assurance is becoming more and more sophisticated with various new and improved trends, methodologies, and phases of testing. Be it system verification testing, performance testing, integration testing, or functional verification, almost all categories of quality assurance can be potentially done by remote sites. Many outsourcing companies have been developing focused expertise in testing excellence. However, with multiple teams across geographies getting involved, we have additional complexities and challenges that come into play despite the sophistication.

The general driving factors of GDD discussed in Chapter 1, "Introduction to Global Development and Delivery" on page 3, such as reducing costs, decreasing time to market, and leveraging specific skill sets, are even more applicable to testing projects. The relative independence of the discipline and the specific skill sets available, such as test automation skills or domain expertise, are so well exploited that we often see remote testing teams as one of the earliest forays a company makes into GDD.

In this chapter, we discuss the most common issues in most distributed test teams, how tool selection can be done to alleviate the pain points, best practices, and case studies.

8.2 Challenges in testing for GDD

General best practices, such as effective test management, selection of appropriate tools, uniform processes implementation, focus on test automation, and so on, bring added complexity to GDD. In this section, we see some of the specific challenges of testing in a distributed environment.

8.2.1 Distributed test management

Effective test management is an important aspect of overall governance and it is a crucial factor in assessing the project health. Various challenges are associated with the different aspects of test management.

Process

One of the many challenges of testing is justification of the investment proportional to the other disciplines. While distributed testing addresses the cost component, it exposes inherent testing challenges even more so. It further shows that testing and development do not work well together, that status reporting on testing is time consuming, and that collaboration is weak. Testing is difficult to do in parallel, and no change management is in place for any organization in testing.

Distributed testing teams highlight the need for a formalized test process to be in place to help overcome these challenges and others. A successful GDD solution should provide a streamlined approach to collaborative test asset management with alignment for testing processes that are already in place. Planning, authoring, execution, and reporting need to work in orchestration of the process.

Planning

Planning is the first step for testing activities, either centralized or distributed. However, the way the test plan takes shape is important for GDD. The following questions should have clear and precise answers documented during test planning and should be available to all team members throughout the testing cycle.

► What to test?

Scope assumptions that can be clarified quickly in a single site can cause delays and unnecessary repetition in a distributed environment. Each and every small role and responsibility should have a place in the test plan. Along with scope, defining the test focus, that is, at what levels are the distributed teams testing and at each respective level, and what type or types of tests are being conducted is another important challenge. Planning for test focus is challenging in a collocated environment; it is even more challenging in a GDD environment in which the GDD landscape can be quite complex.

► Who owns what?

A plan should clearly indicate primary component or module ownership of various distributed teams. It should also be clear in regard to which testing activities are being done by which group or groups of owners and any considerations that may exist for sharing these responsibilities across geographies.

► How to test?

Testing activities should be standardized across all teams. This helps to ensure that the same process is followed everywhere and affirms uniformity and equality across geographies. If the same set of processes, tools, and methodology is implemented across all teams participating in GDD, it is convenient for management to compare various distributed teams in terms of competency, performance, and results.

► How to share artifacts?

Artifacts, such as test suites, test scripts, logs, and so on, should be accessible for teams across geographies. Most testers ensure that the test scripts and other artifacts are reusable. However, since there is no team to validate the transparency, all test artifacts develop a tight coupling to the geography over a period. By the time this coupling is detected, often the situation becomes difficult to manage simply because the artifact base becomes so huge that decoupling becomes a job in itself.

Building test artifacts for reuse is also a major challenge in this respect. Using test planning to identify areas of initial test asset reuse, although requiring more time up front, can lead to major efficiency gains in terms of ease of test artifact sharing later in the development life cycle.

Test authoring

Tracking the level and types of tests that are being authored at various sites can be a challenge in distributed teams. Without a test management repository to manage this test authoring information as formal test assets visible to the distributed testing environment, it is difficult to track test progress and communicate this to the wider development team environment. In addition, without having some way to run test reports at the test authoring level, it is difficult to provide the benefits resulting from evaluation of test reports throughout the test life cycle.

Test execution

There may be a necessity for test case execution in remote machines and sharing of results across teams. Thus, the artifacts used during the execution should be accessible from any distributed location.

The decision on the infrastructure and the way the tests will be executed should be well thought and have input from multiple constituencies who are involved in the effort, such as members of the IT, networking, quality assurance, and other infrastructure groups. Access to testing artifacts might be location agnostic given that the environments are in full collaboration from a connectivity and integration standpoint.

Moreover, the execution strategy should be manageable, repeatable, and transferable across geography. This is important so that one geography can supplement the others in need. We recommend that test teams participating in GDD should swap testing activities (unless technically impossible) for a period ranging from a week to maybe a month once in every test cycle. This not only ensures that all artifacts are in good condition and operational, but also works as a peer review of test artifacts by other distributed test teams. In many cases, offshore models that are starting require a more intense degree of collaboration in the beginning, where test and development resources are in close contact. As the model begins to unfold, utilization drops. Sharing environments must support utilization capabilities at both ends of the spectrum.

Test reporting

A testing effort is only useful if it can convey the testing status and measures of quality for the product. Generating reports is simple enough, but presenting the right information, at the right time, to all the appropriate people can be trickier than it seems for several reasons:

► If there is too little information, then management will not fully understand the issues affecting quality and there will be wasted communication cycles between teams.

► If there is too little information, then the meaning and impact of key information might get diluted or lost.

► There might be regional or other technical issues that affect sharing of information between distributed teams.

Another consideration in reporting results is how the information is arranged, and in what formats (that is, the information can be tool based, browser-based, or in documents). Management's understanding of the testing and quality information will be reduced if there are technical or other restrictions limiting the arrangement, format, speed, and ease of access of reports. Data should be presented in a clear and logical design that conveys the appropriate meaning, not in a layout constrained by tools or technology. It is therefore essential for test management to consider the need for flexibility and capability in providing a wide range of reporting format.

A common method and format of test reports should be followed by all test teams so that results can be collated, understood, and compared easily. Synchronization intervals for communication among stakeholders must be set appropriately. It is also important that test execution be consistent from each geography to prevent data loss. For example, if there is a lack of consistency, some geographies may execute test assets from point products as opposed to the central harness, such as a test management tool.

Finally, since testing may be distributed in many different ways, one challenge particular to GDD testing is providing an efficient reporting capability throughout the test life cycle. It is one thing to have test reporting for test execution, but it is another to have a test reporting capability that provides test reporting for each major phase of the test life cycle (that is, planning, authoring, and execution).

Tracking and traceability of testing cycle

All phases of the testing cycle should be trackable and traceable at all times. This is important to fix the gaps whenever teams depend on each other. Tracking and traceability should be implemented through a tool (not just a process) so that engineers save effort by not doing the job of the tool manually every time a trace is needed. At the same time, management should also have a tracking and traceability console or dashboard that reflects the latest set of data with mapping to the overall project plan.

8.2.2 Integration testing

One area of test focus that is of particular concern for GDD is integration testing. In scenarios where individual components are distributed across geographies, one of the biggest challenges is to coordinate availability of all components in order to perform integration tests. Unavailability of even the smallest piece can delay integration testing and push back already committed product delivery time lines. A contingency plan to support manual distribution of shared assets should be high in the list of mitigating factors for all facets where integrations are of concern.

There are also issues of coverage and division of responsibility among the various QA teams on who is responsible for the integration between two components. This issue worsens when the components do not follow the same release train. Without effective processes, a distributed team might not even be aware of a potentially problematic change in another product that would affect the integration.

8.2.3 Test tools training

For any team to be successful, the right set of environment and appropriate selection of tools is important. Selection of tools should cover almost every aspect of product testing sufficiently in depth and breadth. Availability of the test tool is necessary not just for better productivity, but also to make sure that the team is using their time and energy at the right place and not in doing repetitive and exhaustive tasks over and over. Built-in integrations between tools are especially useful to optimize collaborative efforts and to enable a streamline approach for information reporting and sharing.

8.3 Rational test tools for GDD

For any team to be successful, the right environment and the appropriate selection of tools is important. The selection of tool(s) should be such that it covers almost every aspect of product testing sufficiently in depth and breadth. The availability of the test tool is necessary not just for better productivity, but also to make sure that the team is using their time and energy at the right place and not just repeatedly doing an repetitive and exhaustive task.

8.3.1 Functional, regression, and performance test tools

The test tools market is currently flooded with a wide range of tool offerings. However which tools are most suited for the product under test is not the only factor for choosing the right tool. The "eco-system" that a test tool brings with it is as important as the core testing functionalities that empower the tool. For example, suppose a hypothetical tool 'X' can test any application, on any platform, for any custom control, but does not provide any mechanism to report the results, or provides test results that are in an unusable form. That tool is unsuitable for our needs.

The following is the list of other parameters that should be considered for selecting tools suitable for distributed test teams:

► Scripting with no or a minimal learning curve or industry standard scripting

This is one basic and important requirement considering the dynamic structure of teams. Testers change teams, products, companies, and even geographies during their service period, which makes them experts in a few industry standard scripting languages. The minimal learning curve helps set up and run a remote site testing team much faster. Rational Functional Tester, for example, supports industry standard Java and VisualBasic technology-based scripting. Avoid tools that promote proprietary languages and other aspects that do not support open standards. ·

► Scalable data pool support

The datapool provided should be able to scale in terms of data access and speed over LAN and WAN. RFT provides a public datapool mechanism where distributed teams can access the same project and use the same set of data. Data pools should have flexibility and simplicity and provide standard methods to access datasets, such as Open Database Connectivity (ODBC).

► SCM integration capabilities

The tool needs to provide integration with industry standard SCM tools simply because tracking changes is important for the maintenance of test scripts, especially when its performed by several different teams. RFT, RPT, and RMT have integrations with Rational ClearCase that allows users across distributed teams to share and track changes in test scripts effectively.

8.3.2 Test management tools for GDD

IBM Rational ClearQuest Test Manager, the test management package applied on top of ClearQuest, leverages ClearQuest's multisite capabilities to support distributed test planning, authoring, execution, and reporting. In this section, we highlight some of the features.

Plan, author, and execute

The following features of ClearQuest Test Manager help address the pain points in test management in GDD:

▶ ClearQuest Test Manager, with its integration with Reqpro, allows better traceability from requirements to tests and defects and helps address test management from the overall life cycle perspective. This is especially handy when the teams are distributed across geographies (Figure 8-1).

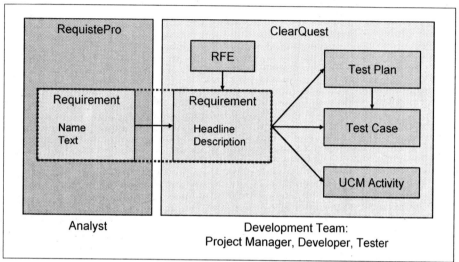

Figure 8-1   Test traceability using RequsitePro, ClearQuest Test Manager, and Rational test tools

▶ Throughout the test cycle, thorough coverage of the requirements is crucial. This is more complicated when business analysts and testers are in different locations. Built-in coverage tracking capabilities of ClearQuest Test Manager help address this challenge. Reqpro requirements can be mapped to test plans, test cases, and configured test cases.

▶ ClearQuest Test Manager provides a graphical display of the test plan hierarchy. This helps team members with a clear understanding of how the tests are organized.

▶ ClearQuest Test Manager integrates with the functional testing tools, such as RFT, RPT, Rational Robot, and so on.

▶ ClearQuest Test Manager automates sharing and reuse of test assets. ClearQuest Test Manager allows you to log in to any project and execute the test scripts associated with it. A remote user can leverage this to share or to supplement execution of test cases.

▶ ClearQuest Test Manager provides Web-based test planning, reporting, and high scalability.

Figure 8-2 illustrates a simple test planning in distributed teams.

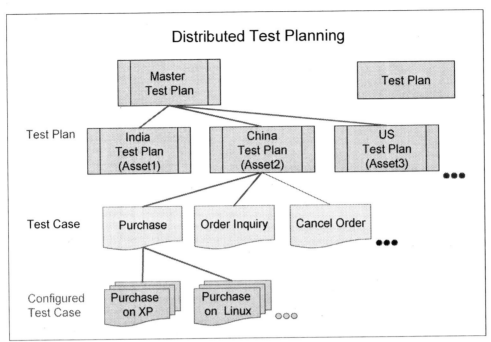

Figure 8-2   Sample test planning in distributed teams

Common repository

With a single project view, ClearQuest Test Manager allows multiple users to get a real time view of the entire project status. It also allows traceable, auditable relations between development, test, and project artifacts.

Its centralized user management with LDAP user authentication support resolves GDD challenges that are related to the accessibility of the tools from anywhere and addresses security concerns.

Reporting

ClearQuest Test Manager provides effective reporting that allows better tracking of test case definition for your requirements, creation and association of test scripts with test cases, and test case execution. When different teams execute tests at different locations, it is important to collate the results and then publish them to depict the overall status of testing. ClearQuest Test Manager can consume various test management related reports and present it in a single view.

ClearQuest provides querying capability that allows the testers to search for specific test cases based on the filters. Built-in queries give information about coverage, status such as planned versus failed, planned versus implemented etc. In addition, it allows customization of reports as well. Test management and overall project management of deliverables from distributed teams are simplified.

Quality dashboard

Using Rational ProjectConsole (PJC) and its integration with Rational tools or other third-party tools, you can automate the measurement of process execution against the defined plans. The results of these measurements can then be used to improve the plans and the processes incrementally. The tool can publish and show results in a Web browser without any necessity for client install (Figure 8-3).

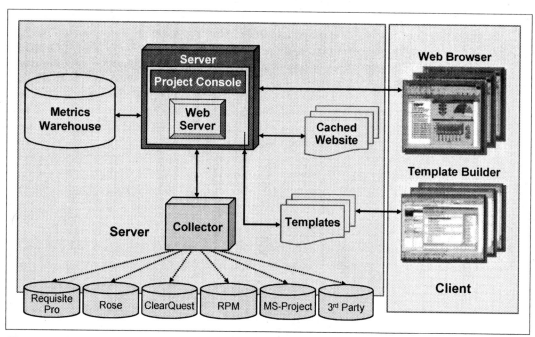

Figure 8-3   Quality dashboard using PJC

8.3.3 Requirements gathering for integration testing

Effective integration testing mostly depends on better collaboration among the teams. The distributed test teams have to share the test cases, changes that can potentially affect integration, release vehicle information, and so on.

Some simple best practices can help in resolving conflicts:

► If release cycles and streams are different, the product that is released later should sustain integration testing.

► Treat it as a requirement gathering exercise and assign ownership. For example, in ITSO Inc., Rational Reqpro was used to collect information about the integration points and ownership was assigned appropriately. This helps all teams clearly understand what needs to be tested and by whom.

► Make sure changes that affect integrations are communicated ahead of time so the testing teams can plan appropriately.

8.4 Case study

ITSO Inc. has testing activities that are distributed primarily between two locations (Beijing and Santa Clara). Natural language testing support is provided by a team in Dublin. Figure 8-4 illustrates the relationship between these sites.

Teams at all the locations use IBM Rational Functional Tester and IBM Rational Performance Tester for component unit testing, integration testing, and performance testing. IBM Rational Manual Tester is used for logging the results of all manual test cases. The test results at all the locations are imported into Rational ClearQuest Test Manager. ClearQuest Test Manager consolidates all test results into a single test report and sends it to the entire team through e-mail.

At the start of the product release cycle, the Santa Clara and Beijing teams do one round of buddy testing, that is, the Beijing team tests components developed by Santa Clara using their test harness and other test artifacts and vice-versa. This way, teams make sure that everything is documented and is accessible across the geography. Also, having this activity at the test cycle provides enough time to teams to update artifacts where gaps were found during this buddy testing.

The YBJ consulting team in Dublin can submit, validate, and close TVT- and GVT-related defects in ClearQuest. Being a remote untrusted site, YBJ has read-write access to ClearQuest for only those records that are for "TVT" and "GVT" components. This is needed because they do not require information on other defects filed on the product because that is outside the scope of their job. Also, since Dublin is an untrusted remote site, it is a good practice to give access to product artifacts on a "need to know" basis.

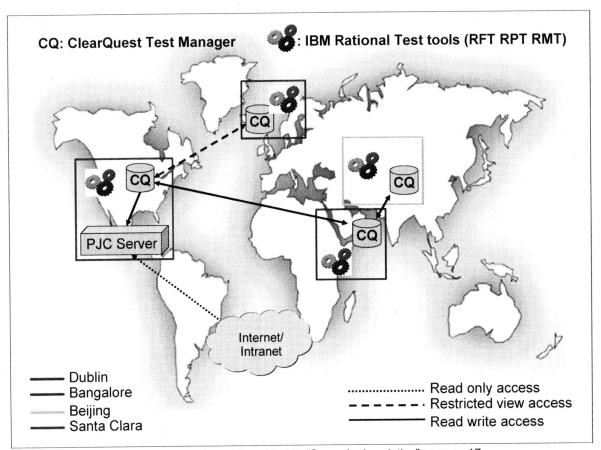

CQ: ClearQuest Test Manager   : **IBM Rational Test tools (RFT RPT RMT)**

──── Dublin
──── Bangalore
∙∙∙∙∙∙ Beijing
──── Santa Clara

∙∙∙∙∙∙∙∙∙∙ Read only access
– – – – – ∙ Restricted view access
──────── Read write access

Figure 8-4   Case study of the scenario mentioned in 1.7, "Scenario description" on page 17

Weekly status reports are sent automatically by the ClearQuest Test Manager to the team. A Quality dashboard for day-to-day tracking is implemented by using IBM Rational Project Console, as shown in Figure 8-3 on page 175.

Every defect in ClearQuest is traceable back to the requirement. Therefore at the end of the release cycle, it can be evaluated easily as to which components are less stable and which ones are robust. This type of release postmortem report helps in planning subsequent release iterations.

8.5 Conclusion

Team coordination, test planing, execution, and reporting are important aspects of the test management cycle. The effective method to control all these parameters is to have a quality dashboard that is capable of gathering accurate data, extracting useful information from it, and presenting it in a Web-based form for universal access.

Test management challenges in GDD are similar to that of overall project management challenges. Planning across distributed teams, getting appropriate status, managing human resources, and so on are applicable more in this discipline than in any other discipline in the overall project life cycle.

Part 3

Connecting the dots

This part is about some behind the scene GDD requirements. These requirements are spread across all phases of distributed software development. People and portfolio management, security, compliance, and other key factors are discussed here.

Success factors for GDD

In this book, we have reviewed the various challenges encountered in Global Development and Delivery (GDD) throughout the software disciplines of product development. We talked in detail about the tools setup, configuration, samples, best practices, and so on. In this chapter, we take a high-level look at some of the key success factors for GDD, such as global project management, collaboration across distributed sites, and global access to artifacts.

9.1 Introduction to key success factors

Several key factors can help facilitate and manage the effectiveness of a geographically distributed organization. The ability to govern and execute the global development process and the final product outcome depends on decisions that the organization makes regarding issues such as distributed project management, effective collaboration across teams, and global and secure access for all sites.

Part 2, "Running the show" on page 57, provides details about how Rational tools can help address specific challenges around GDD. As we come to the conclusion of the book, we tie together the product features that have been elaborated on previously with the concerns that we indicated.

9.2 Project management in GDD

One of the biggest issues for companies with a distributed development strategy is effective project management across geographies. Project management in GDD must account for new risks such as:

► Providing consistent communication across various sites

► Enabling a sufficient information exchange to manage the project

  Members of distributed teams frequently represent diverse language groups, cultures, and time zones. If not properly understood and managed, these factors can lead to miscommunication on many levels, from how to establish project requirements to how to transfer defect data when a bug has been fixed.

► Unifying the process across sites and managing expectations across sites (methods, process, culture, and so on)

► Cross site dependencies not defined and late delivery impacts not communicated

► Costs of multisite project underestimated (travel, education and training, and infrastructure)

► Sites managing their own risks without considering the overall project risks

  A risk may not warrant a response when considered at a site level, but may be disastrous for the overall project.

► Difficulty in achieving global visibility of project measurements across distributed teams

The following sections provide an overview of various products from IBM to support Project Portfolio Management (PPM).

9.2.1 IBM Rational Portfolio Manager

IBM Rational Portfolio Manager governs portfolio and project management with a framework to define and evaluate GDD project plans and initiatives into measurable global programs and projects. It provides a way to effectively plan, track, and manage all aspects of GDD project and resource portfolios. With extensive collaboration features, Rational Portfolio Manager connects distributed team members to form a virtual team, where all members are aware of and engaged in project decisions, schedules, discussions, meetings, and knowledge bases. Establishing a globally connected team fosters responsiveness among colleagues, speeds group decision making, and provides additional avenues of communication to share ideas and problems. It does all of this while keeping team members up to date with the latest project news and activity so all members are in sync.

Key features to support project management for GDD

Rational Portfolio Manager captures project and proposal scope, schedule, financial, and resource details, thus helping project managers to visualize and set the desired investment balance of projects and people and helping the entire organization to remain synchronized with the strategic objectives. Here we focus on the Rational Portfolio Manager features that are important from a GDD perspective.

> **Note:** For more details about IBM Rational Portfolio Manager, see:
>
> `http://www.ibm.com/software/awdtools/portfolio/index.html`

Ensure consistent processes across geographies

Optimal and efficient execution starts with having a standardized, understandable, and repeatable process. Rational Portfolio Manager provides integration with Rational Method Composer. Using Rational Method Composer, you can customize, integrate, and configure the process for your global teams to follow, right down to a work breakdown structure (WBS). You can then export your process and WBS into a template that Rational Portfolio Manager can import. Your project's WBS reflects the process, helping to automate a consistent process across geographies.

The tight integration between Rational Method Composer and Rational Portfolio Manager means that distributed teams can take advantage of process deployment features. For more details about Rational Method Composer and Rational Portfolio Manager integration, see:

`http://www.ibm.com/developerworks/ibm/library/ar-rmcrpm/index.html`

Rational Portfolio Manager extends worldwide

Rational Portfolio Manager delivers worldwide access to the centralized data repository and addresses the following GDD challenges:

► Build secure and customized user-based access from anywhere, anytime

► Enterprise roll up of all projects based on common standards and metrics irrespective of their geographies

Rational Portfolio Manager has three-tier architecture that leverages several technologies and concepts to provide global secured access, for example:

► Allows for multilingual, multicurrency capabilities

► Secured access from anywhere and anytime

   – Resource security controls system-level permissions.

   – Role-based assignment security controls the ability to view, create, and modify information at the data level.

► Leveraging technologies, such as HTTPS (SSL) and XML to enable the open flow of information between systems

IBM Rational Portfolio Manager provides a centralized repository that contains detailed and consolidated data to assist you in your GDD efforts when prioritizing, planning, managing, and measuring your project portfolio. Having all project information integrated in one centralized repository creates huge efficiency improvements for most organizations. For example, project measures, roll-ups, and status can be reported in real time. Project teams can work together better, and historical data can aid in the estimation of future projects.

Global resource assignment

Global planning for delivery based on resource availability, estimates, and inter-project dependencies is one of the biggest challenge in execution of GDD projects. IBM Rational Portfolio Manager provides the ability to forecast, plan, and assign resources in a global environment based on estimates and inter-project dependencies. Rational Portfolio Manager features a powerful resource-scheduling engine that analyzes bottlenecks, available slack, over-allocated resources, and due date constraints in an iterative process. It helps you find the best solution available across a multi-project environment so that all globally distributed team members are effectively used on the right project with the right skills, which contributes to a greater return on investment (ROI). The following RPM features can be used for global resource assignment:

► Rational Portfolio Manager helps you understand forecasted resource capacity based on incoming demand by time period and by skill set. Figure 9-1 represents a resource pipeline along a timeline, giving you a visual representation of planned, proposed, and available resources. This can help you schedule demand more effectively based on resource availability. It also helps you recognize and plan for high demand.

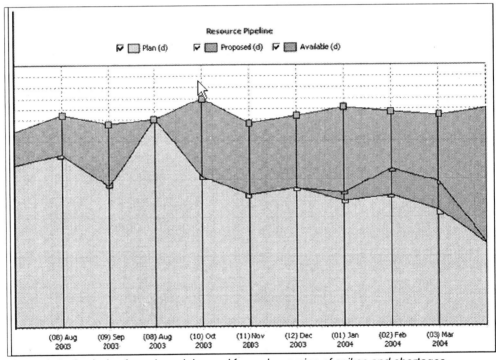

Figure 9-1   Analysis of supply and demand for early warning of spikes and shortages

► Rational Portfolio Manager helps you optimize resource allocation by allowing you to analyze multiple what-if scenarios to understand the impact on resources of different scheduling options, which leads you to the optimal mix of resource utilization and demand management. Figure 9-2 depicts one of the what-if scenarios for Net Availability/Year. Vertical bars represent demand, supply, and net availability of skilled resources in hours.

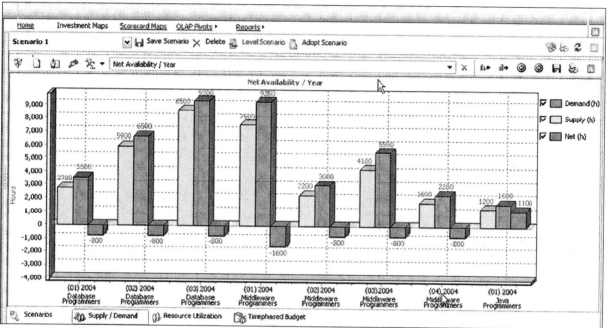

Figure 9-2   Optimizing resource allocation and demand using What-if analysis

► Rational Portfolio Manager makes resource search identification and assignment quick and easy, even in globally distributed teams. Figure 9-3 shows the resource search and assign interface from Rational Portfolio Manager, where resources can be searched and assigned from a geography, organization, or pool with specific competencies or skills.

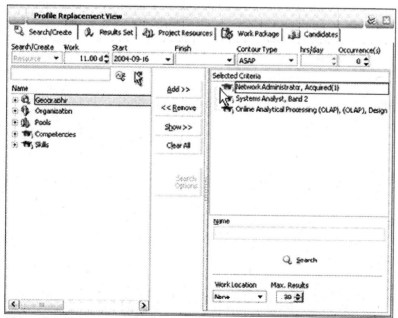

Figure 9-3   Locating and assigning globally distributed resources in real time

Automated workflow and processes

Multiple teams, locations, languages, and disciplines equate to mass confusion when work is transferred between disciplines within the development life cycle. Any number of questions can arise: Has our offshore development team fixed the defect? Has it been passed to quality assurance (QA) for testing? Who has been assigned the latest change request introduced in the triage meeting? Are there any new requirements? When left unanswered, these types of questions can have a significant impact on your project, such as delays in project delivery and poor quality.

Rational Portfolio Manager helps to increase productivity through process automation with an efficient and effective workflow that addresses the following key GDD challenges:

► Ability to establish and re-use best practice templates across all geographically distributed sites

► Define workflows based on project or activity types and automate flows based on dynamics in order to unify the process across sites and managing expectations across sites

Rational Portfolio Manager manages, automates, and tracks the flow of all project work, using its integrated collaboration workflow engine. Project processes are configured and automated into a fluid knowledge-enabled work stream that is ubiquitously present and accessible throughout the project life cycle. All workflow requests and related outcomes are recorded and stored in the repository against the originating project element. This ensures complete process traceability and allows process review and audit.

Figure 9-4 shows the workflow for processing funding request. A step in the workflow can have associated checklists. For example, *Step - Develop Funding Request* has a checklist that includes such items as "Quantify business benefit", "Fill out Service Funding Layout", and so on. It is also possible to define a voting step, such as *Step - Funding Quality Vote*, where various people from a distributed team can vote and the decision about the next step is based on voting results. Rational Portfolio Manager also tracks the workflow execution and stores its history making them audit-ready. For example, Jennifer is working on the *Develop Funding Request* step and history stores all the information about the completed items in the checklist.

Rational Portfolio Manager provides integrated scope management for keeping track of issues, risks, requirements, and changes. Each of these elements can be assessed, can have a workflow for approval, and can connect directly to the WBS so the impact to the project is clearly tracked. Rational Portfolio Manager uses project-configured state notifications and triggers. When specific changes or events occur, relevant participants are alerted via e-mail notifications. Therefore, Rational Portfolio Manager enforces processes across distributed teams by streamlining workflows through automation and results in improved collaboration in a global team.

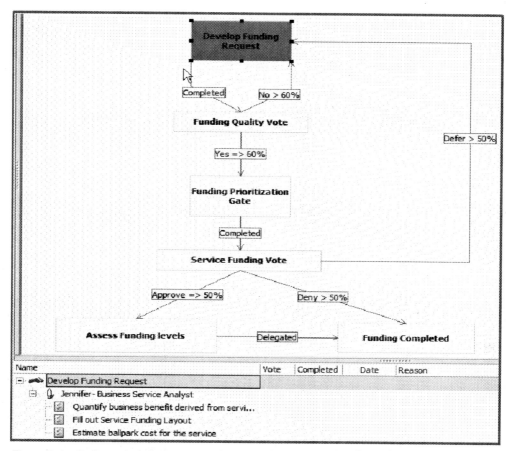

Figure 9-4   Audit-ready automated workflow to enforce decision rights and responsibilities

Portfolio budgeting and planning at the enterprise level

There can be a significant benefit to organizations that have a single source of project performance information for all sites across various geographies. It enables an organization to select, plan, and budget for global projects and programs on an annual and periodic basis.

Using a financial module in Rational Portfolio Manager, project managers can estimate capital costs and consumable budgets. Then over time, they are phased across the life of the project. For example, to facilitate the capture and tracking of incurred or committed expenses, Rational Portfolio Manager enables users to easily enter time and expense information against the appropriate accounting charge codes via an intuitive expense entry and reporting interface. The benefit of this integrated capture is that time and expense can be seen in the context of project tasks and activities. By centralizing project expense, reporting and cost variances are calculated in real time, so you can reduce potential project risk and contingency utilization. As project participants incur expenses, Rational Portfolio Manager calculates the remaining expense budget for each charge code and displays the associated budget variance. This helps to provide real-time visibility into ROI and can provide early warnings against cost overruns.

Dynamic scorecard capabilities for decision making

Rational Portfolio Manager has a scorecard view implemented through Key Performance Indicators (KPIs). This view helps you to make strategic decision and selections based on objective criteria. It also allows for tracking of global projects and their ranking.

Scorecards can also be used to assess compliance risk and remediation as well as business benefit. Figure 9-5 shows sample scorecards defined for the "Mainframe upgrade" initiative. A scorecard determines a quantitative result (% score) from qualitative information. Categories, questions, and answer are weighted to determine the score calculation.

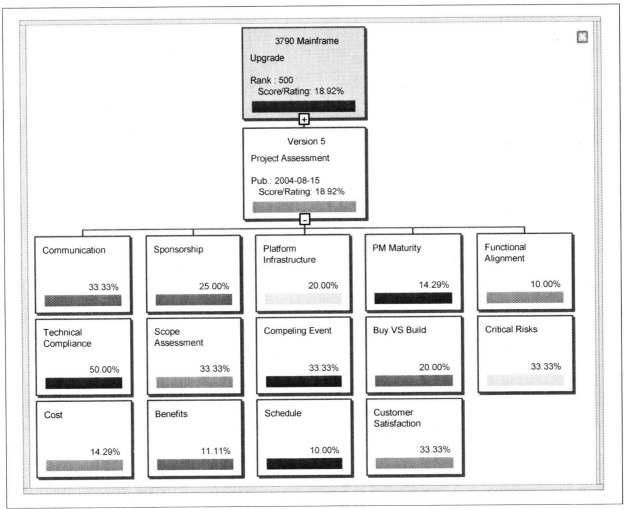

Figure 9-5   Assessing organization- and project-level compliance using scorecards

Managing risk and change

To prevent uncontrolled changes from taking place over the life of the GDD project, an overall change control and issues management system must be developed, agreed to, and implemented with discipline. Rational Portfolio Manager addresses overall change control and issues management by centralizing all exceptions with their assigned owners, priority, and status in the issues repository. This ensures that all issues that pertain to the project are identified, logged, and responded to by generating resulting actions or tasks. For each issue, the team member can define proposed actions, identify the impacted areas, and quantify the impact.

Rational Portfolio Manager also provides organizations with a standardized and automated mechanism to manage, track, and monitor the different changes and change requests resulting from the eight possible project areas. All change requests are centralized in one repository. They are prioritized and classified either as a new request, a change request generated from a risk event, or a change request generated from an issue. The team members may propose resulting actions or tasks. This centralizes all project activities.

Instead of managing four task lists that result from project issues, changes, risks, and the project schedule, Rational Portfolio Manager ensures that all work is consolidated and viewed in one location.

The risk management module in Rational Portfolio Manager includes a PMI risk ranking matrix and workflow abilities. Rational Portfolio Manager enables the project team to collaborate on risk management by ensuring that all risks are catalogued and responded to from one central repository. Each potential risk event is described and measured based on its impact, probability, and precision rankings in the provided Risk Ranking Matrix (see Figure 9-6).

The Rational Portfolio Manager Risk Database identifies each risk and describes its impact on each of the project areas. In addition, the trigger that identifies how you know when a risk even occurred is provided. Using Rational Portfolio Manager, risk owners can also set the "closure criteria" that describes what must happen in order for the risk to be considered closed. Furthermore, it provides an organization with a risk response mechanism. Risk owners can identify acceptable levels of risk, avoid a risk even, or mitigate it. Based on the selected course of action, the risk owner can generate actions or tasks.

The Rational Portfolio Manager Risk functionality provides a repository for all of your risk management data. Included in this functionality is a method for monitoring and keeping track of Risk ID/Description, Trigger/Detection, Risk Attributes, and Closure Criteria. The risk management plan also provides the procedures for effective risk management in the project.

In summary, managing exceptions in one place in Rational Portfolio Manager has following benefits:

► Contingency planning for time and budget overruns can be instituted.
► All elements that can impact scope creep are managed through an automated process.

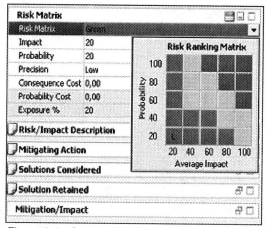

Figure 9-6 Systematic risk management at the organization, portfolio, and project level

Improved governance with Rational ClearQuest integration

IBM Rational Portfolio Manager integrates with Rational ClearQuest providing improved governance and increased effectiveness of managing globally distributed teams by adding project visibility into activities that are managed in Rational ClearQuest. Using Rational Portfolio Manager, a project manager can know at any moment whether the project is on time and in budget based on having the most current information about all of a team's work items in ClearQuest. Team members can track and update the project records or tasks in either IBM Rational Portfolio Manager or Rational ClearQuest.

Service offerings for IBM Rational Portfolio Manager

IBM professional services provide three service offerings for developing and deploying the IBM Rational Portfolio Manager solution:

- ► Project and Portfolio Management assessment
- ► Rational Portfolio Manager fast-track deployment service
- ► Rational Portfolio Manager standard deployment service

PPM assessment offering

The first step before deploying IBM Rational Portfolio Manager software is the PPM assessment. This is an independent evaluation of your PPM practices, measured against IBM best practices in project and portfolio management. The PPM assessment can require as few as two days or as many as 10 days of consulting effort, depending on the scope and complexity of the assessment. Given your desired results and your current situation, it provides recommendations for deploying IBM best practices that offer the greatest business value.

Rational Portfolio Manager fast-track deployment service offering

The fast-track deployment service is scoped to be completed after 25 to 30 days of consulting effort. Fast-track services focus on deploying a basic set of processes and metrics, with minimal customization for capabilities such as portfolio analysis and reporting, new-project initiation request, business-case review approval, project planning, project execution, and project closeout.

Rational Portfolio Manager standard deployment service offering

The standard deployment service offering is used to deploy Rational Portfolio Manager software to one or more project teams from one or more organizations that require customization of the tool to meet specific requirements for processes and metrics. This service offering can deploy any of the IBM best practices in project, program or portfolio management, encompassing any functional area of the Rational Portfolio Manager solution. Typical standard deployment can take 60 days or more. We recommend standard deployment for GDD customer because it offers services for teams from more than one organization.

9.2.2 IBM Rational ProjectConsole

The IBM Rational ProjectConsole tool collects actual development data from products within the IBM Software Development Platform along with third-party products, presenting the results graphically so that you can easily and quickly assess project progress and quality. This capability allows you to objectively measure and better predict those areas that will require special attention. Rational ProjectConsole helps answer various types of questions: Where should I focus scarce resources in order to stay on schedule? What trends are occurring that could affect cost and schedule? As a Web-based solution, Rational ProjectConsole can help keep your projects on schedule and on budget.

Key Features to support GDD

Here we focus on the ProjectConsole features that are important from a GDD perspective.

Ability to measure progress and quality

There are two types of metrics of particular importance to GDD projects: portfolio management metrics and project development metrics. Development metrics are efficiently handled through Rational ProjectConsole. Project data is collected from each development discipline and displayed graphically using charts, tables, and indicators, showing you the true status of the project in an instant. The advantages of using ProjectConsole are:

▶ Automatically collect data

Rational ProjectConsole extracts data from Rational Suite® (CQ, ReqPro, TM, and so on) and third-party tools and store it in a Measurement Warehouse.

▶ Instant status recognition and analysis capabilities

You can then analyze the data, and display measurements based on this data. Each team member can now view the measures, and drill down to better understand the underlying data, making sure that they have the information they need for decision-making.

▶ Correlate measures across projects, products, and time

Use and apply experiences from one well managed GDD product to other ongoing ones or planned ones.

Integration with Rational Portfolio Manager

This integration allows you to collect information about the general health of projects and general scope elements from Rational Portfolio Manager and store this information in the Rational ProjectConsole warehouse. You can also associate software development information to projects in Portfolio Manager. This association only affects the data that is stored in Rational ProjectConsole and does not modify any data in the source tools. The integration allows you to create charts in Rational Portfolio Manager by accessing the data stored in Rational ProjectConsole. With this integration, you can now do trend analysis on the health of your projects and scope elements, in addition, it gives ProjectConsole a much richer charting widget to display metrics (Figure 9-7).

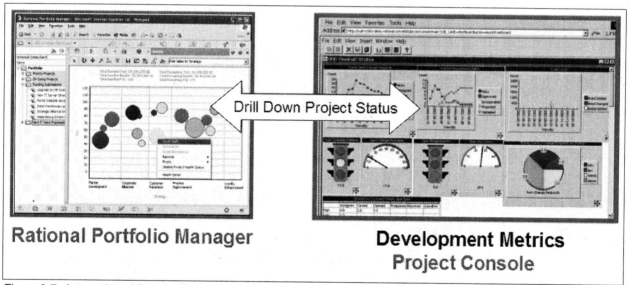

Figure 9-7   Integration of Project Console and Rational Portfolio Manager

9.2.3 Iterative development

Many of the business, project, and technical risks associated with the GDD project can be mitigated with iterative development. The benefits of iterative development are well-documented. There are areas unique to iterative development that advance GDD enablement phase strategizing approaches, such as:

▶ Incremental phase plan (loading more iterations in the construction phase)
▶ Incremental delivery phase plan (loading more iterations in the transition phase)
▶ Evolutionary phase plan (loading more iterations in the elaboration phase)
▶ Hybrid phase plans (combining the two above approaches)

There are three main ways that GDD risks can be reduced:

► Iterative development is based on a continuous assessment of the risks projects are facing.

► High priority risks can be tackled in the early iterations in the project life cycle.

► Finally, because an iteration involves a little of each discipline (requirements, architecture and design, implementation, testing, deployment, and so on), GDD technical risks can be addressed incrementally and early in the life cycle. Since an iteration plan attacks each aspect of the development disciplines, these plans effectively bring the distributed team together to address risks, as opposed to waterfall development where risks associated with different development disciplines are dealt with sequentially.

Communication is difficult for various reasons. In GDD projects, communication can be complicated by delays in feedback processing due to different time zones, different cultures, and so on. Iterative development can help improve communication by making the feedback continuous. Unlike waterfall projects, where communication can be periodic and all-at-once, iterative project management engages all aspects of the development to some degree for every iteration.

Iterative development delivers value incrementally. This allows the distributed team(s) to communicate the progress of their aspect of the project (for example, requirements, architecture, programming, testing, and so on) based on incremental builds of the software product itself, since each iteration results in a build of the software. Every iteration therefore represents review points that can bring early and continuous communication from the entire distributed teams. In conventional waterfall managed projects, the problem of limited periodic communication and feedback is exacerbated in a GDD project context where teams may not be involved in the project until much later in the life cycle and where the ability to address certain project issues may become impractical later in the life cycle.

9.3 Collaboration

Collaborating across geo-political boundaries involve effective processes, tools, and mature communication levels. In this section, we summarize how Rational tools help in collaboration, and we discuss some of the prominent people issues we have encountered in our experiences.

9.3.1 Collaboration with Rational tools

As we have seen in Part 2, "Running the show" on page 57, lack of effective collaboration is one of the major inhibitors of success for a GDD organization. An informed collaborative relationship with the team, stakeholders, and the customer solidifies the trust necessary for a successful project in both good and difficult times. If not properly understood and managed, diverse cultures and languages, different time zones, and working across the world can lead to miscommunication on many levels, from how to establish project requirements to how to transfer defect data when a bug has been fixed.

Team collaboration can be achieved through effective tools that equip distributed teams with the infrastructure, processes, and integrations they need to work together more efficiently.

The IBM Rational tools addresses communication and collaboration challenges by accelerating project success through a collaborative team-based development and workplace environment. The chapters in Part 2, "Running the show" on page 57 discuss most of this in detail; we present a summary here:

► The Rational Unified Process provides a unified process, which improves team communication, enabling development teams to collaborate effectively, work more efficiently, and decrease time to market.

► Rational RequisitePro improves global requirement communication and interpretation.

► Rational Software Architect provides collaboration by communicating systems/application architecture and design using the Universal Modeling Language (UML).

► Through flexible workflow management and activity-based change and defect tracking across the life cycle, Rational ClearQuest facilitates communication, collaboration, and coordination between all stakeholders across the enterprise.

► Rational Performance Tester integration with ITM and ITCAM improves team productivity in deployment and problem diagnosis.

► Using IBM Workplace™, virtual development teams can be created using with team spaces, learning, calendaring and scheduling, awareness, instant messaging, Web conferencing, and e-mail.

► IBM Lotus® Quickr™ provides ways to define content libraries and team spaces for sharing information.

► IBM Rational Portfolio Manager provides powerful collaboration capabilities, such as workflow collaboration, re-use of best practices and templates, and evolution of models as maturity increases.

9.3.2 People management

The inconsistency and unpredictability people bring and how important it is to manage people issues has been written about extensively. Inability to collaborate, resolve conflicts, and inspire and motivate people all result in spiraling costs and poor product quality. Understandably, issues are compounded due to time, space, and cultural distances, and have to be dealt with carefully.

In a GDD environment, cultural issues are often cited as causing a lot of frustration. However, we have to be cautious about categorizing any people-related issues as a result of cultural differences or for that matter attributing GDD as the cause of all people issues. We would have enough variation in behavior because of personality issues and personal issues as it is.

In this section, we try not to talk about generic people issues but mainly about those that can be with confidence stated as due to the effect of GDD. The diversity that GDD brings to the workforce is a major potential for shared best practices, innovative thinking, and so on, but is also a major potential for misunderstandings, miscommunication, and missed opportunities.

Local project management

One of the foremost problems that a central project manager might face is to understand and manage all remote sites with their diverse issues. Unless there are local project managers who can guide the team, a significant amount of time would be lost on the team that is waiting for clarifications and on rework. It is preferable to work with a local leader who can guide and provide clarity. Based on the complexity of the project and the size of the remote teams, the experience and skill level of the leader may vary.

Conflicts and resolution

In this section, we discuss some of the examples of conflicts and how different teams have resolved them.

Status tracking

Projects are managed through one core site. Teams may be made up of team leads and team members co-located at the core site, team leads and team members co-located at a remote site, or team leads at one site with team members located at any one of the remote sites. In any of these cases, unless there is clear communication of the goals and status of the project, there is potential for risks and conflicts. The core site may feel like the project is out of control due to a lack of accurate and current status updates from the remote sites. The remote sites may feel like they are being too tightly controlled by the core site.

Another problem often reported is a tendency on the part of the remote sites, especially in countries such as India or China, to not flag potential delays, setbacks, and difficulties ahead of time. The teams are often considered to be reluctant to impart bad news. In fact, in our conversations, this has come up as one of the top issues that must be addressed, because of the impact it would have on the project deliverables.

Some of the best practices to be followed while reporting and getting status are:

► Make status reporting more quantitative. Qualitative goals could be open for interpretation while quantitative goals put things in clear perspective.

► Make status reports comprehensive. Talk about what was achieved, for example, the previous week, what the team hopes to achieve next week, and make sure issues and dependencies are listed. Listing dependencies explicitly again helps the project manager to track potential delays.

► Have more frequent milestones. An iterative process with smaller and frequent milestones makes it easier to track delays. Some project managers have milestones as short as every week.

► Have incremental milestone builds that get tested daily/weekly. Use builds as checkpoints on current status. The milestones should be in terms of working code, a document, or any other tangible artifact.

► Clearly define the scope of the milestones so there is no confusion on what is expected.

► Explicitly review upcoming milestones and ask for any potential delays in status meetings.

► Identify a liaison with a similar cultural background if possible to aggregate and summarize informal status checks better.

Participatory culture

Many times, a change in design, feature, or even the idea for a feature is often inspired near the company coffee machine. Features are dropped or included based on informal discussions. While most companies have processes to take minutes of or record formal meetings, often the explosion of information that is exchanged during such informal meetings are lost to remote sites. The remote sites are left to play catch up. Remote sites are also the ones with the burden of trying to get the information. In some cases, the remote site finds itself having wasted resources on features that have been dropped or descoped.

Communication of overall business vision and goals to remote sites is also critical. Remote sites may not be aware of overall program status, priority of open issues, and so on.

A conscious effort on the part of the core site to keep the remote site informed of such information is critical. If a remote site is not properly informed, resources at a remote site may be either underused, or used in a counter-productive manner.

Although these problems exist for all geographically distributed sites, they are magnified when the distance between sites spans large time-zone differences. When sites are far apart, it becomes much harder to use modern communication techniques such as e-mail, instant messaging, or phone conversations to have real-time discussions.

In short, each of the sites, especially the core site, has to take the initiative and interest in ensuring a participatory culture.

- Record meetings whenever possible, so that the remote sites can understand the thinking behind a decision.
- Capture and distribute meeting minutes when recording is not possible.
- Include relevant whiteboard content in the meeting minutes.
- Capture changed requirements, or design or functional specification in the appropriate tool or artifact as soon as decisions have been made. Sharing technical details is a major motivator.
- Arrange for important meetings with business goal announcements at an appropriate time for all sites. If a shared time cannot be arranged, repeat the meeting for each distributed site. Strategy and product direction must be given to each of the distributed teams so the goals are aligned and are not undermined by local culture or bias.
- Determine a process for geographically distributed team to be able to participate in "water cooler" design discussions so that all team members can participate in informal design discussion.
- Identify a team culture and look for ways to strengthen it.
- Build sustained relationships.
- Rotate senior management staff.
- Resist us versus them mentality; each of the sites combine to form one team.

Empowerment

Often in remote sites there is a perceived or real feeling of inequality. When the company has invested energy and money on hiring and training, it also has to make sure such perceptions are corrected. A conscious effort on the part of the core site to empower the remote site employees goes a long way in reducing conflicts and attrition.

Building trust is the core priority. This is especially a burden on the remote site, because in most cases the decision making authority is with the core site by default and the remote site is new to the product. While it can be difficult for certain personalities, it is better in the long run to make a conscious effort. Similarly, the core site has the burden of being open and acknowledging the efforts and making sure the subsites have more and more decision making authority as time goes by.

While this is often a challenge in emerging centers, in our experience, it is perceived in sites at distance from decision making authorities as well. It is also more apparent where the remote site has been set up in a "follow the sun" model with management in the core site. The feeling of inequality increases as the site matures in terms of skill and experience levels but does not have proportional modular responsibilities, insight into organizational goals, and a forum for voicing their concerns.

Most of the GDD literature on people issues is written predominantly from the point of view of the core site; the last two points are almost a sidebar. Those two factors are, however, major challenges with the remote sites and are often reasons for lower morale and demotivation.

- Make sure the success of the GDD environment is a measurable goal for the individuals on all sites involved.

- Educate members with the perception of threat.

- As a core site. be prepared to have a lack of visibility into day to day work allocations and resources. As a subsite, be more proactive in reassuring the core site's project deadline concerns.

- Communicate project details early on, so the subsites have sufficient time and information to be part of decision making.

Language and expression issues

It is inevitable in geographical distribution to encounter problems due to language usage or fluency. It is important to carefully differentiate a lack of fluency and possibly hesitancy or delay on the part of the speaker from a lack of technical ability. The possible natural tendency on the part of the native speaker to take charge and assume opinions, status, and results can cause tangible effects in the project.

Lack of documentation may not be a problem when you can pick up the phone and explain the reason. Both sides have to make extra efforts to document when there are expression, language, and accent issues. It is critical that at each remote site, there is a member of the team that can act as a liaison during technical exchanges to ensure that cultural or language differences do not get in the way of program goals.

When teams are co-located, questions about requirements or design can be easily resolved using traditional communication systems (face to face, e-mail, IM, phone, and so on). When teams are geographically distributed, this becomes more difficult. Therefore, clear and accurate documentation must be maintained to ensure that each of the development sites has an equal understanding of the program goals, requirements, and milestones. In cases where there are language or fluency issues, each site must make extra efforts to identify where expression, language, and accent issues are resulting in a misinterpretation of program objectives.

In some cultures, a mistake or even a potential mistake is identified in the form of a polite question. Because of a hierarchical nature, a junior member might not speak up against a senior member in a common conference call. Without an understanding of the differences, there is the danger of underestimating people or misunderstanding someone's intention. This invariably leads to personality issues and cascades eventually into every little detail of the product where the situation becomes unworkable.

Much has been written about the language and hierarchical relationships in different cultures, mostly from the American perspective. Most product development companies are a culture within the culture of other geographies, emulating their core site's cultural preferences and undergoing adaptations to suit the other culture as well. There is already an extra effort on the part of both sides wherever they may be to bridge the gap. Senior members, engineers, and managers who have had work experience in the U.S. or U.K. disperse the lessons learned to new engineers in China and India, for example. Similarly, in some cases, an explicit cultural liaison is selected to interact with the team.

Getting past people issues

Sometimes what may initially be perceived as a people issue may turn out to be due to ineffective tools or processes. It is difficult to get past the personalities and look for tangible causes outside, especially when one is dealing with a relatively alien culture. We look at some examples in our case study.

► Broken build

In ITSO Inc.'s release 9.0 development work, it turned out that changes developed at the India site were breaking the build. Initially it was perceived as a people issue, that is, a lack of skills or cooperation on the part of the engineer, who insisted repeatedly that a local build was performed before checking code into a common build stream. But it turned out due to an insufficient replication process, the India site did not always have the latest code base. Apart from fixing this, which significantly reduced the build breakages, the engineer also set up automated builds on India time as well. These two solutions stabilized the product considerably and increased the perception and respect for the engineers at the India site.

► Quality of code

This often becomes a problem when the core site perceives that the remote site's code is not of the same quality. Due to working in the same product for a long time and due to working as a team for a longer time, core sites have some standards that are not well documented.

Remote sites, in the initial days, are often a team of engineers who have been brought together for a project for the first time. Often operating under tight schedules due to hiring and retention constraints and turn over, there is a mismatch on the skill level, while there is no corresponding adjustment on expectations. This is compounded by the distance and lack of rapport.

After the coding standards are put in place and expectations clearly articulated, and a local lead goes through a prior level of reviewing, such issues are resolved. In the ITSO Inc. India team, Jay made sure the code got reviewed by Uma first. Uma was one of the senior engineers who had been part of the team since the beginning and was also aware of the informal standards. A new hire went an extra step and documented the standards as well.

Multiple teams that have also expressed an interest in an onsite visit by the key engineers have always played a positive role as well. In the case of ITSO Inc., there were visits arranged from U.S. to India and China as well.

► Uniform processes

Sometimes the processes followed may have suited one location but may cause problems for another location. It is worth assessing and resolving processes that do not make sense. ITSO Inc. had set up a data center and expected its engineers to log in to that system for their daily development and testing tasks. While the Santa Clara employees did not have a major problem with this setup, the China Development center, due to latency issues, found it thoroughly frustrating to use the same for GUI intensive IDEs. This was resolved by having one centralized local server that was synchronized often until the connectivity improved.

Motivation

A well motivated workforce makes major contributions to the product. In a GDD environment, groups are fragmented. Apart from this situation, the skewed work hours and the cultural differences can cause emotional detachment. They may not feel like they are working in the same team.

Other than normal techniques, such as good pay packages, training, and competency development, one of the issues that come up is career planning. In many cases, because the project management work is controlled by a core site, the remote sites do not have a clear management career path. Similarly, because the transitioned work is often maintenance, major technical challenges and growth in the technical side are also not apparent.

ITSO Inc. made a conscious effort to empower the local managers to make product related decisions. The remote site management in one case decided to give up some of the work they were sharing with Santa Clara for fully owning another component, which was predominantly in maintenance. This showed a path for management growth. On the other hand, because they were still following a 24X7 model and sharing some of the work with Santa Clara, some engineers had an opportunity to work on cutting edge technology. ITSO Inc. also made a conscious effort to implement the same technical growth path available to its Santa Clara employees to the India and China employees.

While the remote sites struggle with such issues, the core sites also have to grapple with threats of work force reduction. This can only be addressed by a genuine interest and investment in the employee's long term growth. Reinforcing the one team spread across geographies goes a long way in creating rapport and motivation.

Other areas that have to be concentrated on are education, training, and professional development. Another point to consciously stress is work-life balance so that the employees do not get demotivated and burned out.

Communication

Collaborating across geographies requires innovative skills, techniques, and effective tooling. Many surveys have repeatedly pointed out how the ability to make collaborative decisions diminishes without visual cues and diminishes further without aural cues.

This is one of the reasons why such methods as Agile programming place much importance on face-to-face communication. In the absence of visual cues, a telephone conversation can compensate but the loss of visual contact is noticeable. When the communication method involves e-mail exchanged over a period of days, the delayed response due to time differences can cause additional frustration. Some general best practices are:

► Ability to work from home so they can collaborate with people in different time zones without getting tied to office

 This provides the ability to use instant messaging and voice communication, but does not address the loss of visual queues.

► Allow flexible work hours to compensate for out of office hours

► Make an effort to get to know the person beyond the status reports

 Create a rapport.

► Maintain wiki pages or team rooms where information is shared

 This is a good place to have a short cultural orientation as well. Some information about the general work timings, day-to-day climate issues that they face, vacation plans, and so on, can help the other sites understand what is appropriate and what is not.

In our case study, the China testing team set up a team room with pictures and brief descriptions of each engineer on both sides. They updated the site with documents, interesting conferences, papers, and so on. They used the site for posting informal blogs. They had frequent meetings and rotation of engineers. This made the China testing team and the Santa Clara testing team bond well and have a more of a one team feeling.

Audio conferences

In a GDD environment, audio conferences are a day to day occurrence. If there is a good overlap of time zones, then audio conferencing is a good collaboration technique if done effectively. Audio conferences create faster resolution than multiple rounds of e-mail. Some of the best practices to be followed are:

► Make sure employees can attend calls from home so that it becomes easier during odd hours.

► Local numbers or toll free numbers are helpful.

► Have a strong moderator or chair for the call who will not allow the meeting to be derailed by arguments and off topic conversations.

► Have a moderator or chair for the call who can ensure language issues do not get in the way of meeting the conference objectives.

► Plan so noise levels and disturbances are low.

► Publish agendas and stick to them. Long drawn meetings are often inconsiderate of sites in off-office hours.

► Follow up with minutes so everyone is on the same page.

► Try experimenting with tools that help capture the white board if it is chalk-talk intensive meetings.

► Choose an appropriate time for calls.

► Give audio feedback over phone even if it is a simple assertion like "I am listening". A dead silence from remote sites is often cited as something that is uncomfortable and confusing.

► Informal conversations increase trust.

Chat

Chat clients such as IBM Sametime® offer assistance as an informal and immediate communication tool. They are also nonintrusive.

Here are some best practices that can be followed:

► Reinforce something that is being said in the meeting using chat if someone in a remote site is having difficulty following.

► Use chat for shorter conversations.

► Use chat away messages as a "how to reach you" indicator.

► Emote icons help convey thoughts better.

Web conference

Web conferences are handy ways to do presentations and demos while having the audio conference. Used effectively, this can address most of the needs of any physical meeting except perhaps capturing the board.

Web conferences are often used to run a demo and a presentation:

► Make sure you send setup details ahead of time.
► Plan for a setup time before everyone gets online.
► Make sure the bandwidth is good enough so that window refresh is adequate.
► Send presentations ahead of the meeting time if possible.

As the GDD models across countries mature, most project managers start the projects with a clearer understanding of what to expect with respect to their geographically distributed teams. Finally, how good your product is should depend on the quality of the management and development teams and should not be a factor of whether the team members are co-located or distributed.

9.4 Global and secure access

One of the key GDD requirements is that, users must be able to access any asset from any location as and when necessary. Software development assets, test assets, metrics collected, defects, and project status should be available for teams located anywhere.

Rational tools provide options for access from different locations. In addition to native local clients for LAN-connected users, ClearCase, ClearQuest, and RequisitePro all provide Web-based clients for remote access to data. ClearCase and ClearQuest also offer replication across servers, so users in different locations can have local access to a server with the replicated data. The Rational Portfolio Manager client functions across either a LAN or WAN connection.

9.4.1 Security

To deliver higher quality software, standard processes, best practices, and tools that focuses on data integrity and security are a must. In this flattened world, with development spanning geo-political boundaries with specific laws and untrusted sites, security becomes a crucial factor.

One of the important goals of security in a GDD environment is to centrally specify and enforce a uniform security policy across teams. Because outsourcing and engaging with untrusted sites introduces risk and is especially a major security concern in GDD, it is important to have uniform policies in product development across subsites as well.

Some of the best practices are:

- ▶ Have a clear understanding of what needs to be controlled and what can be allowed. This concept is best viewed in a matrix where you specify the kinds of permissions in one axis (for example, read only/read+write/layout view) and on the other axis you can either have groups or components of the application you want to restrict. Figure 9-8 shows where the X-axis is components and the Y axis are the permissions. Note in the example below each cell has the list of groups that can perform those actions in those components.

In our case study, for example, the Dublin site for ITSO Inc. Corporation is an untrusted site, and has been given access only to the files required for translation (Figure 9-8).

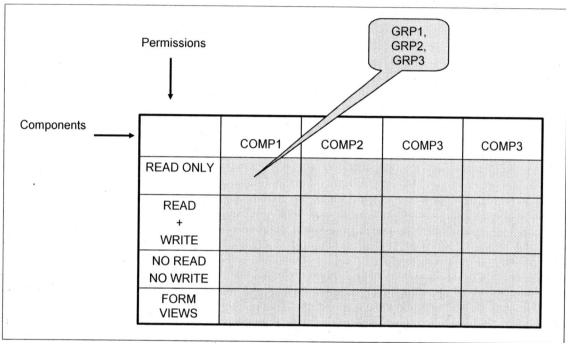

Figure 9-8   Security Matrix for an application in an organization

A good case study on implementing such security restrictions for a change request can be found in 5.1.2, "A case study on security" on page 90. In this case study, we show you how Rational ClearQuest can help you enforce fine-grained security restrictions in your change management space.

Rational Portfolio Manager also helps you enforce fine-grained security restrictions. The screen capture in Figure 9-9 shows how you set up the Rational Portfolio Manager security privileges. In Rational Portfolio Manager, security settings are granular, and permissions are based on groups and a person's role in a group. For each component, you can configure the layout (for example, how the form appears for a particular user) or you can configure the pivot settings (pivot is a reporting mechanism for Rational Portfolio Manager data) for a particular user. In Rational Portfolio Manager with the power of layout, you can even prevent visibility of certain fields for certain users. Figure 9-9 shows how you can configure the access rights.

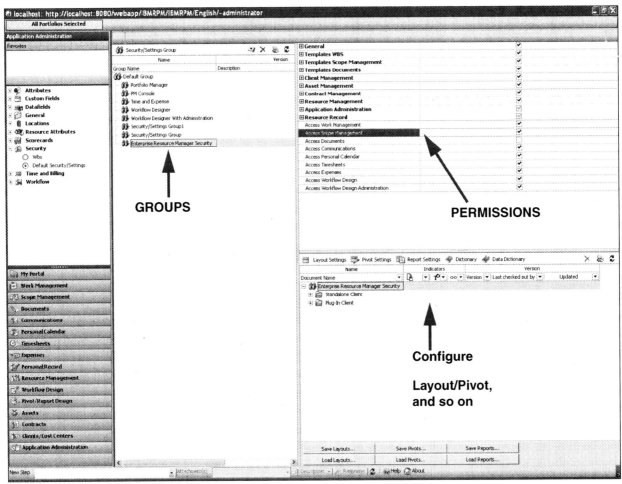

Figure 9-9   Security settings in Rational Portfolio Manager

► Decide on the process of handing off and getting back artifacts. For example, in SCM tools, it is important that files get accessed by the groups you want to authorize. Currently in ClearCase, you can restrict access to file systems at the VOB level.

► Establish Authorization and access controls using LDAP authentication. Currently, ClearQuest and Rational Portfolio Manager are LDAP enabled. This also helps in single sign-on within the organization for different applications.

► Have a secure access for the database that the application uses, with different access levels for different types of users (trusted and untrusted). It is important that the defect data or project data is not hacked by somebody outside the organization.

9.5 Enterprise-level concerns

This book focuses mainly on the product development aspects and the issues discussed above mainly deal with the success factors at the project level. However, it is worth mentioning briefly there are various other factors, such as Portfolio Management in GDD and Governance.

9.5.1 Governance

Governance in a software development organization defines and directs the desired behaviors of development teams, often in ways that improve predictability and ensuring a positive business impact by controlling changes, measuring adherence to process, and validating business alignment and results. Some of the basic goals of development governance are:

▶ Clear ownership of development assets and approval processes

▶ Feedback mechanisms that help manage variance, improve predictability, and validate the delivery of business value

▶ Traceability to validate that the planned scope aligns with the business goals

Governance becomes difficult when the assets and processes being managed are distributed across the globe. Establishing responsibilities across distributed development organization, enforcing focused measures, and traceability needs effective tooling.

Some best practices for governance across geographies are:

▶ Avoid sharing Responsibility and Role assignments for tightly-coupled work products that span more than two time zones. Where possible, keep responsibility for work products that address a given area of concern within the same geographic site.

▶ Carefully control variations to process definitions between sites. Minimize variations as much as possible. Maintain models for each variant, but track as a single Business Use Case specification, indicating variations to flows according to the sites requiring the variations.

▶ Facilitate communication and collaboration by defining extensive guidelines and quality criteria for each work product and then verifying adherence through quality gates. Track deviations to process as a root cause of defects, and provide feedback mechanisms that allow team members to recommend process improvements

▶ Include business alignment as a key aspect of scope review and approval processes.

Compliance, the demonstration of conforming to a regulatory framework, is another important dimension of governance and represents behaviors defined by external agencies to which the development organization must conform.Organizations with compliance requirements should include checks for compliance in their governance frameworks to ensure that compliance is being addressed uniformly across projects and locations and to avoid negative consequences of non-compliance. Penalties for violating certain regulations, such as Sarbanes-Oxley, can be severe, including imprisonment and other legal actions. Others, such as Occupational Safety and Health Administration (OSHA) or European Agency for Safety and Health at Work (EASHW) violations can carry heavy fines and bad publicity. By being proactive and establishing a governance framework that validates compliance can substantially reduce the risk of experiencing these types of consequences.

In a GDD environment, compliance becomes even more important as the number of regulatory authorities, standards, and policies increases and the complexity rises across geo-political boundaries. Thus, distributed teams require tools that can manage and enforce regulations in a way that is specific to the site.

Governance with Rational tools

Rational solutions help in effective governance and compliance in and across the various phases of development life cycle. This section summarizes the benefit. Refer to Part 2, "Running the show" on page 57, for details.

Rational Method Composer and Rational Unified Process (RUP) allow you to integrate and tailor your processes for global software development. The RUP for Compliance Management plug-in tailors RUP to help define, enforce, and audit a compliant process. You can then export that process and use it as the basis of the WBS in your Rational Portfolio Manager project plan.

As described previously, Rational Portfolio Manager provides global management of projects and resources. Its Web-enabled, audit-ready workflow capabilities can help you manage process and regulatory compliance.

With RequisitePro, you can establish traceability between requirements within both your project and other projects. You can track requirements volatility and preserve baselines. The ReqPro-CQ integration enables you to associate test artifacts and change requests with specific requirements, so you can demonstrate test coverage and defect status. You can also associate requirements with model elements from both your business process models created in WebSphere® Business Modeler and your architectural models in Rational Software Architect and Rational Software Modeler. This enables you to create traceability from your business needs to your requirements to your implementation model.

ClearCase, with its central repository capabilities and maintenance of revision history, also helps with compliance, especially when used with UCM. You can track changes back to the requirement or change request that they address, the artifacts that were altered, and the author of the change.

Build Forge helps to automate builds that can be run from anywhere. It allows workflow to be defined, which helps in better metrics for milestones and improved predictability of the project status.

ClearQuest, with its distributed capability, helps in assigning defects to individuals in any location, helps in tracking the status of the defects by a project manager irrespective of the location, and helps in notification and reporting. Such features as automatic notifications, audit trails, electronic signatures, querying implemented across team locations help in traceability, predictability, and tracking of the overall status of the project. ClearQuest test manager provides traceable, auditable relationships between development, test, and project artifacts across a global team. The Build Tracking and Deployment Tracking features enable you to track build status and content. They also enable you to create workflow and approvals to recommend builds for deployment to different environments.

Rational solutions improve IT governance and management through IT lifecycle integration.

References for compliance and governance

Refer to the following sources for more information about compliance and governance:

- Establishing portfolio management governance: Key components

  `http://www-128.ibm.com/developerworks/rational/library/oct06/hanford/index.html`

- Resource Library

  `http://www-306.ibm.com/software/info/developer/solutions/compliance/resources/index.html`

- Managing compliance with RUP: A starter plug-in

  `http://www-128.ibm.com/developerworks/rational/library/dec06/paradan-mueller/index.html`

- Establishing compliance using Rational tools: *Rational Business Driven Development for Compliance*, SG24-7244

9.5.2 Portfolio management in GDD

A project portfolio may be seen as a simple inventory or list of all the projects in the company, or, at a higher level of conceptual maturity, as a balanced collection of projects aligned with strategy, for optimum value. PPM aligns projects and resources with business priorities. It is about planning and managing projects individually and as a comprehensive portfolio of assets, which must meet enterprise objectives. The union of portfolio management and project management helps people at all levels of the organization work together collaboratively towards a common cause.

Why do businesses need a PPM strategy? Let us look at some of the strongest reasons:

- Limited IT budgets and resources: Most organizations need to improve the way they use their existing resources in order to maximize productivity. This applies to both people and tools.

- Need for better IT governance: Many IT organizations lack a consistent, accountable body for decision-making. PPM provides a decision-making framework that helps ensure IT decisions are aligned with the overall business strategy; IT participates in setting business goals and directions, establishing standards, and prioritizing investments.

- Need to improve the project success rate: According to the latest Standish Group survey, executive support and clear business objectives are among the top ten success factors for application development projects. PPM includes approaches for achieving both of these requirements.

- Difficulty in achieving global visibility.

One of the biggest challenges for companies with a distributed development strategy is effective management of individual projects as well as the full project portfolio. Management needs timely and accurate information to make strategic business decisions, and defining performance metrics for all facets of distributed projects is a critical enabler. The goal is to quantify the culture of the organization, that is, to measure what is important to you. From a

GDD perspective, Portfolio management metrics is one of the metrics that is important for GDD projects. Portfolio management metrics capture data to prioritize and assess the risks and benefits of each project in your application portfolio. It can help you make better decisions, and make faster decisions based on facts, so that you can drive toward a consistent, predictable business plan moving forward.

Key benefits of PPM

As with any new strategy, introducing PPM into an organization requires an investment of time and effort. However, this investment yields proven benefits:

► Closer alignment of IT with business: With an easily digestible, holistic view of their entire project portfolio, executives and managers can more readily understand where IT dollars are being spent and which projects continue to be worthwhile. The complete visibility in to the entire portfolio results in effective GDD planning and execution.

► Better IT governance: PPM helps managers monitor project progress in real time and provides detailed data to help in achieving compliance.

► Cost reductions and productivity increases: PPM helps managers identify redundancies and allocate resources appropriately; it enables them to make better IT staffing and outsourcing decisions, and to spot opportunities for asset reuse.

► Business-based decision-making: By viewing projects as they would view components of an investment portfolio, managers can make decisions based not only on projected costs, but also on anticipated risks and returns in relation to other projects/initiatives. This leads to improvements in customer service and greater client loyalty.

► More predictable project outcomes: A PPM strategy bridges the gap between business managers and the practitioners who deliver the projects; it ensures consistent processes across all sites and helps managers assess a project's status in real time, predict project outcomes, and identify inter-project dependencies and cross-site dependencies.

Planning, managing, and aligning IT projects and investments with business goals is the first step to a successful GDD implementation strategy. Visibility into the portfolio to align projects, resources, and priorities, and the ability to perform ROI, payback, or break even analyses help to provide the guidance and structure needed to effectively coordinate which projects are best suited for a GDD strategy.

A project management tool, such as IBM Rational Portfolio Manager, provides an overarching view of project portfolios, resulting in a closed-loop portfolio management process that combines top-down portfolio analyses with bottom-up project management. Rational Portfolio Manager captures vital project data and helps evaluate, calculate, and communicate all dimensions of a portfolio to help assign resources within distributed structures and measure project cost, quality, and completion time. These capabilities are essential to assessing and balancing the risks and benefits of GDD efforts while ensuring they are aligned with business priorities and creating business value.

Key features to support portfolio management for GDD

Rational Portfolio Manager helps to achieve global visibility for distributed teams, using metrics and reporting tools to effectively manage the progress and status of individual projects, as well as the entire portfolio. Aligning IT projects and investments with business priorities requires strategic focus and discipline. Part of this discipline includes measuring the process improvement for each stage in the development life cycle.

One of the important metrics from the GDD perspective is portfolio management metrics. Capturing portfolio and project data is the first step toward using metrics effectively, and one of the most important factors is establishing an accurate baseline. You have to know where you started in order to know whether you are improving. Often, managers get overwhelmed by the idea of defining and creating metrics, but the key to successfully using metrics is to measure the right things, not everything. When it comes to metrics, less is definitely more.

Portfolio data and metrics are handled by Rational Portfolio Manager, and cover areas such as earned value, budget variance, and schedule variance. Capturing this information allows you to protect the bottom line, because management has a clear view of dollars and resources consumed by the project, as well as the expected, versus actual, cycle time. Established guidelines allow you to monitor progress, and alert you when a variance you have established is exceeded, so you can make adjustments proactively, before a problem becomes too large and expensive to fix easily. As you develop and execute your GDD strategy, Portfolio Manager can help you understand, prioritize and assess the risks and benefits of each project in your application portfolio. It can help you make better decisions, and make them faster. These decisions based on facts result in moving toward a consistent, predictable business plan. They also achieve the following actions:

► Align IT investments with business goals
► Increase IT business efficiency
► Consistently plan, execute, and manage your distributed projects
► Match the right skills, to the right job, at the right location

A case study for project and portfolio management

ITSO Inc. is using Rational Portfolio Manager to do project and portfolio management. The Rational Portfolio Manager server is set up in Santa Clara, U.S. that can be securely accessed from geographically distributed ITSO Inc. sites. Rational Portfolio Manager operationalizes your business strategies by automating the complete portfolio management life cycle step-by-step, from opportunity identification through project execution and closure.

Opportunity assessment

A recent market survey by ITSO Inc. discovered a growing industry in supply chain management. The expected industry revenues are over USD1.5-2 million per year. Therefore, ITSO Inc. is planning to take up an initiative for developing a product for supply chain management named "ITSO Inc. Supply Chain".

Initiation

John is the project manager for ITSO Inc. Supply Chain. In order to start the initiative for ITSO Inc. Supply Chain, John completes a scorecard that describes the business case and enters the financial information in Rational Portfolio Manager. His high level estimate for product development is approximately one year with a team size of 30 members.

Portfolio analysis

Rene is the Portfolio manager for ITSO Inc. Rene is responsible for reviewing the proposals across enterprise to achieve business vision. Using investment maps (Figure 9-10), Rene reviews various initiatives started in various geographies. In the investment map, analysis of various proposals shows that ITSO Inc. Supply Chain will give a maximum ROI. The green color and size of bubble indicates proposal alignment with business strategies. However, from market analysis, Rene realizes that to maintain a competitive edge in a retail sector solution, the time to market of product should be not be more than six months, which is nearly half than what is estimated. To achieve this, he needs to double the resources, which doubles the cost. Using a "what if" and "resource supply/demand" analysis, Rene decides to go for GDDof the project to increase ROI and decrease the time to market.

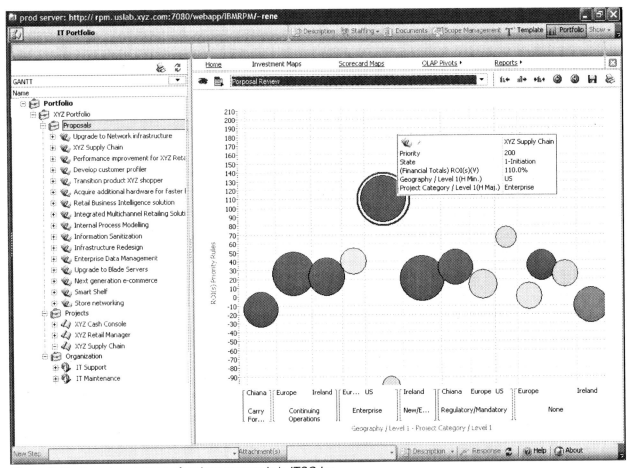

Figure 9-10 Investment maps of various proposals in ITSO Inc.

ITSO Inc. has defined a workflow that is automatically instantiated for a processing funding request (refer to Figure 9-4 on page 187). A team of reviewers accesses the quality and prioritization using the voting functionality available in a Rational Portfolio Manager workflow and decides to approve the funding. After approval of funding, John converts the corresponding proposal to a project in Rational Portfolio Manager.

Planning

John defines a project plan by tailoring a project template of a previous RUP technology-based successful project, which is similar to ITSO Inc. Supply Chain. He moves ahead and assigns resources for the project. Using Rational Portfolio Manager, he is able to search and assign resources from any geography based on the project's skill needs, implied schedule, and resource availability. (Refer to Figure 9-11.). He publishes the project, so that individual team members can see the project tasks.

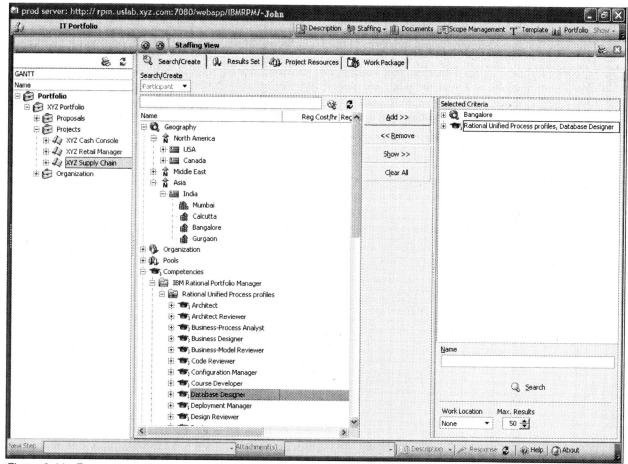

Figure 9-11   Resource assignment for ITSO Inc. Supply Chain

Execution

To achieve effective communication and collaboration in geographically distributed teams, ITSO Inc. has established their entire standard processes such as requirement management, defect management, and so on using various Rational Portfolio Manager workflows.

ITSO Inc. has projects spread across many sites. Each team member enters information about their work into Rational Portfolio Manager, irrespective of their geographies. Using Rational Portfolio Manager, John is able to plan, optimize staffing profiles, and use resources. He can now work collaboratively with Rene to ensure the financial health of his project. Rational Portfolio Manager helps Rene to monitor, manage, and compare all projects and proposals from ITSO Inc. Portfolio. Using the Rational Portfolio Manager Portfolio Dashboard, Rene is enable to work with executives to view project execution and financial investments, ensuring expected ROI.

9.6 Conclusion

We now come to the conclusion of our book on GDD. Geographically distributed development is no longer a buzzword, but much the way forward. Many other companies are opting for distributing their development work either for tactical or strategic reasons. There is still more to learn as we go down this path, encounter new challenges, and help evolve this approach as a sustainable model. In this book, we have shown how Rational solutions can be applied to manage product development that is distributed across geopolitical boundaries. We have not treated in as much depth or have omitted altogether some topics, such as open source based development or outsourcing to an untrusted site due to scope constraints.

This book has been based on our experiences in distributed development, and on information gathered from partner labs within IBM and from some of our clients who practice distributed development. For each phase of distributed development, we have added detailed scenario descriptions and tool recommendations. We hope that the suggested techniques, tools, and processes help you as you go down the GDD path, encounter new challenges, and evolve this approach as a sustainable mode.

Mapping and terminology of the IBM Rational product set

This appendix provides additional information about ClearCase derived objects (DO). It also explains the terminology for Base ClearCase, Unified Change Management (UCM), and ClearQuest.

ClearCase derived objects

A derived object is a file created in a VOB during a build or build audit with `clearmake` or `omake`. Each DO has an associated configuration record (CR), which is the bill of materials for the DO. The CR documents aspects of the build environment, the assembly procedure for a DO, and all the files involved in the creation of the DO.

> **Note:** All derived objects created by executing a build script have equal status, even though some of them may be explicit build targets, and others may be created as side effects of the build script (for example, compiler listing files). The term siblings describes a group of DOs created by the same script and associated with a single CR.

Derived objects sharing (ClearCase winkin)

In a parallel-development environment, it is likely that many DOs with the same path name will exist at the same time. For example, suppose that source file msg.c is being developed on three branches concurrently, in three different views. ClearCase builds performed in those three views produce object modules named msg.obj. Each of these is a DO, and each has the same standard path name, for example, \proj\src\msg.obj.

> **Note:** Symbolic links created by a build script and files created in non-VOB directories are not DOs.

In addition, each DO can be accessed with ClearCase extended names (Figure A-1 on page 213):

► Within each dynamic view, a standard Windows path name accesses the DO referenced by that view. This is another example of the ClearCase transparency feature.

– msg.obj

  The DO in the current view

► You can use a view-extended path name to access a DO in any view:

– M:\R1_integ\proj\src\msg.obj

  The DO in view R1_integ

– M:\R2_integ\proj\src\msg.obj

  The DO in view R2_integ

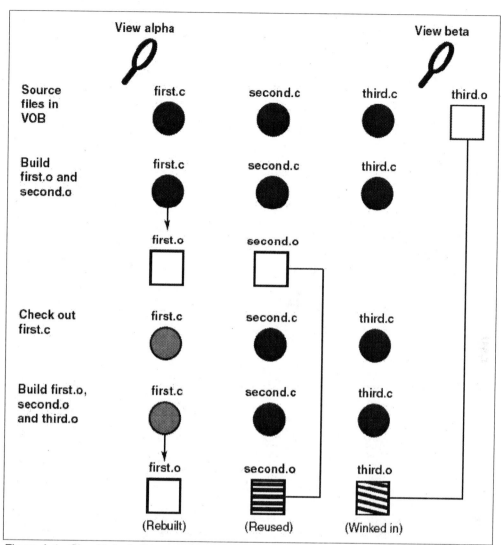

Figure A-1   ClearMake build scenario

Base ClearCase terminology

With Base ClearCase, we mean using the ClearCase product without UCM.

Branch

A *branch* is an object that specifies a sequence of versions of an element. Every element has one *main branch*, which represents the principal line of development, and may have multiple *subbranches*, each of which represents a separate line of development (Figure A-2).

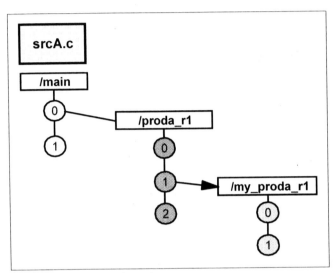

Figure A-2   Element branches

The concept of branches and branching is central in ClearCase. Branching is done in order to provide work areas for development. It is not uncommon to have dozens of branches active at a time. The ClearCase naming convention for branches is to use lower case alphabetic names.

Because branching is done on a low level, it also becomes important to find a branching strategy that works from all level of perspectives and abstractions. There are some general rules that applies for ClearCase:

► The main branch should not be used for development work, but should be reserved for major milestones or released versions.

► All major development is done on branches.

You can use ClearCase branches non-exclusively for various purposes:

► Physical: For components and subsystems
► Functional: For patches, fixes, releases, enhancements, and features
► Environmental: For different operating systems, platforms, and tools
► Organizational: For teams, programs, projects, work activities, and roles
► Procedural: For processes, policies, and states

Each branch in ClearCase is an instance of a *branch type* object. This allows you to attach attributes to the branch types, which can then be used to mark the purpose of the specific branch, and thus enables you to ensure that the right type of branches are being used.

Version label

A *version label* can be attached to any version of an element to identify that version in an easy to remember way. A single version of an element can have several different labels. Labels are usually applied to a set of elements to mark important project milestones or the starting point of a branch (Figure A-3).

A *label type* is an object that defines a *version label* for use within a VOB. Labels can be easily queried, and are useful in tracking which version of an element goes with versions of other elements.

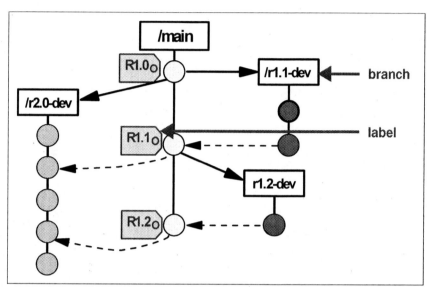

Figure A-3   Version labels

Labels can only be attached to an element version, and by default, only one instance of a label type may be attached to any version of an element tree. However, you can define a label type so that one instance of a label type can appear once on each branch of a tree. But this is definitely not recommended, and there are drawbacks to using the same version label several times in the same element tree, for example:

► It is potentially confusing.

► In a version-extended path name, you must always include a full branch path name along with the version label, which overrides the whole purpose of using a label in the first place.

Labels work best as a *snapshot* of your system, for example, marking specific release versions, or specific builds. Labels should be more or less static in nature and, once attached to a particular object, they should not be moved.

Configuration specification

A *configuration specification*, or *config spec*, contains the rules used by a view to select versions of elements. The rules are flexible, and you can use various specifiers to indicate which versions to select. A view has exactly one config spec.

For example, a config spec for a view used in ongoing development would contain rules that select the latest version in the my_r1 development branch (Figure A-4):

```
Element * .../my_r1/LATEST
```

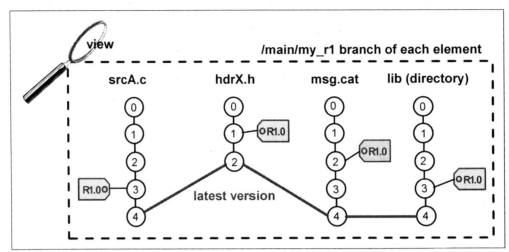

Figure A-4   Configuration specification: selecting latest versions

To examine the versions that were included in a particular release, you would use a config spec that uses a label rule to select the versions that were labeled for that release (Figure A-5):

```
Element * R1.0
```

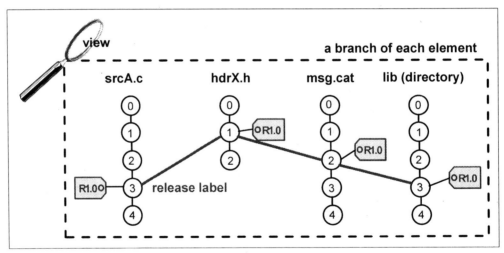

Figure A-5   Configuration specification: selecting a specific release

UCM terminology

UCM simplifies development by raising the level of abstraction to manage changes in terms of activities, rather than manually tracking individual files. Let us start with the UCM terminology.

Project

A UCM *project* is a logical unit that is mapped to the development structure of an application or system. A project contains the configuration information (for example, components, activities, and policies) needed to manage and track the work on a specific product of a development effort, such as an auction Web site or an order fulfillment process for an e-business. A basic UCM project in ClearCase consists of one shared work area and many private work areas (one for each developer).

Component

A *component* is a group of file and directory elements (source code and other relevant files, such as a a customer GUI) that are versioned together. The team develops, integrates, and releases a component as a unit. Components constitute parts of a project, and projects often share components. Components provide separation of concern and organize elements into well defined entities.

A VOB can host one or more components, but a component without any elements does not have to be in a VOB.

Figure A-6 shows the convention used in ClearCase to represent a component.

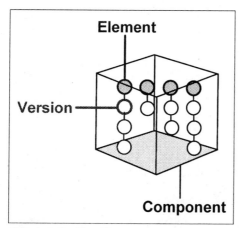

Figure A-6   ClearCase component

Activity

An *activity* is an object that records the set of files (*change set*) that a developer creates or modifies to complete and deliver a development task, such as a bug fix (Figure A-7). Examples of other activities include an update to a help file or the addition of a menu item to a GUI component. The activity title usually indicates the cause of the change (or is a link to ClearQuest).

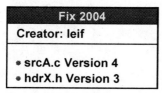

Figure A-7   Activity

Work areas and streams

A *work area* is a development area associated with a change (Figure A-8). In Base ClearCase, a view is a directory tree that shows a single version of each file in your project, and the view is your *work area*. In UCM however, a *work area* consists of a view and a *stream*.

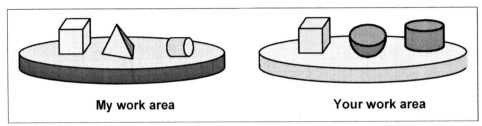

Figure A-8   Work areas

A *stream* is a ClearCase object that maintains a list of activities and baselines and determines which versions of elements appear in your view. In UCM, streams are layered over branches, so that you do not have to manipulate the branches directly. Figure A-9 shows the ClearCase convention of representing streams.

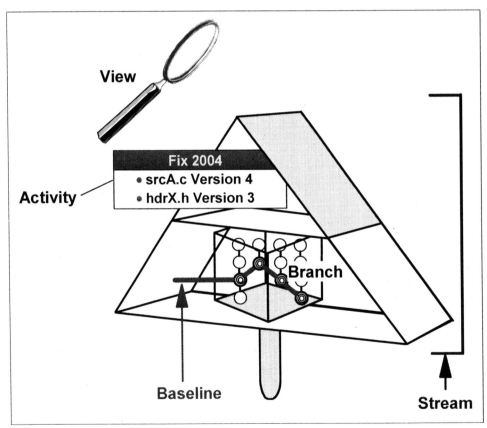

Figure A-9   Stream

A project contains one main *project integration stream* that records the project's *baselines* and enables access to the shared elements at the UCM project level. The integration stream and a corresponding integration view represent the project's primary shared work area.

Baseline: A starting point; see "Baselines" on page 219.

In most projects, each developer on a project has a private work area, which consists of a *development stream* and a corresponding development view. The development stream maintains a list of the developer's activities and determines which versions of elements appear in the developer's view.

Development streams can be created from the project integration stream recursively and hierarchically. This partitioning can be for functional, organizational, or procedural reasons.

Although the integration stream is the project's primary shared work area, project managers can designate a development stream to be a shared work area for several developers who are working on the same feature.

The terminal (lowest level) development streams are used by developers as a private work area. The changes and activities flow from terminal development streams to the next higher level to form a shared work area.

Baselines

A *baseline* identifies one version of each element in a component that represents the integrated or merged work of team members (Figure A-10). It represents a version of a component at a particular stage in project development, such as the first design, a beta release, or a final product release. Throughout the project cycle, the project manager creates and recommends baselines and changes their attributes to reflect project milestones.

A baseline is the means of communication between team members, allowing them to share new changes developed in the development streams.

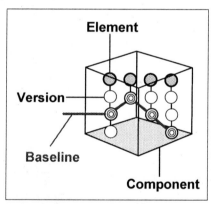

Figure A-10 Baseline

When developers join the project, they populate their work areas with the versions of directory and file elements represented by the project's recommended baselines.

Alternatively, developers can join the project at a feature-specific development stream level, in which case they populate their work areas with the development stream's recommended baselines. This practice ensures that all members of the project team start with the same set of files.

Composite baselines

If your project team works on multiple components, you may want to use a *composite baseline*. A composite baseline is a baseline that selects baselines in other components. In Figure A-11, the ProjBL1 composite baseline selects baselines BL1 and BL2 of components A and B, respectively.

The Proj component does not contain any elements of its own. Its sole purpose is to contain the composite baseline that selects the recommended baselines of the project's components. By using a composite baseline in this manner, you can identify one baseline to represent the entire project. A new composite baseline is created whenever a new contained baseline is created.

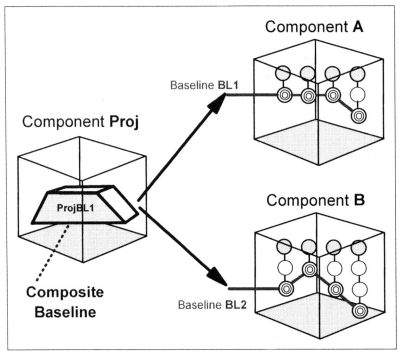

Figure A-11   Composite baseline

ClearQuest terminology

The ClearQuest product provides activity-based change and defect tracking that can manage all types of change requests, including defects, enhancements, issues, and documentation changes with a flexible workflow process. The process can be tailored to the organizations specific needs and the various phases of the development process.

When you use ClearQuest, you work with a variety of objects, including:

▶ ClearQuest databases
▶ Schemas
▶ Schema repositories
▶ Database sets
▶ Connections

The following sections define these components and explain how they work together as part of a change management system.

Schemas

A ClearQuest *schema* is a complete description of the process models for all the components of a user database. This includes a description of the *states* and *actions* of the model, the structure of the data that can be stored about the individual component, *hook* code or scripts that can be used to implement business rules, and the forms and reports used to view and input information about the component. ClearQuest provides out-of-the-box schemas that can be customized for a client installation.

A schema is a pattern or blueprint for ClearQuest user databases. When you create a database to hold records, the database follows the blueprint defined in a schema. However, a schema is not a database itself: it does not hold any records about change requests, and it does not change when users add or modify records in the user databases.

Schema repositories

ClearQuest stores schemas in a special type of database called a *schema repository*, which is also sometimes referred to as a *master repository* or a *master database*.

A schema repository can store multiple schemas, for example, one schema for defect change requests and another schema for feature enhancement change requests.

In Figure A-12, the schema repository stores both Schema A and Schema B. The schema repository can also include multiple versions of the same schema. A new version is created each time changes are made to a schema, for example, by changing an action or adding a new report definition. In Figure A-12, the schema repository stores three versions of Schema A and two versions of Schema B.

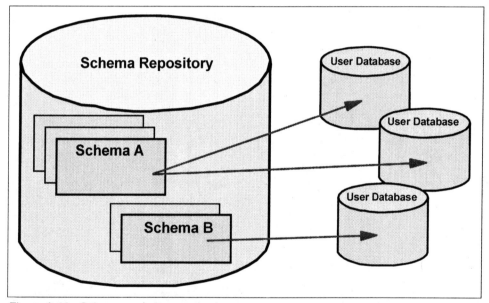

Figure A-12 Schema repository and schemas

User databases

A *user database* in ClearQuest is a collection of user data for one process model. You associate each user database with a specific version of a specific schema. For example, in Figure A-12, each user database uses a version of a schema stored in the schema repository. The schema defines the way the data is stored and changed in that database (that is, the database is an instance of a version of a schema). Users change data in the databases when they add or modify information about change requests, but these changes have no effect on the schema.

Databases contain a record for each change request. As the change request moves through its life cycle, the data stored in this record changes accordingly.

You can create and associate multiple databases with a single schema. For example, if you have three projects that use the same process model for correcting defects, you could create one database for each project and associate all three with the same schema. In Figure A-12 on page 221 two user databases use the latest version of Schema A.

Database sets and connections

A *database set* (dbset) is one specific schema repository and all of its associated user databases (Figure A-12 on page 221). A *connection* is the set of credentials that allow access to the database set.

All of the schemas and databases for one project are included in one database set. However, one database set can support multiple projects, or one project can have multiple database sets.

State transition model

A *state transition model* is a systematic representation of the possible steps in one change request life cycle. The state transition model represents a change management process model. The model defines the change request life cycle in terms of the *states* that the change request passes through, the *actions* that are taken to move between the states, and the *rules* that define when and how the actions can be taken.

The *state* of a change request is its current status. Typical states include submitted, assigned, opened, postponed, duplicated, resolved, and closed.

An *action* is an activity that moves a change request from one state to another (a state transition). Typical actions include assign, reject, open, postpone, duplicate, validate, resolve, and close.

Rules define when and how an action can be taken. For example, the ability to use a validate action to move a change request from a resolved state to a closed state might be restricted to quality assurance engineers.

A process model can be illustrated in a diagram, as shown in Figure A-13. In this diagram, states are shown as ovals and actions are represented by arrows.

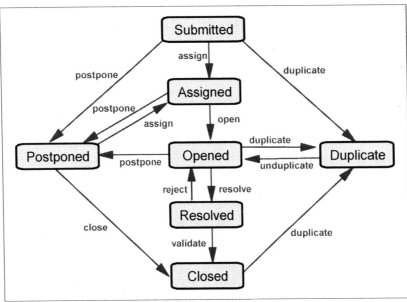

Figure A-13   A state transition model

Related publications

The publications listed in this section are considered particularly suitable for a more detailed discussion of the topics covered in this book.

IBM Redbooks

For information about ordering these publications, see "How to get IBM Redbooks" on page 224. Note that some of the documents referenced here may be available in softcopy only.

► *Rational Business Driven Development for Compliance*, SG24-7244

► *Software Configuration Management: A Clear Case for IBM Rational ClearCase and ClearQuest UCM*, SG24-6399

Online resources

These Web sites are also relevant as further information sources:

► Establishing portfolio management governance key components

  `http://www-128.ibm.com/developerworks/rational/library/oct06/hanford/index.html`

► Managing compliance with RUP: A starter plug-in

  `http://www-128.ibm.com/developerworks/rational/library/dec06/paradan-mueller/index.html`

► Resource Library

  `http://www-306.ibm.com/software/info/developer/solutions/compliance/resources/index.html`

► Geographically distributed development: IBM's unified lifecycle approach

  `http://www-128.ibm.com/developerworks/rational/library/content/RationalEdge/sep04/cammarano/index.html`

► IBM Geographically Distributed Development Information Kit

  `http://www-306.ibm.com/software/info/sdp/gdd/en/index.jsp`

► Geographically Distributed Development (GDD) - SCM Community of Practice Page - w3ki

  `https://w3.webahead.ibm.com/w3ki/pages/viewpage.action?pageId=272770`

► Forrester Research: Globally Distributed Development Defined

  `http://www.forrester.com/Research/Document/Excerpt/0,7211,38099,00.html`

► Borland: Globally Distributed Development (GDD) Solutions

  `http://www.borland.com.tr/tr/solutions/compliance_solutions.html`

► CM Crossroads - Geographically Distributed Development: How to Keep Control Across the Globe

  `http://www.cmcrossroads.com/content/view/7191/164/`

- ► TTPCom Deploys Perforce To Enable Globally Distributed Development

  http://www.perforce.com/perforce/press/pr46.html

- ► EnableNow I Rational Tech Chat: GDD Green Threads Overview

  http://w3-03.ibm.com/software/xl/enablenow/en.nsf/doc/CPHE-6UQVZX

- ► IBM Rational Software - Global development and delivery

  http://www-306.ibm.com/software/info/developer/solutions/gdd/index.jsp

- ► Viewtier Technical Articles - Addressing Performance Problems Of Integration Builds

  http://www.viewtier.com/support/articles/addressing_performance_problems_of_int
  egration_builds.htm

- ► Test management best practices

  http://www-128.ibm.com/developerworks/rational/library/06/1107_davis/

How to get IBM Redbooks

You can search for, view, or download Redbooks, Redpapers, Hints and Tips, draft publications and Additional materials, as well as order hardcopy Redbooks or CD-ROMs, at this Web site:

ibm.com/redbooks

Help from IBM

IBM Support and downloads

ibm.com/support

IBM Global Services

ibm.com/services

Index

A

access control privilege 76
action 222
activity 116, 217
architecture models 36
artifacts 36
assessment 26
assets transfer 36
associated risk 60
auditability 90

B

Base ClearCase 116
    deployment example 144
    terminology 214
baseline 218–219
    composite 219
branch 214
    type 214
branching strategy 144, 214
buddy testing 176
build 151
    automating the build system 153
    challenges in GDD 152
    deployment 155
    local availability 154
    management solution with Rational Build Forge 157
    Rational solution 155
    reduction and tuning of build time 153
    strategy solution with IBM Rational ClearCase 156
    Web interface 154
Build Forge 139
    architecture 161
    console 139
    solution for build management 157
building block 45
business factors 7

C

capability patterns 52
case study
    build and deployment 165
    GDD process 53
    project and portfolio management 207
    requirements management and design 73
    security 90
    test management 175
    triage 99
CCRC 118, 123–124
CCWeb 123, 131
central repository 60
change management 60, 83–84
    infrastructure 88

    system 84
change set 116
chmaster 149
ClearCase
    component 217
    derived object 212
    MultiSite 121
    multisite setup for GDD with ClearQuest 120
    solution for build strategy 156
    stream 218
    winkin 212
ClearCase Remote Client (CCRC) 118, 123–124
ClearCase Web (CCWeb) 123, 131
clearmake 156
ClearQuest
    deployment tracking 164
    integration 141
    multisite setup for GDD with ClearCase 120
    schema 93
    terminology 220
ClearQuest Test Manager 78, 86
code visualization 72
collaboration 7, 14, 61, 192
    with Rational tools 192
collector 161
communication and governance 88
component 217
composite baseline 219
config spec 215
configuration specification 215
connection 222
construction 45
content element 45
coordination problems 13
core site 11
cost benefits 7
coverage analysis 65
CQWeb client 85
CreateView script 146
cultural differences 15
cumulative decision making 99

D

database
    set 222
    user 221
dbset 222
defect
    density 109
    distribution across geographies 107
    management charts 106
    resolution rate 108
delivery 38
    processes 52

W